ASSET PROTECTION MADE E-Z!

by
Arnold S. Goldstein, J.D., LL.M., Ph.D.

E·Z LEGAL FORMS®

Deerfield Beach, Florida
www.e-zlegal.com

Asset Protection Made E-Z™
Copyright 1999 E-Z Legal Forms, Inc.
Printed in the United States of America

E·Z LEGAL FORMS®

384 South Military Trail Deerfield Beach, FL 33442
Tel. 954-480-8933 Fax 954-480-8906
http://www.e-zlegal.com/
All rights reserved.
Distributed by E-Z Legal Forms, Inc.

1 2 3 4 5 6 7 8 9 10   CPC   R   10 9 8 7 6 5 4 3 2

This publication is designed to provide accurate and authoritative information in regard to to subject matter covered. It is sold with the understanding that neither the publisher nor author is engaged in rendering legal, accounting, or other professional services. If legal advice or other expert assistance is required, the services of a competent professional should be sought. From: *A Declaration of Principles jointly adopted by a Committee of the American Bar Association and a Committee of Publishers.*

Asset Protection Made E-Z™

Written by Arnold S. Goldstein, J.D., LL.M., Ph.D.

Limited warranty and disclaimer

Table of contents

How to use this guide 7

Introduction 9

1 Essential steps to lifelong financial protection...................11

2 Creating a creditor-proof plan......................................25

3 How creditors discover assets....................................39

4 Laws that shield assets..55

5 Wealth-saving strategies with co-ownership 69

6 Trusts that protect assets..85

7 Build a financial fortress with limited partnerships..........107

8 Asset protection with an LLC...127

9 Any corporation can protect wealth 139

10 Protecting your assets offshore 163

11 Bankruptcy: Keep your assets, lose your debts.............187

12 Strategies that stop the IRS...205

13 Protecting your assets in divorce................................227

14 Strategies to stop foreclosures and repossessions........255

15 Creditor and disaster-proof your business....................273

Glossary of useful terms..293

Index 299

How to use this guide

E-Z Legal's Made E-Z™ Guides can help you achieve an important legal objective conveniently, efficiently and economically. But it is important to properly use this guide if you are to avoid later difficulties.

◆ Carefully read all information, warnings and disclaimers concerning the legal forms in this guide. If after thorough examination you decide that you have circumstances that are not covered by the forms in this guide, or you do not feel confident about preparing your own documents, consult an attorney.

◆ Complete each blank on each legal form. Do not skip over inapplicable blanks or lines intended to be completed. If the blank is inapplicable, mark "N/A" or "None" or use a dash. This shows you have not overlooked the item.

◆ Always use pen or type on legal documents—never use pencil.

◆ Avoid erasures and "cross-outs" on final documents. Use photocopies of each document as worksheets, or as final copies. All documents submitted to the court must be printed on one side only.

◆ Correspondence forms may be reproduced on your own letterhead if you prefer.

◆ Whenever legal documents are to be executed by a partnership or corporation, the signatory should designate his or her title.

◆ It is important to remember that on legal contracts or agreements between parties all terms and conditions must be clearly stated. Provisions may not be enforceable unless in writing. All parties to the agreement should receive a copy.

◆ Instructions contained in this guide are for your benefit and protection, so follow them closely.

◆ You will find a glossary of useful terms at the end of this guide. Refer to this glossary if you encounter unfamiliar terms.

◆ Always keep legal documents in a safe place and in a location known to your spouse, family, personal representative or attorney.

Introduction to Asset Protection Made E-Z™

Big lawsuits, business failure, tax troubles, divorce, catastrophic illness. The list of potential threats to your financial security is endless. There are just too many ways to get into financial trouble-unless you act now to protect what you own.

This book is not only for the rich and powerful. It is essential for everyone—mainstream Americans from a thousand different occupations who get up each morning to do a day's work. Their only goal is to build a safe and secure nest egg.

Whoever they are, whatever their backgrounds, however great or small their wealth, most believe our society is dangerous to their pocketbook. They no longer believe our legal system protects their wealth. They see friends, neighbors, business associates, employees, and even family members as potential litigants. The dangers lurk everywhere.

No matter how careful or honest you may be, you can never achieve financial security. One poor decision or being in the wrong place at the wrong time can destroy you financially. One mistake can cost you everything you worked years to build.

You may not like the world as it has become. But, you cannot change it. However, you can protect yourself so that you can survive in the world as it is if you have your very own financial self-defense plan, a plan that shelters everything you own against any financial or legal threat.

You cannot afford to settle for less. The probability is that you now have absolutely no wealth protection plan. Asset Protection Made E-Z is for you. You will see how to legally safeguard your wealth and property from lawsuits, creditors, the IRS, divorce, bankruptcy, probate, or any other financial disaster that can unexpectedly wipe you out. Discover the little-known secrets and strategies that can give and your family a lifetime of financial security starting today!

Wishing you many more assets to protect!

Arnold S. Goldstein, J.D., LL.M., Ph.D.

Essential steps to lifelong financial protection

1

Chapter 1

Essential steps to lifelong financial protection

What you'll find in this chapter:

⟶ Why you need asset protection

⟶ How to recruit the best advice

⟶ The scope of your plan

⟶ Why time is of the essence

⟶ How to learn more about asset protection

We live in a lawsuit-crazy and financially risky world where we may easily and unexpectedly lose our assets. Each year, more families, individuals and businesses are suddenly and devastatingly bankrupted. And, it may happen to you!

Like so many others, you may wonder what you can do to protect your wealth from these mounting dangers. How can you achieve the lifelong financial security and peace of mind you need and deserve? What must you do to defend yourself financially? These are important questions, and this first chapter highlights the key steps to sound asset protection planning. Good planning in asset protection, as with most things, is the foundation for success.

Step #1: You are the next target

Face one unfortunate reality as your first important step—regardless of how safe and secure you now feel, without advance asset protection, your hard-earned wealth may well end up in someone else's pocket. There are simply too many ways in our over-litigious, over-regulated and overly hostile society to encounter nightmare financial troubles. Consider a few of the more obvious dangers that may impoverish you next month or next year:

> *note* Everyone will flirt with liability and financial disaster, regardless of lifestyle, occupation or caution. Dangers can be minimized but never entirely avoided.

1) A whopping tax bill.

2) A costly accident and negligence claim.

3) Breach of an important contract.

4) A lawsuit for professional malpractice.

5) Creditor claims from a failed business.

6) Nursing home or catastrophic medical bills.

7) Lawsuits from disgruntled business partners or employees.

8) Huge fines for violating a federal or state law.

9) A lawsuit for defamation.

10) Divorce.

11) Governmental seizure and forfeiture of your property.

These only exemplify the many mine fields that can unexpectedly wipe you out. And until it happens, you seldom realize how vulnerable your assets and your family's financial security really are. Until you do understand your vulnerability, you will probably take your financial stability for granted.

If you are still unconvinced that a wealth-shattering event can happen to you, then consider the eye-opening odds:

1) Ninety million lawsuits will be filed next year in the United States. The odds that you will be the target of a lawsuit next year are one in four (a scarier one in two probability if you earn over $50,000 a year). Statistically, you are virtually guaranteed to be targeted by at least one devastating lawsuit within ten years. Lawsuits are now the American way of life and our courts are a glorified crap-shoot with 700,000 lawyers looking for deep-pocket defendants. You may be their very next target.

2) Divorce? You may be very happily married today. Still, the odds are that you will someday divorce. Depressing? No more so than the likelihood that the divorce will financially cripple you, whether you are husband or wife.

3) Own a business? Here's more unpleasant news. If your business is under five years old, it has an 80-percent likelihood of failing. What personal liabilities will this create? What assets will you lose?

> **note** Are you under age 30? Prepare to defend against no less than five major lawsuits over your lifetime, and most likely many more.

4) Tax problems? Our crazy, unpredictable and unfair tax laws and an increasingly aggressive IRS will make tax troubles more and more common. Twenty million Americans are now on the run from the IRS collection corps. What will they lose? What would you lose if the tax collector suddenly appeared at your door?

5) Then there are the unexpected bills. Can you afford enormous hospital or medical bills if you or a family member needed uninsured catastrophic care? What would happen if you lost your job, bills mounted and creditors came calling? U.S. bankruptcies have skyrocketed to a record 1.25 million annually, and they continue to soar. Two million Americans may soon go bankrupt annually. Will you become another statistic? And what would you then lose?

These and other dismal facts prove one point: Everyone is vulnerable to countless and unforeseeable legal or financial disasters. There is no surefire way to escape liability or losing your assets without smart planning.

> **note** Four million Americans are audited annually. Most are clobbered by huge tax bills. But there are many other opportunities to get into big trouble with the IRS. When you owe the IRS you will most likely see how quickly assets can vanish.

Step #1 then is to adopt a defensive and realistic philosophy: Don't wonder if you will someday face these financial dangers. *Ask when.* Since you can never predict the answer, the only logical option is to anticipate financial crisis and build the strongest possible asset protection fortress before it's too late. Remember—financial crisis may strike tomorrow.

Step #2: Protect your assets

Many people feel uncomfortable with the objectives of asset protection. They believe asset protection is either illegal or immoral, a device to cheat creditors of their rightful due. You may see this book as nothing more than a guide for certified deadbeats. But this is not the case.

note Asset protection, when properly practiced, is certainly not illegal. Of course, you cannot commit illegal acts, such as perjury, violate bankruptcy laws or fraudulently conceal assets from creditors. However, legitimate asset protection planning neither encourages nor permits these or other illegal acts. You can and must implement your asset protection plan, complying with all laws. This is the underlying rule to sound planning.

The ethical question is considerably more difficult to discuss. Many people consider it improper to shelter assets from those who may assert a rightful claim. Yet, others believe there is no ethical obligation to expose or lose assets you can legally protect. Too many claims are unjustifiable, inequitable or frivolous, even those that result in a court judgment. Americans are victimized by too many unfair and baseless claims. These unfortunate folks prove that while life cannot be without its risks, it is illogical to needlessly participate in a legal lottery where you can unjustly lose all that you own on a spin of roulette-wheel justice. To survive, you must adopt this same pragmatic attitude.

note **People seeking protection are neither crooks nor immoral. They are savvy souls with a strong survival instinct. They are taking advantage of the laws designed and intended to protect against life's financial vagaries.**

Asset protection is financial self-defense in its purest form. It combats the frivolous and harassing lawsuits against our most productive and affluent citizens and companies, the "deep-pocket" defendants who become perennial targets only because they have exposed wealth.

You join the growing ranks once you protect your assets. Only the poor or hopelessly oblivious are not protecting their assets or at least thinking about it from time to time. And, many more attorneys enthusiastically, if not always competently, happily assist them. This is why so many corporations, trusts, limited partnerships and a variety of other asset protection devices designed to achieve that mission flourish. The law endorses asset protection as a permissible and even desirable pursuit, as evidenced by the many laws created solely to protect assets.

note If ethical or moral issues surrounding asset protection still concern you, take Step #2 and try this practical solution: Protect yourself! If you feel morally bound to pay a future claim, then surrender your assets to appease your conscience and sense of fair play. Asset protection gives you that option.

Step #3: Organize your team

Your asset protection plan necessarily involves those most intimately involved in your finances. Building your team is important Step #3. For example, you cannot ignore your spouse who will rightfully become alarmed when you suddenly and inexplicably re-title marital assets for unknown and suspicious reasons. Anticipate and allay those fears and uncertainties. Involve those entitled to know the reasons for changing your financial affairs. With candid explanation comes understanding and cooperation. Use close family members and trusted friends to administer your financial game plan as trustees or executors.

The well-protected are less inviting targets for a lawsuit. The bottom line is that wealth is good. Vulnerable wealth is bad.

Be careful about disclosures even within your team. Your spouse may understand asset protection is a key objective, but why needlessly reveal this to friends, relatives or others who should instead believe your goals involve good tax or estate planning? While asset protection is legal, your actual intent may become an important factor if an asset transfer is later challenged by creditors. You then gain no advantage if a friend or associate testifies that asset protection was your only objective.

Your team should include only people you can unquestionably trust to faithfully implement your plan. Cautiously evaluate the extent each can be trusted, and whether they will remain trustworthy under stressful circumstances. And can they professionally handle their responsibilities? Asset protection planning requires you to objectively evaluate others, and this is as critical as selecting the right legal strategies.

Step #4: Prioritize your objectives

The primary purpose of asset protection is to shelter all assets from all financial and legal threats. How you protect your assets partly depends upon your other financial goals and objectives. For example, how will your asset protection plan enhance or hinder your tax objectives? Estate plan? Must you sacrifice good investments for better protection but poorer investments? What about control when controlled assets are less safe from creditors? So, begin Step #4 planning by understanding the inevitable conflicts and trade-offs. Discuss them with your spouse and others affected by your plan. Your professional advisors should explain the trade-offs, the possible alternatives, and how to best reconcile conflicting objectives.

17

note Asset protection does not always produce negative financial consequences. The opposite is often the case because timely and well-designed asset protection plans may encourage superior investments, lower taxes and a sounder estate plan. Asset protection planning oftentimes spurs the comprehensive and balanced financial plan every individual, family and organization needs.

E-Z TIP Your business partners or key business associates are examples of potential asset protection teammates. But, confine individuals narrowly involved in your financial affairs only to the financial matters that specifically involve them.

Still, you must anticipate the advantages and disadvantages that may arise from each possible asset protection plan. Have your advisors explain anticipated consequences from each strategy. You must ultimately choose the one plan that is most consistent with your overall and sometimes contradictory objectives.

You may, of course, achieve good asset protection through many different strategies. Ten asset protection specialists will suggest ten different plans. Why? Variations in state law is one reason. What is ironclad protection in one *note* state may produce no protection in another state. Thus, asset protection planning is greatly influenced by state laws.

CAUTION Your advisors cannot always sense your priorities or what outcomes you consider most important. You may sacrifice certain financial benefits for greater financial security, but it is always a modest price for the peace of mind that only comes from finally achieving true lifelong security for you and your family.

Your plan also reflects your attorney's own background and experience with the various options available. An attorney inexperienced with limited partnerships may suggest using a less-effective but more familiar trust.

Cost also shapes your plan. Asset protection can be expensive. Complex asset protection plans may cost thousands of dollars. Even modest plans may consume huge professional fees. A plan to match your pocketbook may provide effective protection. Discuss fees with your attorney before you plan so your advisor designs an affordable plan.

Timing is yet another factor. A plan designed to successfully defend against a future liability may greatly differ from one crafted to stonewall a present creditor. Asset protection planning considers prospective claims. The creditor and his commitment to pursue assets are key ingredients. As assets influence the plan so will the creditors.

Finally, and perhaps most importantly, you must be comfortable with your plan. Many highly effective strategies, such as offshore trusts, can cause discomfort. Alternatives that cause less anxiety while providing acceptable safety must be your compass for direction.

Asset protection plans seldom share identical facts, family relationships or potential hazards. Design the plan that perfectly fits your situation.

Step #5: Asset Protection—A lifelong commitment

Finances change. Obligations change. Laws change. Legal and financial hazards change. Financial goals change. Asset protection plans must also change.

Step #5 then is to make asset protection planning a continuous process. Review your plan at least once a year, and more frequently with each major event: a windfall inheritance, threatening lawsuit, relocation to another state or family change. Each trigger the need to review. Updates ensure your plan is continuously the best for your situation.

> **⚠ CAUTION** Asset protection erodes when it is no longer a prime objective. Once a financial threat passes, you may consider asset protection less important. You again become vulnerable.

It involves time, expense and effort to enjoy strong protection. But, giving protection priority over more attractive, but vulnerable, financial opportunities is part of that commitment.

Step #6: Recruit asset protection pros

Asset protection planning also requires the right professionals to balance your team. Finding these professionals is Step #6. Lawyers and legal considerations most influence your plan, but other factors are also important. For safe and sound tax planning, your accountant must participate. Achieving your investment objectives—liquidity, yield, safety and growth—require a good financial planner or investment advisor. For instance, you need your banker to refinance your assets or your bank's trust department to become the trustee of your new trust. Your insurance agent becomes another important professional when annuities or insurance are part of your plan.

Successful asset protection plans depend less on the number of advisors than on choosing the right advisors. A skilled asset protection attorney is absolutely essential. Unfortunately, few attorneys have the background or training in asset protection. Your family lawyer may be proficient in routine legal matters yet know little about asset protection.

DEFINITION

Fortunately, you can find good legal talent. Most asset protection lawyers originate from within the legal specialties of bankruptcy, corporate law and probate. *Bankruptcy lawyers* reconcile disputes between debtors and creditors and either chase or protect assets. Corporate lawyers are familiar with the numerous asset protection entities—corporations, limited partnerships, limited liability companies—and commonly handle asset protection. Probate lawyers are especially expert with the various trusts, gifts and other asset protection structures also used for estate planning. Usually they have a knowledge of asset protection.

Interview a prospective attorney very carefully:

1) Check references from other asset protection clients.

2) Evaluate all of the attorney's answers to your questions, as well as the questions posed by the attorney.

3) Discuss fees and costs.

4) Determine whether you are comfortable or not with the attorney.

5) Determine if the attorney will design and implement your plan and defend it should it be challenged. Whether your plan withstands a creditor attack is its acid test. Your lawyer must be confident that he or she can win that contest.

To find a good attorney, call your local bar association or clerk of your local bankruptcy court. They know the veterans who can best help you.

A good financial planner, in many instances, is no less important than a good lawyer. Most families must balance asset protection along with their other financial objectives. To achieve this balance requires a well-qualified financial planner. Financial planning is a new profession and so it is difficult to determine competency. Check memberships and affiliations. *Chartered Financial Consultants (CHFC) and Certified Financial Planners (CFP)* are important designations.

Step #7: Become proactive

Professionals won't have all the answers. You must take your own counsel. Step #7 requires that you learn at least the fundamentals of asset protection, just as you mastered the basics of sound investing or tax planning.

Why this advice? First, only through personal knowledge can you measure the competency of a prospective asset protection lawyer. Second, when you stay abreast of asset protection strategies, you maintain the

note Close professional coordination is most necessary when you have a significant net worth, diverse assets or complex investment objectives. Those with modest wealth may need only their attorney and accountant.

best asset protection. Third, you may implement many asset protection strategies yourself, while your attorney handles the complex procedures. A knowledgeable client immeasurably adds to his asset protection plan in many different ways.

Step #8: Measure your wealth

E-Z TIP Your financial planner should have some asset protection experience and also understand its importance to your overall plan. This professional may even refer you to a good asset protection lawyer.

A good asset protection plan protects everything you own. And it is common to overlook valuable assets. You may, for instance, mistakenly believe certain assets are automatically protected or overlook future assets, such as an inheritance. This may require your parents to revise their estate plan to protect your future inheritance from their creditors and your own. One goal of Step #8 then is to protect both your present and future assets. What assets must you

21

protect? Estimate the value of each item and how each asset is presently titled (individually, tenants by the entirety, joint tenants, tenants in common, in trust, etc.). Specify your ownership interest in co-owned assets.

Review every sale or transfer of significant assets over the past five years and help your advisor to decide whether these transfers may be recoverable by creditors. Always anticipate inheritances or other prospective windfalls that may come your way and thus require protection. Finally, list all liens or encumbrances against each asset to determine the net equity remaining to protect.

> **E-Z Tip**
>
> Learn! Read other books about asset protection. Attend asset protection seminars sponsored by professional organizations. You can't be a bystander on the important mission of ensuring your financial security.

Next, add your assets and subtract your liabilities to calculate your net worth. You may be considerably wealthier than you had estimated. But asset protection is not only for the wealthy. It is for anyone with assets that they would hate to lose. Wealth is relative. People with modest assets find it is no less devastating a loss.

Step #9: Protect yourself before it's too late

Step #9 means that you must judgment-proof yourself before trouble strikes. Courts can unwind last-minute transfers that defraud existing creditors. Asset protection should occur before serious problems arise.

Most people quickly seek asset protection only when prompted by a lawsuit or other temporary crisis. And the perceived need for asset protection usually vanishes with the threat. Most procrastinators eventually get hit with a financial disaster that never vanishes as easily as does their hard-earned wealth.

ACT NOW—are the two most important words in this book!

Planning Pointers

◆ Good planning is essential to a sound asset protection plan.

◆ You must start with the reality that you can at any time face a wealth-robbing crisis from any direction. Without an asset protection plan you are vulnerable.

◆ Asset protection is legal and ethical financial self-defense using structures and strategies approved for that purpose by our legal system.

 You must first anticipate financial trouble and accept your vulnerability. Only then will you take asset protection seriously.

◆ Asset protection planning requires you to involve family members and other trusted individuals who will play a role in or be affected by your plan.

◆ Prioritize your financial objectives so your plan properly integrates tax, estate planning and investment goals.

◆ Make asset protection a lifelong commitment. It is too easy to relax your protection once a danger passes—and that only makes you vulnerable once again.

◆ You need asset protection professionals to design your best plan. That means involving your tax advisor and financial planner as well as an attorney who specializes in this field.

◆ Protect yourself before it's too late. The time to protect assets is before you have creditors.

Creating a creditor-proof plan

2

Chapter 2

Creating a creditor-proof plan

What you'll find in this chapter:

- ▶ What is a fraudulent transfer?
- ▶ How to spot a fraudulent transfer
- ▶ The dangers of fraudulent transfers
- ▶ Fraudulent transfers and the IRS
- ▶ How to arrange safe transfers

Your one asset protection goal is to ensure that your creditors cannot seize your assets. When a creditor can successfully claim that assets were disposed of in a fraudulent manner, the creditor may recover the assets.

Will your creditor prevail? The answer depends upon whether your creditor can convince the court that your transfer was a mere sham to unfairly and fraudulently place your assets beyond the creditor's reach. The acid test of any asset protection plan is whether the creditor prevails.

Perhaps you scurried to transfer assets shortly after a lawsuit or creditor claim. You possibly tried to salvage whatever possible from the grasp of your creditors through helter-skelter disposal of assets to friends and relatives. Your assets may have been sold for less than fair value, or gifted to a trusted friend or relatives who dutifully would return your property once your financial threat disappears. Or, you may be that financially

> ⚠ **CAUTION** You cannot escape debts by simply gifting assets to friends or relatives, or via other equally transparent attempts to shield assets from creditors.

---

troubled businessman who transfers assets to his wife before filing bankruptcy. These are typical knee-jerk reactions once trouble strikes, but they seldom work.

Transferring assets to a seemingly safer haven may seem the smart way to protect them, but it seldom stops the more determined creditor. Nor will gifting property to a relative or friend succeed. Will your asset protection plan keep your assets 100-percent safe from creditors? Unless your plan can pass the fraudulent transfer test, it is a faulty plan.

Primer on fraudulent transfers

Creditors can successfully recover a debtor's assets by proving the transaction was fraudulent because it hinders or delays their rights as creditors to obtain the debtor's property. To overturn a fraudulent transfer, the creditor will invoke either the *Uniform Fraudulent Conveyance Act (UFCA,* followed in most states), or the comparable *Uniform Fraudulent Transfers Act (UFTA,* found in eight states). Several states still observe English common law, which closely parallels the American fraudulent transfer laws.

Fraudulent transfers are either:

1) fraud-in-law (constructive fraud), or

2) fraud-in-fact (actual fraud).

A fraudulent transfer occurs when:

1) you transfer your property

2) for less than fair market value, and

3) the transfer rendered you insolvent or unable to pay your creditors.

Each element is necessary for it to constitute a fraudulent transfer. But the creditor need not prove that the debtor actually intended to defraud. The transfer, for instance, may have happened before the debtor knew of the claim or underlying liability. The fact that the creditor had the right to make a claim is sufficient to set aside a later non-fair value asset transfer that renders the debtor insolvent and unable to satisfy this creditor.

Fraudulent transfer laws are based on the premise that the property of an insolvent debtor constructively belongs to his creditors. Should the debtor, however innocently, transfer the property without receiving in exchange assets of approximately equivalent value, his present creditors can recover the transferred property. This remains true even without proof that the transfer was intended to deprive creditors recourse to the assets when transferred. A fraudulent transfer even exists notwithstanding the debtor's charitable objectives for the transfer, or even that a charity received the asset.

There are two central questions in establishing a fraudulent transfer:

1) What constitutes fair consideration or fair value? and

2) When does a debtor become insolvent?

DEFINITION

In answer to the first question, *fair consideration*, or *fair value*, exchanged for property is the price a reasonably prudent seller could obtain for the asset using commercially reasonable efforts. That price, however, need not equal the exact fair market value. Cases suggest that a price equal to 70 percent of the actual market value may be sufficient consideration for many assets. The law recognizes that certain assets are difficult to sell under distress for their actual worth. Assets such as publicly listed securities can be sold for an established price on any business day; therefore, a debtor who sells securities for considerably less will fail the fair consideration test.

> *note*
>
> Fair value consideration can be money, property or services. Courts closely examine service agreements to establish their true value. A mere promise to furnish future services will not qualify, only services previously or simultaneously rendered.

When assets are sold for less than fair value, the transferee may be forced to return the property upon repayment to him of the purchase price. Or, the transferee may be ordered to pay the difference between the price paid and the asset's fair value. This is an appropriate remedy when the asset is no longer recoverable. A transferee, however, is fully protected if he acted in good faith and without knowledge of fraudulent intent when accepting the asset and also paid fair value.

DEFINITION

The second question was: When does a debtor become insolvent? No conveyance is fraudulent if the debtor retains sufficient assets to satisfy the creditor. You are *insolvent* within the meaning of this law only when your remaining property is insufficient to pay existing debts when they become absolute and due. *Liabilities* encompass all debts, including contingent or disputed debts. The law does not prevent you from gifting assets if you remain sufficiently wealthy to fully pay your present debts. But whenever a transfer of property for less than fair consideration causes your liabilities to exceed your assets, the courts will infer the transfer was fraudulent and the assets recoverable.

> **CAUTION** You cannot safely transfer assets for less than fair consideration if your remaining non-exempt assets (and liability insurance) will not fully cover your known or unknown present liabilities when they fall due.

With actual fraud cases, your creditor must prove you actually intended to hinder, delay or defraud. The relationship between transferor and transferee, whether the transfer included all or only part of the debtor's assets, whether the transfer was concealed, and whether the transferor had knowledge of the claim are all factors the court will consider.

These, and other factors, can only imply fraudulent intent and raise the presumption of fraud. Still, such transfers can often be successfully defended as advancing legitimate estate planning, tax investment or business objectives. The court may be more lenient concerning such transfers even though their transfer nevertheless hindered the creditor.

> **note** Since a creditor cannot easily prove your state of mind or force you to confess such fraudulent intent, they usually prove fraudulent intent through circumstances or factors that suggest such intent.

The creditor can even then recover the assets under a constructive *fraud claim*, or so-called *fraud-in-fact claim*. The creditor can then ignore the question of actual intent and need prove only that the creditor either had a present or foreseeable claim, the transfer was for inadequate consideration, and the transfer rendered the debtor unable to satisfy the creditor.

When fraudulent transfers become uncontestable

The time period within which creditors must challenge a fraudulent transfer is governed by the state's statute of limitations. This time period is usually four years after the transfer, or one year after actual discovery of the transfer could have been reasonably made by the creditor, whichever date came later. Under this common rule, a fraudulently transferred asset is never completely safe as a creditor can always argue the recent discovery of the earlier transfer. This allows the creditor one more year to set aside a transfer that may have occurred many years earlier.

States with fraudulent conveyance statutes generally impose the more strict five-year statute of limitations. Later claims are not allowed regardless of when the creditor discovered the transfer. This is the prevailing rule as most states have the stricter fraudulent conveyance statutes. But do check the laws in your state so you know when creditor recovery claims become barred.

Fraudulent transfer actions are very frequently initiated by a trustee in bankruptcy who will claim the bankrupt fraudulently transferred assets before the bankruptcy. Under bankruptcy law, the trustee has two years from the first meeting of creditors to commence a fraudulent transfer claim.

Under the Bankruptcy Code, a fraudulent transfer must occur within the year preceding the bankruptcy. But earlier transfers are not necessarily safe because the trustee can elect to sue under the state's fraudulent transfer laws rather than bankruptcy law, because the state statute of limitations extends beyond the shorter one-year statute of limitation under bankruptcy. The bankruptcy court can also refuse to discharge debts when a debtor engaged in a fraudulent transfer or other inequitable conduct.

Why fraudulent transfers are dangerous

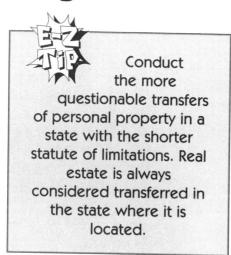

Conduct the more questionable transfers of personal property in a state with the shorter statute of limitations. Real estate is always considered transferred in the state where it is located.

In a fraudulent conveyance case, the debtor's conduct receives very close attention. But what about the transferee who received the property? What rights does he have to keep the property? What liability can the transferee suffer for participating in the fraudulent transfer?

If the transfer is fraudulent, the transferee can be compelled to re-transfer the asset for the benefit of the debtor's creditors. A transferee, innocent and unaware of any fraudulent intent, can impose a lien on the asset for the price he paid for the asset. The transferee is then reinstated to his original position as he surrenders the asset and any benefit of the bargain. If the transferee previously sold the asset, and the second transfer was also in good faith, and the second transferee also innocent, then the second transferee regains the price he paid for

> **E-Z TIP**
>
> Delay bankruptcy as long as possible if you have questionable transfers in your past. Avoid bankruptcy for at least one year.

surrendering the asset. But any transferee who conspires to commit a fraudulent conveyance may be forced to reconvey the asset without receiving repayment. That is why all transfers should be arms-length to avoid conspiracy or bad faith claims against the transferee. Civil or criminal sanctions may be possibly imposed on a transferee, as well as the transferor, and this can bring serious sanctions. If the bad faith transferee further transferred the assets beyond creditor reach, the transferee may become accountable to the creditor for the value or equity in the property that would otherwise have been available to the creditor.

Criminal penalties for fraudulent transfers are also possible in several states, where a transferor or transferee who knowingly is a party to a fraudulent transfer commits a misdemeanor. This can include attorneys and other professionals involved in the fraudulent transfer. An attorney so involved may also be professionally sanctioned under Bar ethics rules in effect in certain states.

While many transfers are voided as fraudulent transfers, only the more blatant dispositions attract prosecutorial attention, and these cases usually involve acts of actual fraud or deliberate concealment.

Because a fraudulent transfer can be troublesome, you should never transfer property to someone who would react poorly to a fraudulent transfer claim made against him. Few individuals will loyally attend depositions and court hearings without eventually sacrificing your

> **note**
>
> In practice, criminal sanctions are rare in fraudulent conveyance cases because there is a very fine line between lawful or at least well-intentioned asset redeployment and criminal fraud.

assets to your creditors. Respect your transferee's position if there is any possibility of a fraudulent transfer claim. Never involve friends or relatives whose association you value. Involving them in a fraudulent transfer case can destroy relationships.

How creditors recover fraudulently transferred property

A creditor who suspects a fraudulent transfer has several remedies. The precise remedies will partly depend upon whether the claim has reached judgment or is a pending or future claim.

A judgment creditor who suspects a fraudulent transfer can file suit directly against the transferee and have the court:

> ⚠️ **CAUTION** As a civil remedy, the courts can hold both the transferee and the transferor jointly and severally liable for attorney's fees and costs incurred by the creditor to recover fraudulently transferred property.

1)   set aside the transfer and restore title to the original owner-debtor for seizure by the creditor;

2)   enjoin further transfer, encumbrance or depletion of the asset (freezing the asset), pending the outcome of the fraudulent conveyance action;

3)   award damages from the transferee and supplemental damages from the transferor (equal to the legal costs to recover the asset);

4)   appoint a receiver over the conveyed asset if the asset may disappear or be dissipated;

5)   recover from the debtor the proceeds received when the property was sold (but the creditor cannot void the sale to a subsequent good faith purchaser who paid fair value).

note

While these and numerous other remedies are available to a creditor in a fraudulent conveyance case, a court, to the extent practicable, will simply attempt to restore the creditor to his position before the fraudulent transfer. Whether this can be practicably accomplished, of course, depends largely on whether the transferee still holds the asset and whether it has been since altered, destroyed or sold.

> **E-Z TIP** For additional protection have your transferee's independent attorney review any proposed transaction. This strengthens your argument that the transfer was arms-length and helps insulate you from criticism should the transfer be later challenged.

A non-judgment creditor has considerably greater difficulty, but even the non-judgment creditor has his remedies. For instance, he can challenge the transfer and freeze the assets still in the hands of the transferee if he can convince the court:

1)   there is reasonable expectation of a future judgment,

2)   other assets are unavailable to satisfy the prospective judgment, and

3)   the transfer will probably be found fraudulent.

The creditor's case strengthens when the court sees a pattern of fraudulent transfers, and that the creditor will lose any future rights to recover unless the remaining assets are attached for the benefit of the creditor.

Special IRS asset recovery rules

The IRS has special remedies to assert when it encounters a fraudulent transfer. The IRS may assess and collect estate, gift and income taxes due from the transferor, or assess these taxes directly against a transferee who received the fraudulently transferred property for less than fair consideration. And, the IRS may directly assess the transferee without court action. The liability of the transferee then essentially becomes that of a *jeopardy assessment*, as the IRS then proceeds directly against the transferee and the transferor to recover the overdue taxes.

DEFINITION

note The IRS uses the fraudulent transfer laws in the state where the action is filed because no federal statute or IRS regulation specifically provides for fraudulent transfer actions by the IRS.

The IRS may also file a court claim against the transferee for the transferor's estate, gift and income taxes, although this is not technically required. The court may: 1) set aside the fraudulent transfer or 2) impose transferee liability. In the first instance, the IRS has the court void the transfer so the IRS can directly seize the asset. In the second, the IRS seeks a monetary judgment against the transferee equal to the value of the fraudulently transferred asset.

Despite its broad recovery powers, the IRS infrequently chases fraudulently transferred property. This is probably because the IRS requires a cumbersome bureaucratic process to initiate and recover a fraudulent conveyance, unless the IRS filed a lien before the transfer. The IRS must otherwise litigate the case through a typically short-staffed regional counsel. Only more substantial cases are litigated.

Tell-tale signs of a sham transfer

What badges or indications of fraud signal a fraudulent transfer or sham deal? Fourteen clues courts look for include:

1) Transfers not in the debtor's ordinary course of business or usual pattern for disposing of assets.

2) Transfers of assets for inadequate consideration when the transfer creates or adds to the debtor's insolvency.

3) Secrecy in the transaction.

4) An unduly hasty transfer.

5) Transfer to a family member, friend or close business associate.

6) Where a buyer of a business allows the seller to retain managerial control, or a home buyer allows the seller to remain in occupancy.

More caution should be exercised when the IRS is the creditor as the IRS may invoke obstruction of justice or money-laundering statutes in certain fraudulent conveyance cases.

7) Failure of the parties to use independent counsel on transactions where independent representation is customary or reasonable.

8) Extraordinary or superficial attempts to make the transfer appear fair and reasonable.

9) Unusual possession or use of the asset by the seller after the transfer.

10) Transferring assets outside the debtor's jurisdiction.

11) Failure to promptly record deeds or title documents.

12) Mortgages or liens for services rendered in the past, or where such services have questionable value.

13) Failure of the debtor or transferee to accurately record loan transactions or repayments.

14) Failure by the transferor to collect overdue loans secured by the property.

These badges of fraud simulate an actual transfer of property, but are not intended to legitimately divest the transferor of his property. Commonly, a transferee holds title in his name with the tacit understanding that title will be later reconveyed when the creditor threat passes. Meanwhile, the transferee usually allows the property to be used as the transferor wishes.

These factors alone do not conclusively prove fraud or a fraudulent transfer; however, they may easily persuade a court to find such a questionable transaction a fraudulent transfer and hence recoverable by the creditor.

E-Z tips for safe transfers

To help avoid fraudulent transfer claims, follow these important pointers:

• **Protect your assets before a claim exists.** There cannot be a fraudulent transfer on a transfer that occurred before the liability. That is why it is so important to judgment-proof yourself in advance of any financial or legal difficulty. The safe strategy is to be liability-free when you protect your assets.

• **Smaller incremental transfers** attract less notice than transfers of significant assets.

• **Avoid any insider transactions to family or close business associates.** Even completely innocent transactions are often suspicious to courts and creditors. Involve non-family members as trustees or corporate officers in transferee entities. A brother-in-law with a different surname is preferable to your same surname brother. Make all transactions appear arms-length, even when they are not arms-length.

> **E-Z Tip**
> Avoid transfers of all or most of your assets to one transferee. Eggs in one basket are more easily attacked. Assets widely scattered require a creditor to file numerous fraudulent transfer lawsuits. The cost and effort may discourage such actions.

• **Establish the transfer for purposes other than sheltering assets from creditors.** Your attorney's correspondence may, for instance, show that you were instead engaged in estate planning when your irrevocable trust was prepared. And this can be persuasive. Document recitals or preambles that state an innocent legal purpose for the conveyance. And what the instrument is designed to accomplish is strong evidence of innocent purpose.

• **Carefully document everything that you receive for your property.** What services were actually performed? Why are they worth their stated value? If you borrowed money, can you show canceled checks or other customary documentation to prove the debt?

• **Avoid circumspect actions.** Selling your home? Avoid becoming its tenant. People seldom buy homes to rent. Selling your business? Think carefully about remaining in control as its manager. Selling a boat? Think twice about keeping it at your dock.

• **Verify the value of your property.** Establish fair consideration. Have your home appraised by local real estate agents. Prove you received at least 70 percent of its appraised value. If you sell an asset for a low price, obtain photographs or appraisals to show defects or other reasons to justify the lower price. Assume the value of a recently transferred asset will be questioned. Be prepared!

note Transferees to questionable transfers must understand that a claim may arise and must be willing to defend against such a claim.

• **Choose your transferees carefully.** If a creditor attacks your transfer, your transferee must defend the transfer. A friendly "straw" with title to your property may not act as you want when facing litigation. He may then quickly surrender your asset or otherwise not cooperate. You then forfeit the asset by default.

• **Never publicize your transfers.** Why alert your creditors when you rearrange your financial affairs? This only encourages creditors to move more swiftly to protect their rights.

• **Employ multiple asset protection strategies.** Why simply deed your home to one party when you can also mortgage it to a friend owed $100,000? Your creditor must then challenge both the transfer and the mortgage. This may be too ambitious and expensive a proposition.

• **Don't overplay your hand.** It is not always smart to be completely judgment-proof. Creditors forced to search too strenuously for some asset to recover may target your more valuable assets. Detract creditors with more reachable, but less valuable, assets.

Planning pointers

◆ Creditors do have rights and they must be respected. A creditor can recover assets that you transferred for less than fair value and which rendered you unable to pay your creditors.

◆ Generally, only existing or foreseeable creditors can recover property that had been transferred. An existing creditor is any creditor to whom you have a present liability, whether known or unknown, actual or contingent.

◆ Actual intent to defraud the creditor is not a necessary element for the plaintiff to prove. It is sufficient for the creditor to prove that the transfer had the effect of rendering the debtor unable to pay the creditor.

A fraudulent transfer can impose liability on the transferee, and in some states it is a criminal offense.

◆ Creditors usually have five years to commence a fraudulent transfer case. In some states it is four years, or one year after the transfer was discovered.

 ◆ The best protection against a potential fraudulent conveyance claim is to shelter assets before you have creditors.

How creditors discover assets

3

Chapter 3

How creditors discover assets

Now more than ever, you must include financial privacy as a key ingredient in your asset protection planning. Those who observe your wealth may also see you as a tempting target for a lawsuit. Unfortunately, it is more difficult today to hide wealth. And the greater your wealth, the greater your need for privacy. One goal of asset protection then is to invest in more secretive assets or wealth that cannot be so easily discovered.

> *note*
>
> In our America, information about your finances is more accessible than ever before as computers feed financial data about you to countless organizations, governmental agencies, credit bureaus, banks, insurance agencies, health providers and virtually everyone else with a linkage to you.

A major lawsuit is a frightening experience, particularly when it is your first encounter with litigation. More distressing is a creditor scrutinizing your financial and legal records to discover assets to satisfy his claim. Still more devastating is the creditor actually seizing your home, car, life savings, investments, business and other hard-earned assets. You must then understand how creditors find and seize assets and how to legally protect yourself in both situations.

Secrecy is not asset protection

The most common mistake is to confuse secrecy or concealing assets with asset protection. In fact, secrecy has less connection with asset protection than with lawsuit discouragement, which is its true function. The reason is because a creditor can eventually compel you to disclose your finances. We cannot rely on secrecy under oath. Answer truthfully and you destroy secrecy. Lie

note Remember: Once that creditor obtains the judgment, the creditor is entitled to honest answers concerning your assets. Secrecy then is no longer a protective device.

and conceal your assets is to commit perjury, which is a serious crime. This point was emphasized before. Your goal is to achieve legitimate asset protection. This allows you to disclose your assets, assured that they will remain safe from your creditor.

Secrecy, then, has only two legitimate roles in asset protection:

1)   to keep wealth less visible so that it will not attract potential litigants

2)   to prevent a creditor from attaching your assets before judgment

Poverty can be power

When assets are well protected, it can be counterproductive to keep the financial arrangements secretive.

note Remember, asset protection must not only protect assets but also discourage others from pursuing them.

When you are armed with a good asset protection plan, you should publicize it to potential or present litigants. Make them realize that they cannot easily collect even if you do have considerable wealth and they do win their lawsuit.

It makes little sense to engage in protracted litigation because the plaintiff believes you have "deep pockets," when you can stifle his enthusiasm by revealing assets fully protected from potential judgments. Early disclosure of this financial protection will discourage litigants from starting lawsuits or quickly end those cases now pending.

When you must disclose your assets

Creditors generally cannot demand information concerning a defendant's assets until they have a judgment because assets relate only to the ability to pay and are irrelevant to the issue of liability, which must first be decided. Under the rules of evidence, irrelevant matters cannot be pursued. But as a defendant, you must timely object if a creditor improperly attempts to discover your assets before judgment. This creditor tactic may encourage you to volunteer information you need not furnish. Creditors are best left blind about your finances unless your "poverty" can be that selling point for diffusing a potential or pending lawsuit.

note

A financial profile that reveals you is critical information to any creditor.

There are two important exceptions to your right not to disclose assets on pre-judgment proceedings. First are the claims of wrongful conduct where punitive damages are recoverable. The court may then compel you to disclose your assets pre-judgment because your net worth helps establish the appropriate punitive damages. Second is when a pre-judgment creditor challenges an alleged fraudulent transfer and sues to set aside the transfer before the underlying claim is won. But even this inquiry must center only on those assets purportedly transferred fraudulently and not other assets. A pre-judgment creditor cannot otherwise compel disclosure of assets. But a creditor can at any time investigate assets, provided the creditor does not breach the defendant's rights to privacy.

Most creditors who contemplate a major lawsuit will not foolishly start without first investigating finances. No creditor will knowingly waste time, money and effort to pursue an uncollectible claim unless the plaintiff wishes to simply prove a point as a matter of principle

note

Proving uncollectibility then is a major objective in asset protection. Without this protection, your assets are exposed. This makes you even more vulnerable and only encourages creditors to vigorously pursue a big settlement or judgment. When assets are properly protected, you and your attorney can convince the creditor to either drop the claim or settle cheaply. But you must deliver this message to your creditor early and forcefully. Poverty is power and will provide the ammunition necessary to send even the most enthusiastic creditor hunting for an easier target.

What creditors ask about finances

A judgment creditor searching for assets can relentlessly probe assets and finances. You must anticipate creditor inquiries. Suppose you will soon face a creditor. How would you answer these questions under oath?

- If employed, what is your full compensation, salary, commission, wage?

- Do you work part-time or full-time?

- Is your spouse employed? (Details)

- Do you have any other sources of income?

- Are you or any family member an officer, director or stockholder of a corporation or similar entity?

- What occupations and business interests have you held or owned during the prior five years?

- What savings, checking or other bank accounts were in your name over the prior five years?

- What bank accounts are now in your spouse's name?

- Identify every source of funds deposited to your spouse's account over the prior five years.

- Do you and/or your spouse have a safe deposit box?

- What accident, health, disability, annuity or income insurance do you own?

- What cash value life insurance do you now own, and what loans are there on these policies?

- Have you assigned or transferred any insurance policies over the past five years?

- Do you or your spouse own an automobile? If so, provide details and list any lienholders?

- Do you or your spouse own a boat? If so, is it mortgaged?

- Do you or your spouse own other vehicles? If so, are they encumbered?

- Do you or your spouse now own or have any interest or have either of you, within the preceding five years, owned or had any interest in real estate, condominiums, time-sharing or cooperative shares? If so, are they mortgaged?

- Do you or your spouse now own or have either of you previously owned any corporate shares, partnership interests, bonds or other securities? If so, are they pledged?

- Do you or your spouse now own mortgages or deeds of trust that are due you? If so, are they pledged or assigned?

- Do you or your spouse own any promissory notes, drafts, or bills of exchange? If so, are they pledged or assigned?

- Do you or your spouse hold judgments or claims against third parties? If so, are they pledged or assigned?

- Do you or your spouse presently have any outstanding insurance claims or have you recently settled any claims?

- Do you or your spouse own jewelry?

- Do you or your spouse own antiques?

- Do you or your spouse own stamp or coin collections?

- Do you or your spouse own patents, inventions, trademarks or copyrights?

- Do you or your spouse own musical instruments? If so, are they encumbered?

- Are you or your spouse a grantor, trustee or beneficiary to any trust?

- Have you or your spouse received an inheritance within the prior five years? Do you anticipate any inheritance?

- Are you a beneficiary under a will or living trust?

- Do you now own or hold any interest in any other asset or property?

- What major assets have you transferred over the prior five years?

- What financial books and records do you and/or your spouse maintain?

- Did you and/or your spouse file tax returns over the prior five years?

- Are you due monies from any governmental agency?

- Who is your accountant?

- What other liabilities do you owe? How many judgments are filed against you?

- Have you or your spouse transferred assets offshore over the prior five years?

- What are your average monthly expenses?

- Are you now paying other creditors?

- What loans or credit have you applied for within the prior five years?

- Are you an endorser, co-maker or guarantor to any loan?

- What financial statements or credit applications have you completed over the prior five years?

- Have you granted mortgages or liens on any property within the prior five years?

- Do you owe any taxes?

- Have you filed all required tax returns? Are any returns under audit?

- Have you made an assignment for the benefit of creditors, or had a receiver been appointed over your property?

- Have you filed for bankruptcy or Chapters 11 or 13 within six years?

- What outstanding orders for payment or supplemental proceedings are pending against you?

- Does anyone else hold property on your behalf?

- Have you made prepayments or repayments over the prior five years?

- Have you held any direct or indirect interest in any other asset over the prior five years not earlier inquired about or disclosed?

What spouses must reveal

As a judgment debtor, you must answer all questions concerning your assets. But must your spouse? Ordinarily, one spouse cannot be forced to testify against his or her spouse because such spousal communication is generally deemed confidential. This marital privilege, however, does not extend to proceedings to discover assets. Most states will allow creditors to interrogate a non-debtor spouse about the debtor spouse's financial affairs. This prevents using marital privilege to conceal assets from a judgment creditor.

> **E-Z TIP**
> Review probable creditor questions with your spouse before an asset discovery deposition. This will ensure both correct and consistent answers. Alternatively, tell your spouse as little as possible about your finances.

How creditors locate assets

A judgment creditor seeking truthful information about finances can use five powerful discovery processes:

1)   *Court examination:* Most states require a debtor to personally appear in court to disclose both assets and income. The court can then determine what the debtor can afford to pay. This supplementary procedure is most frequently used with smaller cases.

2)   *Deposition:* A judgment creditor can also depose the debtor for an office interrogation. This is conducted in a manner similar to other litigation depositions. California and several other states require court authorization to conduct this deposition.

3)   *Interrogatories:* A creditor can submit written questions, or interrogatories, the debtor must answer under oath. Less costly than oral depositions, interrogatories are seldom relied upon to discover assets because a debtor may be either unresponsive or answer vaguely.

4)   *Request to produce documents:* A creditor can require the debtor to deliver specific documents to the creditor for examination. This may be via a deposition or independent request.

5)   *Subpoena duces tecum:* This process compels the debtor to deliver specified documents to the creditor. Because it is more forceful than a simple request to produce documents, most plaintiff attorneys prefer the subpoena.

> **note**
> A Subpoena Duces Tecum can also compel third parties to appear for examination, testify about the debtor's finances and compel the third party to provide specified documents.

Asset discovery procedures are not exclusive. A creditor may use them singly or in combination. For example, a creditor may begin the discovery process with interrogatories and later advance to depositions. These tactical decisions will depend upon the amount of the claim, the debtor's responsiveness, costs, distance and other factors that formulate the most expedient way to discover assets.

Professional asset searches

Because asset protection has become such a widespread activity and because the techniques to achieve it have become so sophisticated, creditors and prospective litigants are turning to professional asset search firms to discover hidden assets. Much of their work reveals whether a prospective defendant has sufficient assets to make a lawsuit even worthwhile. Just as efficiently, these firms track asset transfers from individuals with judgments against them to uncover assets reachable by creditors.

> **note**
> For under $500, a creditor can obtain reasonably accurate financial profiles on most people. Forensic accounting firms involved in larger cases can trace millions in assets (wealth often deployed quite deviously and secretively).

Their detection methods range from laborious audits to linkages with scores of computerized records, interviews and public record searches.

note

Since no true financial privacy exists in America, the asset sleuth's work is less difficult here than elsewhere. Very few asset transfers within the United States cannot be traced. The effectiveness of these firms, however, diminishes considerably when funds or assets are transferred to offshore privacy havens. Their search then may meet with far less success.

You can never safely assume that creditors have not or will not scrutinize your finances under the spyglass of these firms. It is safer to assume that a creditor knows everything about your finances. You will then be less inclined to risk a false statement that can only end with much more serious troubles.

Watch your loan applications

Creditors who investigate assets will review earlier loan applications that may irrefutably highlight assets presently or previously owned. Loan applicants often exaggerate assets on loan applications in order to improve their chances for a loan approval.

What loan applications have you recently issued? What assets are listed? What assets were transferred or do you now intend to transfer? Retrace every step! Incorrect or misleading statements on a credit or loan application must be corrected. An example is real estate listed as a personal asset when you are only the trustee of a trust that owns real estate.

Never apply for a loan or credit if you even remotely anticipate future creditor problems. What you say today may return to haunt you tomorrow.

You cannot easily disclaim ownership to assets you once claimed to own on your loan application. So, think ahead; your loan applications can damage you later.

Avoid a paper trail

A diligent judgment creditor will demand that you produce comprehensive and revealing documents. Each document, in one way or another, may disclose assets you now own and which can satisfy the creditor's judgment. Some examples:

- bank and checking accounts (savings, CDs, checking, money market)

- motor vehicle titles (car, boat, plane)

- promissory notes owed to you

- deeds to real estate

- receipts for property now held by third parties

- insurance policies and special riders

- patents, copyrights, trademarks

- royalty contracts

- bills of sale to personal property

- federal and state tax returns for the prior five years

- applications for credit within the prior five years

- leases to you as a landlord

- trusts to which you are either a grantor, trustee or beneficiary

- Keoghs, IRAs, pensions and other retirement plans

- bankruptcy petitions within the preceding six years

> **note** Review requested documents and other documents in your paper trail with your attorney to determine whether they must be disclosed. The paper trail with the fewest telltale papers will, of course, make it far more difficult for a creditor to find your assets.

- bills of sale or deeds on recently transferred property

- alimony or support orders

- limited partnership documents

- lawsuit documents, whether as plaintiff or defendant

- occupational licenses

- business records

Other documents may be requested; however, the above are those usually most closely reviewed. .

Don't overlook insurance policies

Smart judgment creditors obtain insurance policies. Why? They detail specifically listed and insured valuable assets. Do your insurance policies reveal that you own:

- art?

- antiques?

- musical instruments?

- collectibles?

- jewelry?

Ownership of these and similar assets will be investigated because **they** can be easily moved and secreted from a creditor.

Court records expose assets

A creditor prowling for assets will also check court records for **other** lawsuits against you. Divorces or child support cases, for example, **frequently** divulge valuable financial information. Domestic disputes typically **involve** property issues, requiring the parties to detail their assets, liabilities **and** income. Even an uncontested divorce will require each spouse to file a **verified** and detailed financial statement. Recently divorced? What do the court records reveal about your fiscal affairs?

Other civil actions, while less revealing, may still disclose important financial information. A prior case, for instance, may reveal hidden property or what prior examinations by other creditors, seeking to collect on their judgments, have discovered. This information can greatly assist a **current** creditor.

Does a recent court case reveal your assets? Request the court to seal your file from curious eyes.

Most court records are open to the public and can be freely **inspected**. While creditors cannot remove court documents from the courthouse, **they** can usually be reviewed and copied, except when the case record **and its** documents are sealed by the court.

Bury wealth in bearer investments

An increasingly popular way to privatize wealth is to convert titled **assets** such as real estate or registered stocks and bonds into bearer **investments**. Gold, diamonds, art, stamp collections, coins or other collectibles are **a few** options. You gain more secrecy and asset protection because bearer assets can be easily transported and are completely confidential with ownership frequently anonymous. For even greater privacy, buy and sell collectibles through a third party. Your own private corporation, offshore bank or trust are possible third parties.

Huge fortunes in gold or diamonds, which occupy little space, are easily transported with you and are easily reconverted to cash; all with complete confidentiality and privacy. The one big drawback? Lost or stolen collectibles or bearer investments are forever gone. Insurance is expensive and a give-away that you own such assets. This problem can be partly solved by having these assets owned by a corporation or other entity that can conceal your ownership.

Bearer investments are not only a simple way to privatize wealth, but when purchased wisely they are excellent investments.

Diamonds, gold, art, coins and stamps can, however, dramatically increase or decrease in price. You can also lose money with these investments unless you intelligently invest.

Your best option may be gold bullion or coins stored in an offshore safe deposit box registered to an offshore corporation. Keep buy-sell transactions below several hundred dollars because coin and gold dealers must report suspicious transactions to the federal government. So you should avoid large or unusual deals.

Pay cash for your safe deposit box to avoid the paper trail between you and your safe deposit box containing the collectibles.

Warehouse certificates for precious metals safely stored in Swiss or Austrian banks are also good investments. Swiss certificates are registered to the buyer who is usually a corporate or trust intermediary. Swiss certificates have a steady market and are available through several Zurich precious metals wholesalers. As the certificate holder you can always demand delivery of your precious metals to guarantee liquidity.

What percentage of your assets should you invest in bearer collectibles? The answer, of course, depends upon both your investment savvy and your need for financial privacy. If you are confident you can profitably trade and are not risk-adverse, then invest more. On the other hand, if you are inexperienced with collectibles, then you need a professional to invest for you, or you should ignore collectibles as an asset protection option. In the hands of the uninitiated, they are even less safe than if exposed to creditors.

Thirteen steps to financial privacy

To build stronger financial privacy and greater asset protection, faithfully follow these thirteen essential strategies:

1) Never disclose your social security number unless it is absolutely vital. No law requires disclosure although no U.S. bank will open an account for you, nor employer hire you, without one. And the IRS closely investigates taxpayers without a valid social security number.

2) Use a corporation or another entity for more-sensitive transactions. For multiple transactions use several companies.

3) Avoid excessive or unnecessary checking account transactions. Cash, money orders or credit cards are safer because they create a less visible paper trail.

4) Be cautious when investing offshore. Observe all currency reporting laws and other mandatory reports.

5) Limit the financial information you disclose on credit, bank or brokerage applications. Provide only essential information.

6) Increase the bearer transactions that are not reportable under your name.

7) Hire only accountants, financial planners and investment advisors who can and will hold your financial information confidential. They also should agree to notify you upon any request or subpoena for financial or other information about you.

8) Have your accountant work through your lawyer to insure confidentiality, and use a post office box or mail drop to obtain more confidential legal or financial correspondence.

9) To gain even more privacy, use a Nevada or Wyoming corporation. Nevada and Wyoming corporations offer more privacy than do other U.S. corporations—including Delaware. Offshore companies in privacy havens are considerably more secretive.

10) Use private vaults, not bank safe deposit boxes, for your cash and valuables.

11) Prepare living trusts to bequeath property. You avoid probate and its inevitable financial disclosures and publicity.

12) Borrow only from lenders who demand the least amount of information about you.

13) Deploy assets and structure investments to legitimately provide less detailed financial information on your tax returns.

Planning Pointers

◆ Never consider secrecy or concealment of assets as a way to protect assets from creditors. Eventually you will be forced to testify under oath, and to deny or conceal ownership is committing the crime of perjury.

◆ There is little opportunity to keep assets private within the United States. Through sophisticated computer searches an asset investigation firm can uncover most assets with little difficulty. Privacy can be obtained offshore; however, a creditor can probably trace the expatriation of funds from the U.S. to a privacy haven.

◆ You need not voluntarily disclose assets until a creditor obtains judgment and is entitled to collect. Two exceptions: a) when a plaintiff sues for punitive damages, the discovery of assets and income is relevant to an appropriate award, and b) when the litigation involves allegations of conversion or fraudulent conveyance and the discovery centers on those assets.

◆ When your assets are well protected, it may be worthwhile to voluntarily disclose your assets and how they are titled either before or during litigation for purposes of discouraging the litigation.

◆ Creditors entitled to discover assets have wide discretion in the questions used to examine debtors, as well as the procedures used to discover assets.

◆ The spouse of a defendant can be forced to disclose her finances to a judgment creditor even when she is not involved in the litigation.

◆ Loan applications and insurance policies can both disclose assets.

◆ There are many ways to limit your paper trail and make it more difficult for a creditor to find assets. Privacy in the ownership of assets can discourage litigation when you appear to have fewer assets, but it is not as important once the creditor has the right to collect.

Laws that shield assets

Chapter 4

Laws that shield assets

What you'll find in this chapter:

▪▶ Protecting your homestead

▪▶ Protecting your paycheck

▪▶ Protecting your pension

▪▶ Protecting annuities and insurance

▪▶ Protecting proceeds from exempt property

Your wealth may already be partly or fully protected by an array of federal or state laws that automatically shelter certain assets from creditors. Federal and state creditor exemption laws are specifically designed to ensure basic financial security, and, most commonly, partly or fully protect retirement funds, annuities, insurance, wages and home equity.

To gain maximum advantage from these laws, first understand the assets protected in your state, and then how to shelter as much of your property as possible under their protective umbrella.

Will homestead laws protect your home?

Forty-five states feature so-called homestead laws. The laws fully or partly shelter the family home from creditors. Homestead exemptions usually extend only to real estate owned and occupied as the debtor's principal residence; however, the property eligible for homestead protection is not always clear. Some states, for instance, limit homestead protection to single-family residences and exclude duplexes, triplexes or apartment buildings where only

CAUTION

---

one unit is debtor occupied. When the debtor's personal residence cannot be legally segregated from the remaining building, the entire property may be homestead disqualified. If you own a multifamily residence, check this point carefully.

> **E-Z TIP**
>
> Homestead protection can even apply to mobile homes or boats when used as a permanent residence. This will also vary among states and must be carefully checked. You may also lose homestead if you title your home in another entity, such as a living trust.

Homestead protection generally extends to condominiums, as a condominium is considered property legally independent of other real estate. Ownership in a cooperatively owned building may not always qualify for homestead protection because the debtor does not own real estate, but only shares in a corporation that owns the building, coupled with exclusive rights to occupy a specific apartment. New York cooperatives are popular and are homestead protected under New York law.

Because homestead laws can be unclear, never assume that your home is protected. Also remember that five states provide their homeowners absolutely no homestead protection, leaving the entire equity in the family home vulnerable to creditors. Most states protect only nominal equity—$10,000 or less—and thus have negligible value as asset protectors.

How to correctly claim homestead protection

 The requirements to claim homestead protection also vary. Some states specifically require filing for homestead protection in the public filing office where real estate transactions are recorded. Other states automatically grant homestead protection without a filing requirement. You need only prove the property is your primary residence if challenged by a creditor. Several states impose a residency time requirement before you can become eligible for homestead protection.

State laws also differ in who can claim the homestead protection. Several states extend homestead protection only to the head of the household, but most now allow either spouse to claim homestead protection; this is the trend.

Some states cancel all homestead protection when separately applied for by both spouses. Cross-declarations against the same property can cancel each other. Yet other states allow co-owner spouses to apportion homestead protection between their respective ownership interests. Check with the appropriate public officials in your state to ensure you properly qualify for and claimed your homestead protection.

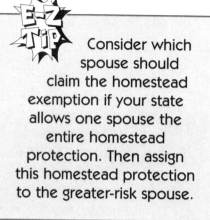

Consider which spouse should claim the homestead exemption if your state allows one spouse the entire homestead protection. Then assign this homestead protection to the greater-risk spouse.

Creditor claims stopped by homestead

Certain creditors can ignore homestead protection. Homestead laws usually protect only against debts that arise after you qualify for homestead. Earlier obligations, whether known or unknown, may not be affected by a later homestead declaration. So claim your homestead protection as soon as possible and before undertaking significant obligations.

Also, homestead protection does not block every type of claim. Homestead usually protects against private claims and lawsuits but not governmental claims. The IRS, for example, is not blocked by homestead, and delinquent taxpayers oftentimes lose their homes to the IRS because they mistakenly believed their state homestead laws would insulate them from the IRS. Certain states allow homestead protection against their own state tax claims, but most do not. Homestead protection usually does not protect against intentional or egregious wrongdoings.

note

State homestead laws cannot protect against the IRS, or other federal claims, because state homestead and other exemption laws cannot supersede federal law or federal claims.

Battery, fraud, civil theft, patent or copyright infringement, RICO claims and civil or criminal fines are common examples of unaffected creditors. Homestead does not apply to mortgage holders as this is a consensual lien. A homeowner may also waive his homestead protection.

Equity that homestead protects

note

Homestead laws seldom provide complete or even adequate creditor protection. The homestead laws, in all states but Texas and Florida, cover only a limited equity. Most states typically protect an amount between $10,000 and $40,000. Example: If your state homestead protects $40,000 in equity, and your home is worth $200,000 with a $100,000 mortgage, then your equity is $100,000. Forty thousand dollars would be homestead protected and $60,000 would remain creditor exposed. If your state offered a $100,000 homestead protection, your entire equity would then be protected.

> *note*
>
> Texas and Florida are the most protective states and shelter an unlimited equity. File bankruptcy in Texas or Florida and you can keep your home regardless of its value.

Several states limit homestead to residences below a specified acreage. Texas protects residences under 200 rural acres, regardless of value. Additional land is unprotected, as is urban property over one acre. In Florida, your residence is generally protected up to 160 acres if outside a municipality and up to one-half of an acre if within a municipality.

Debtor relocations to Texas or Florida have historically been controversial asset protection strategies as assets reinvested in homes in these states thus become fully protected. This remains true in Texas, but not always in Florida.

Since other states are less liberal than Texas and Florida, you must know how much equity is protected under your state homestead laws. If your state has a very limited homestead exemption, leaving substantial equity exposed, then you must protect your home through additional steps.

This nine-point test can help you decide whether your state's homestead law adequately protects your home:

1) Does your state offer homestead protection?

2) Does your residence qualify for homestead?

3) Can you establish this property as your primary residence entitled to homestead protection?

4) Have you properly applied for homestead protection?

5) Where possible, is the homestead protection directed to the greater-risk spouse?

6) Do mortgages against your residence, plus the homestead exemption, equal or exceed the value of your home, or is substantial equity still exposed?

7) Were your debts incurred before or after you claimed homestead and are these debts covered under homestead?

8) Will homestead protect a future equity build-up?

9) Will homestead allow you to sell or refinance your home against a judgment creditor, or will the recorded judgment cloud your title and prevent a sale or refinancing?

Four common homestead problems

1) One problem is that your homestead exemption will not adequately protect your equity. A $10,000 or $20,000 homestead protection is usually meaningless with today's expensive home.

2) Homestead exemptions do not protect against IRS claims, pre-existing debts, divorce, intentional torts or other liabilities, and these may be immediate concerns.

3) Homestead may create troublesome title problems for its negligible benefits. A complex legal process may be required to even temporarily void homestead to refinance property. Homestead technicalities, even when not overly burdensome, can nevertheless still be very inconvenient.

4) Homestead may give you false security. While homestead may protect your home today, it may not protect your home tomorrow when you have more equity or claims that it does not protect against.

Consider this last point on a home presently worth $200,000, with a $100,000 mortgage and $100,000 homestead exemption. The combined mortgage and homestead exemption will presently safeguard your home from creditors, but will it in the future? In several years, the home may be worth $250,000 while the mortgage is reduced to $75,000. This leaves $75,000 in equity seizable by creditors. This is the one major pitfall of homestead: You lose its protection as your home equity increases. One solution is periodic refinancing to continuously limit the exposed equity.

Another chronic problem is that a judgment creditor may cloud the title to your homesteaded home, even when there is no equity to satisfy the claim.

This clouding of title nevertheless can prevent you from selling or refinancing your property. Fortunately, homestead laws seldom allow creditors to file judgments against homesteaded property that have no seizable equity.

Don't lose your homestead protection

You can easily and inadvertently forfeit homestead protection. A creditor, for example, may prove that your homesteaded property is not your true residence. You can have only one domicile, and that is where you presently reside and intend to remain. But how can you prove a residence is your domicile and thus eligible for homestead?

- File all homestead documents and necessary affidavits of domicile in the public records.

- Through what regional IRS office do you file your federal tax returns and what address is on your tax returns?

- Where do you generally receive mail?

- What state issued your driver's license and auto registration?

- Where do you and your family live most of the time?

- Did you file for homestead property tax exemptions on your properties in Florida and certain other states where tax exemptions for residences apply?

> *note*
>
> Acquiring a second home does not automatically disqualify your present residence, as a new residence is not presumed to be your new domicile unless you move.

- Where are you registered to vote?

- What address is in your will, living will and other legal documents?

- Where do you maintain your primary bank accounts?

- Where do you presently maintain church, temple and/or civic memberships?

Other factors may be considered, but these are the most commonly considered factors by a court in a homestead dispute. Your domicile also continues until replaced.

Strategies to maximize homestead protection

There are ways to maximize homestead protection and shelter whatever home equity is possible. A $200,000 home with $50,000 in homestead protection and a $100,000 mortgage still has a $50,000 equity exposed to creditors. How can you shelter this $50,000? One possibility: Increase the mortgage from $100,000 to $150,000, which eliminates exposed equity to your creditors. You can then invest the $50,000 in other exempt assets or protect the cash proceeds following other asset protection strategies.

If you enjoy a substantial or unlimited homestead protection (as in Texas and Florida), another good strategy is to refinance or sell non-exempt assets, such as a vacation home, car or boat, and buy a home. Or you may improve your present home or reduce its mortgage. Your home remains protected by your homestead laws, while these other assets, which were exposed to creditors, would have been either sold or encumbered.

The best strategy to maximize homestead protection is usually to borrow against non-exempt assets and apply the proceeds to the homesteaded property.

Income that is protected

Welfare payments to welfare recipients are entirely protected against creditors in most states. The remaining states either partly protect or provide no protection to welfare payments, including the most common public assistance payments—*Aid to Families with Dependent Children (AFDC)*.

Most states also partly exempt other public assistance payments, such as *Aid to the Blind* and *Aid to the Elderly and Disabled*. These laws prevent creditors from garnishing payments due these debtors and also protect the proceeds received by the debtor if the debtor segregates these welfare payments from other non-exempt funds. Proceeds used to acquire non-exempt assets always lose protection.

Social Security payments and disability income cannot be seized by most creditors. Social Security is not considered a pension under the *Employee Retirement Income Security Act (ERISA)*; however, as with welfare payments, creditors can seize Social Security funds when commingled with non-exempt

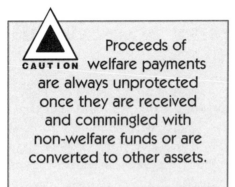

Proceeds of welfare payments are always unprotected once they are received and commingled with non-welfare funds or are converted to other assets.

funds. The IRS can seize Social Security checks.

The *Child Support Enforcement Act of 1975* rejects federal and state income exemptions concerning the enforcement of alimony or child support orders. Conversely, alimony and child support payments are generally not exempt from garnishment by creditors of either the payor or recipient. Creditor garnishments are common after divorce because divorce frequently spawns unpaid bills. Support payments have a limited exemption in several states.

Techniques to protect your paycheck

Federal and state laws protect all or part of your wages from creditors.

The federal wage exemption, established by the *Consumer Credit Protection Act (CCPA)*, states that a creditor may not garnish more than the lesser of:

1) 25 percent of your disposable weekly income, or

2) the amount by which the disposable weekly earnings exceeds 30 times the current federal minimum wage.

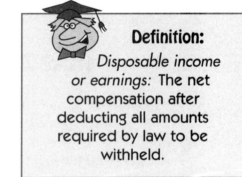

Definition:
Disposable income or earnings: The net compensation after deducting all amounts required by law to be withheld.

Because the Consumer Credit Protection Act is a federal law, it supersedes state laws which may allow more income to be garnished. However, your state may have more protective garnishment laws and this further restricts creditor garnishment of wages. Florida and Texas, the two most protective states, prohibit any wage garnishment against the head of the household. Other states are also very protective. New York, for example, protects 90 percent of wages and California, 75 percent.

Creditors can seize exempt or protected income once it is received. One temporary solution may be to form a corporation and deposit the income directly into the corporation. For tax purposes you may treat this as a loan.

This simple strategy can temporarily shield wages from less-determined creditors, but it is seldom the long-term solution.

Another wage protection strategy is to make a wage assignment to a more friendly creditor who will periodically loan you money. The wage assignment must be in writing and in effect before the creditor garnishment.

How safe is your pension?

Before 1992 there was considerable confusion surrounding the safety of pensions and profit-sharing plans. The U.S. Supreme Court in Patterson v. Shumate, clarified the situation.

> **note**
> To find out whether your pension and profit-sharing plan are qualified under ERISA, and thus protected, ask your plan administrator. Even when your retirement plans are protected, their proceeds are unprotected when commingled with other funds.

Summarily, this landmark case established ERISA-qualified pension and profit-sharing plans as fully protected against all creditors except the IRS and probably other federal agencies. Pension and profit-sharing plans that are not ERISA-qualified are creditor-protected only to the extent state laws protect such plans. This is generally the same as the protection for IRAs and Keoghs.

Protecting IRAs, Keoughs and other non-ERISA retirement accounts

IRAs and Keoghs are less protected than are ERISA-qualified pension and profit-sharing plans. Courts reason that since the debtor can withdraw IRA and Keogh account funds (with a tax penalty), creditors have the same rights.

Other courts allow creditor recourse to IRAs and Keoghs on the question of whether the plan was voluntary or involuntary. Where an employee voluntarily enrolls in an IRA it can be seized by creditors. Employees required to contribute to the IRA as a condition of employment are generally creditor-sheltered.

California, Texas and Florida fully protect IRAs and Keoghs from all creditors except the IRS. All other states only partly exempt IRAs, SEP-IRAs and

Keoghs from creditors. Some states set a statutory protected limit. For instance, $5,000 to $10,000 may be immune; excess accumulations beyond that are vulnerable.

Most states provide only discretionary protection. The court determines that portion of your IRA or Keogh that is reasonably needed for your retirement. Your age, other assets, future earnings and other income sources are a few factors the court will consider. While the amount needed for your retirement is protected (again, except from the IRS), excessive accounts are unprotected.

note Substantial IRAs and Keoghs are as vulnerable as savings. You must then shelter non-ERISA retirement accounts before creditor seizure. Incurring an IRS penalty for early withdrawal may be preferable to losing your entire retirement fund to the creditor.

Annuities and insurance may be your safest investment

Annuities and insurance can be the simplest way to shelter investments from creditors. Most states partly protect insurance from creditors. Life insurance offers more than security. It can also be an excellent investment. Many life insurance policies are now purchased primarily as good investments. While insurance is partly exempt in most states, and probably will remain protected, these states vary considerably in their protection of insurance and annuities.

note Insurance exemptions were known since 1841 and exist to protect dependents of the insured and safeguard their financial stability without state support.

Florida and Texas totally exempt insurance and annuities from creditors. Other states limit their exemption. Protected amounts may apply to each policy or to aggregate policies. With limits applied on a per policy basis, you should spread your insurance over several policies so no one policy exceeds the protected amount.

Insurance exemptions apply universally to policy proceeds payable upon the insured's death. However, some states extend their exemption to the policy's cash surrender value. If your policies have a substantial cash value, check your state laws. Borrow against any exposed cash value before creditor seizure.

There's another excellent solution if your state exemptions do not adequately protect your present investments. Invest in Swiss annuities. You automatically receive full creditor protection. You must own the annuity for at least one year. Swiss annuities also make excellent investments.

How to shelter proceeds of exempt property

How can you protect the proceeds of exempt property from creditors? Example: You sold your homesteaded home and now want to shelter the proceeds.

One excellent strategy is to directly transfer the funds from one exempt asset to another. For example, you may assign proceeds from your homesteaded home to an exempt annuity, to your creditor-free spouse, or to another safe harbor, such as a limited partnership or trust.

> **note** Swiss law protects Swiss annuities against all creditor claims (including divorce, the IRS and bankruptcy), provided your spouse or descendants are beneficiaries, or a third party is an irrevocable beneficiary.

When a judgment creditor patiently waits for you to cash-out, use surprise. You may also mortgage the protected property and invest the proceeds into another exempt asset or some other safe harbor.

Most states automatically protect proceeds from the sale or refinancing of an exempt asset either for a specified time period or for a reasonable time. This protection remains only if the funds are segregated and do not lose their source identity.

You would then become vulnerable to a judgment creditor only during that narrow period when the funds pass from the exempt asset to another shelter, unless you directly assign these funds to your new shelter within the time period the proceeds remain protected. They are then safe continuously.

The one creditor state exemptions cannot protect against

State exemptions offer absolutely no protection against the most dangerous creditor—the U.S. government. The IRS and other federal claimants,

> *note* State laws that partly or fully shelter annuities, insurance, wages, IRAs, Keoghs and other exempt assets are worthless protectors against the IRS and other federal agencies.

including the SEC, FTC and *Health Care Financing Administration (HCFA)*, completely ignore state laws that protect assets. For instance, the IRS can seize a home in Texas or Florida, notwithstanding state homestead laws that fully protect homes from creditors. The only assets protected against the IRS are those specifically exempt under the IRS code, listed in chapter 12.

Planning Pointers

◆ Your home may be adequately protected by homestead. Still, never assume homestead affords you total protection. You may require additional safeguards.

◆ Wages, in most states, are partially exempt. Welfare payments are totally exempt, while Social Security payments can be seized only by the IRS.

◆ IRAs and Keoghs are generally not safe from creditors; however, ERISA-qualified pension plans generally are.

◆ Insurance and annuities are ordinarily partly exempt assets, and they may also prove to be good investments. They can be a wise investment alternative to stocks, bonds and savings that are all protected.

◆ In asset protection planning, a primary step is to convert as many non-exempt assets as possible into exempt assets.

◆ Proceeds from the sale or liquidation of an exempt asset should be directly transferred into another exempt asset, or an entity that provides creditor protection.

Wealth-saving strategies with co-ownership

5

Chapter 5

Wealth saving strategies with co-ownership

What you'll find in this chapter:

➠ Tenancy-in-common is not your best choice

➠ Why joint tenancy may not be right for you

➠ How tenancy by-the-entirety can protect you

➠ The problem with joint bank accounts

➠ The problem with community property

Assets are commonly owned by multiple parties. Joint ownership is particularly common among spouses, whether for titling the family home, bank accounts, shares in family-owned businesses, investments or artworks, collectibles, boats and autos. Co-ownership is also common between other family members. For example, a widowed mother may jointly title her assets with a daughter to avoid probate upon the mother's death. But we also see co-ownership arrangements between very sophisticated corporations.

Co-owning property is an important asset protection strategy. However, incorrectly co-owning property will present greater dangers than owning the property outright or through an entity. The two most important questions when considering co-ownership are:

1) Will co-ownership expand your liability (can you more readily lose your share of the co-owned assets to creditors?

2) Will co-ownership give you the needed protection?

Converting individually owned property outright into assets co-owned with others, most likely your spouse, may be the simplest way to shelter these assets since it requires little effort or cost.

Co-ownership can make sense for reasons other than asset protection. It can help you avoid probate, since jointly owned property automatically passes to the surviving joint owner. Many families protected their assets from creditors only because their home, stocks, bonds or other important assets were co-owned. Asset protection was often the unintended, but welcomed benefit.

note Co-ownership may be one of the first strategies you consider for asset protection. But, it has limitations, and stronger asset protection measures are usually needed.

More knowledgeable individuals realize that co-ownership can also be an effective wealth insulator. Probate avoidance becomes their secondary goal; asset protection, their first!

To fully understand co-ownership strategies for asset protection, you must first understand the four common co-ownerships; their advantages, disadvantages and applications:

1) tenancy-in-common

2) joint tenancy

3) tenancy-by-the-entirety

4) community property

Each of these co-ownerships represents a different degree of creditor protection which also greatly varies by state. Factors beyond asset protection may also influence the co-ownership decision. Estate planning, taxes, the property and the relationship between prospective co-owners are only a few. A fifth co-ownership, *tenancy by partnership*, is discussed in Chapter 7.

Common dangers with tenancy-in-common

DEFINITION

When two or more parties own property together as *tenants-in-common*, each tenant (co-owner) owns a divided interest in that property. That ownership interest is a divisible or dividable interest, and each co-tenant can sell, mortgage, bequeath or dispose of his share of the property without interference or the consent of co-owners.

Since the tenant-in-common's interest in the property is separate and apart from the interests of co-owners, his creditors can reach that divisible interest in the property. The interests of co-owners remain safe from everyone but their own creditors. Tenancy-in-common features absolutely no creditor protection.

Property owned as tenancy-in-common has other hazards. For example, when you own property as a tenant-in-common, your co-owner's creditors can petition the court for permission to sell the entire property through a forced liquidation of your co-owner's interest. You would no longer own a share of the property and instead receive proceeds from the sale that represent your interest. You may always negotiate the purchase of your co-owner's interest from his creditor, but that is not always possible, practical or desirable. Moreover, if the creditor (or any buyer of the debtor's interest in the property) did not want to sell his newly gained interest in the property, you may then end up with a stranger as your new co-owner.

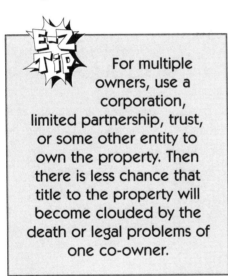

For multiple owners, use a corporation, limited partnership, trust, or some other entity to own the property. Then there is less chance that title to the property will become clouded by the death or legal problems of one co-owner.

Tenancy-in-common is not limited to two individuals. There can be many co-owners with each owning a different share of the property, although it is unwieldy to use tenancy-in-common with more than three or four co-owners.

Your options as co-owner under a tenancy-in-common encountering financial problems are varied. One option is to transfer your interest to the other co-owner at a discount if necessary, before the property is claimed by your creditor. Once the creditor threat passes, the property can be reconveyed to the original co-owner. The purchase price must be sufficient to avoid a claim of fraudulent transfer. The debtor owner may also transfer his interest to a more protective family limited partnership, provided he received in exchange a limited partnership interest that was equivalent in value to the transferred tenancy-in-common interest. The debtor co-owner may also encumber his interest in the co-owned property before a creditor judgment.

Since property under tenancy-in-common is vulnerable to a forced liquidation to satisfy one co-owner's debts, it is important for co-owners under this tenancy to form their relationship confident that their respective finances are stable. This confidence can be misplaced. Parties with financial or legal

> **note**
> Co-owners must always warn each other against foreseeable problems so they collectively and quickly can safeguard the property and their respective interests before they are endangered by a creditor.

problems should avoid a tenancy-in-common. Even with a good financial record, later problems may jeopardize co-owned property.

A tenancy-in-common has no survivorship rights. Each co-owner's interest upon death will not pass to the surviving co-owner, but instead go to his heirs. However, this can cause still other complications since heirs seldom share the surviving co-owner's objectives with the property. A buy-out agreement between co-owners is one solution to this problem, particularly when the buy-out is funded by insurance, an arrangement more common with multi-stockholder businesses.

Joint tenancy: traps and opportunities

DEFINITION

A *joint tenancy* is created when real or personal property is equally owned by two or more parties with the express provision that title is jointly held.

Most states require the joint tenancy to be created by written agreement. Verbal agreement is insufficient. This joint tenancy acknowledgment may be stated in the deed, bill of sale, or other title documents such as a stock certificate. (Example: Mary Doe and/or Ann Smith, jointly, or as joint tenants.) The "or" indicates survivorship rights, which does not apply to a tenancy-in-common. When one joint tenant dies, the surviving tenant or tenants automatically assumes ownership of the deceased tenant's interest, even if the decedent bequeathed his interest in the property to someone else..

> **note**
> Jointly owned property avoids probate (but not estate taxes), and this is its chief advantage and reason for its popularity.

Joint tenancy grants each owner an equal and undivided interest in the property. But this joint tenancy can be terminated if either joint tenant conveys his interest. The joint tenancy then automatically ends and the remaining joint tenants become tenants-in-common with the new owner.

> **note**

How effectively does joint tenancy protect assets? A joint tenancy usually provides little protection over a tenancy-in-common. Creditors of one joint tenant can ordinarily reach his undivided interest in the property by petitioning the court to partition the property and order its sale with the proceeds divided. Several states make it impossible to partition jointly owned property if such an agreement exists between the co-owners. This agreement can be important in asset protection because it defeats the right of the creditor to liquidate the debtor-owner's interest.

Most states allow the debtor-joint tenant's interest to be reached by his creditors during his lifetime. Since each joint tenant, during this period, can freely transfer his interest, his creditors are allowed to reach that same interest to satisfy that joint tenant's debts. The creditor's forced-sale position places the creditor and his buyer in the same position as someone who buys the asset directly from the joint tenant: The joint tenancy is destroyed and the creditor or his nominee buyer becomes a tenant-in-common with other co-owners.

> *note*
> Creditor protection with a joint tenancy can vary considerably among states. So carefully check the laws in your state before you rely upon joint-tenancy as your asset protector.

Creditors generally cannot proceed against jointly owned property once the debtor-joint tenant dies because his interest automatically passes to the other co-owners, but there are four important exceptions:

1) A joint tenancy expressly established to defraud creditors can be set aside; however, a joint tenancy does not evidence fraud.

2) Unlike other debts, federal and state taxes owed by a deceased joint tenant attach to the joint interest and pass with the property of the deceased to the surviving tenant.

3) Several states grant creditors unusual rights against jointly held property. Washington State and South Dakota, for instance, allow creditors of a deceased joint owner the right to reclaim the debtor's investment contribution in the property, although such laws are rare.

4) A creditor's rights against a joint tenant also expand if that joint tenant files bankruptcy. The debtor's entire property becomes subject to bankruptcy, including jointly held property. A bankruptcy trustee may sell all property of the bankrupt co-owner, including jointly owned property. The non-bankrupt co-owners must then protect themselves by claiming their share of the sale proceeds from the property, otherwise all sales proceeds can be applied to the bankrupt's debts.

Joint tenancy is not necessary to achieve asset protection and probate avoidance. For probate avoidance alone, you can title property in a living trust or limited partnership owned by your living trust as the limited partner.

> **note** All assets, except for IRAs, Keoghs and insurance, can be jointly owned. You can also avoid probate when all assets are jointly held.

A creditor's rights against jointly held property ends with the death of the debtor. An attachment during the debtor's lifetime must be liquidated through partition and sale of the property while the debtor remains alive..The debtor's joint interest then automatically passes upon death to the surviving joint tenant, and the survivorship transfer would extinguish the attachment and creditor's rights against that interest. Should the non-debtor joint tenant die first, the creditor would gain the entire property. Survivorship works both ways. Creditors with a judgment sometimes sit on their rights while awaiting the death of the other owner in a winner-take-all, particularly in states where joint tenancy effectively protects against creditors.

How tenancy-by-the-entirety protects assets

DEFINITION

Tenancy-by-the-entirety (T/E) is a unique form of joint tenancy. It is only for a husband and wife. Tenancy-by-the-entirety originates from the theory that marriage unifies the husband and wife, and their property is thus owned by the two by the unity or entirety.

> **note** Thirty-one states allow tenancy-by-the-entirety, although their laws vary. The trend is away from this tenancy, which is considered inconsistent with modern legal transactions and the individuality of husband and wife.

With T/E titled property owned by both spouses in unity, neither the husband nor wife can singly transfer their interest in the property, which is possible with other tenancies. The death of either spouse awards the surviving spouse the entire property. In that respect, a tenancy-by-the-entirety is similar to joint tenancy. The tenancy-by-the-entirety remains until the husband and wife simultaneously transfer the property, they divorce, or one spouse dies.

How effectively can tenancy-by-the-entirety protect assets from creditors? The answer will depend on whether state law treats a tenancy-by-the-entirety differently from regular joint tenancies.

Some states consider the two tenancies the same. A creditor of one spouse can reach the debtor spouse's interest, force the sale of the property and obtain proceeds due that spouse. These few states comparably protect the three tenancies—tenancy-in-common, joint tenancy, and tenancy-by-the-entirety. If you live in one of these states, then titling marital property as tenants-by-the-entirety provides no protection.

Most other states virtually immunize T/E property from creditors of one spouse, but not creditors common to both spouses. Other states protect only certain assets, such as the family home, and others partially protect property. For example, Massachusetts protects the family home from the creditors of one spouse while the other spouse resides there, but not thereafter. Florida, a state with strong tenancy-by-the-entirety laws, protects not only the T/E titled marital home, but also other assets. Real estate and other property, such as bank accounts, stocks, bonds, cars and boats, can all be sheltered through tenancy-by-the-entirety.

One feature of a tenancy-by-the-entirety is that it commonly applies only to the marital home. Second, its creditor protection cannot outlast your marriage. When either your marriage ends through divorce or death, so does the tenancy and its protection. If the non-debtor spouse predeceases the debtor spouse, the protected assets immediately vest with the debtor spouse and become exposed to his creditors. For instance, a husband with a judgment can protect the marital home titled as tenancy-by-the-entirety from his creditor. Upon his death, his interest in the home automatically passes to his wife free of the creditor claim against the husband. However, if the wife died first, the husband's creditor can claim the entire home now fully titled with the debtor spouse. Chances a husband will predecease his wife are about four to one, so it may be a worthwhile gamble to rely upon tenancy-by-the-entirety when the husband has the greater exposure.

note States with tenancy-by-the-entirety laws provide creditors a patchwork of rights. Because tenancy-by-the-entirety laws vary considerably among the states, we cannot generalize their adequacy to protect. You must review this one question with your lawyer.

note   A bankruptcy trustee can usually force a sale should one spouse under a tenancy-by-the-entirety go bankrupt. The non-bankrupt spouse could recover his share of the proceeds, which does not protect whatever equity the bankrupt spouse may have in the property. However, state homestead laws or bankruptcy exemptions may partly or fully shelter this equity.

Tenancy-by-the-entirety protects only against creditors of one spouse. When both spouses are indebted to the same creditor, that creditor can recover property held in the entirety.

A surviving spouse's rights to the entire property upon the death of the other spouse is standard with the tenancy-by-the-entirety. All property under tenancy-by-the-entirety also avoids probate where the deceased

> **E-Z TIP**
> Except for mortgages, spouses should avoid joint obligations, and particularly large business debts. Joint obligations significantly increase the risk of losing marital property to creditors.

note   spouse's creditors must file claims. Vested with full title to the property, the surviving spouse can dispose of the property free of claims against the deceased spouse. Should both spouses die simultaneously, the property would be equally distributed between the husband and wife's estates as it would under tenancy-in-common.

The more powerful IRS cannot as easily be stopped by titling assets as tenants-by-the-entirety. If only one spouse owes the IRS, the property may be

> *note*   Property should expressly state whether it is titled as tenancy-by-the-entirety, or it may be considered a less protective joint tenancy.

partly protected, although a tax lien against one spouse will cloud the property's title. At least one circuit court has allowed the IRS to seize T/E property where only one spouse was a tax delinquent. Protecting property through other devices is recommended where divorce or death of a spouse is foreseeable—if the spouses share common creditors or protection is otherwise questionable.

Joint tenancy and tenancy-by-the-entirety are quite similar except for three important differences:

1) *Tenancy-by-the-entirety can only be between husband and wife.* Unmarried persons may title property jointly or as tenants-in-common. Married couples mostly elect tenancy-by-the-entirety in states where it broadens or completely protects against creditors.

2) *One joint tenant can terminate the joint tenancy* by transferring his interest. Tenancy-by-the-entirety property must be transferred simultaneously by both spouses.

3) *Some states allow a tenancy-by-the-entirety only for real estate*, perhaps only the home, and no other property. Joint tenancy can apply to any property.

Avoid joint bank accounts

How safe are joint bank accounts? This is an important question considering their popularity between spouses, family members and even unrelated parties who live or conduct business together using joint accounts.

Whether creditors of one joint tenant to the bank account can seize all or part of such an account to satisfy the debt rests chiefly upon state law.

A creditor of one joint tenant can usually reach the entire bank account because the creditor's rights to the funds match those of the debtor-joint tenant. Since the debtor-joint tenant can withdraw the entire account, so can his creditor. A joint bank account then becomes dangerous since it is fully jeopardized for the debts of one party. Several states limit creditors of one joint tenant to debtor's fractional share of the bank account, a position that at least coincides with the rights of real estate creditors who risk only the interest of the debtor-joint tenant.

note The risks associated with jointly held properties are not limited to bank accounts. What we say about bank accounts generally applies to such other jointly held property as stocks and bonds, collectibles, autos and boats.

 The Internal Revenue Service is the creditor of greatest concern. Only the IRS can levy a bank without court approval. The IRS requires only notice of intent to levy, after which it can seize the entire joint account. As policy, the IRS will return no more than half the funds to the uninvolved party upon proof that individual contributed at least half the funds to the account.

There are many other ways to lose jointly titled funds. You may, for example, share a joint bank account with your married son. Upon your death, the account avoids probate and automatically passes to your son. But should your son divorce, the wife may freeze the account until the divorce is finalized and the account may be awarded your daughter-in-law. A lawsuit will similarly jeopardize the account.

There is also increased liability with jointly owned property. An auto is an example where both spouses become liable if the auto is involved in an accident. *Avoid expanded liability.* Do not jointly own vehicles and other assets that can create liability. Instead title these assets to the spouse with the fewest assets, or some other entity, such as a corporation, limited liability company or limited partnership.

Co-ownerships avoid probate

Both joint tenancy and tenancy-by-the-entirety conveniently allow a husband and wife to avoid probate. However, there are safer ways to avoid probate. A living trust is one example because a living trust keeps assets safe from creditors of the other higher-risk spouse, except in certain community property states.

There can also be adverse tax consequences when you transfer property through rights of survivorship. Taxes may be eliminated or reduced through more creative trusts. A joint tenancy or T/E may also conflict with how you wish to bequeath your assets. An example is when you have children from a prior marriage to whom you want to leave assets. When you own property jointly with your second spouse, that property will automatically pass to that spouse upon your death, and eventually to his or her family. You may alternatively want to leave property to your new spouse under a life estate. Upon his or her death the assets then pass to your children. Joint ownership defeats such estate planning.

> *note*
>
> Whether joint tenancy is advantageous or disadvantageous can only be determined through a professional evaluation of your financial situation, your state laws, and your wealth-transfer objectives.

You cannot simply assume co-ownerships are always advantageous, whether for estate planning or asset protection. Often it is disadvantageous while other strategies would more effectively produce the right results.

Protecting community property

Nine states have community property laws: Arizona, California, Idaho, Nevada, New Mexico, Louisiana, Texas, Washington and Wisconsin. Originating from Spanish law (which explains their prevalence in southwestern states), community property laws have changed over time and there are now notable creditor protection differences among these states.

DEFINITION

Community property law is best understood by contrasting it with the law in *non-community property states*. In non-community property states, if the husband owes an obligation, his property can be seized to satisfy his obligation. Conversely, the wife can lose her assets to satisfy only her debts. If the husband and wife are both liable, the property of either or both spouses can be seized by the creditor. In sum, because two defendants are married neither affects the liability for their respective debts nor limits the property that may be seized by creditors.

note

Unlike non-community property states, marital status becomes key in community property states for determining both the liability for obligations and the property that may be seized by the creditor to satisfy those debts. In community property states, you determine a creditor's rights by answering three questions:

1)   Did the debt arise before the marriage, during the marriage, or after the marriage ended?

2)   Is it a debt of one spouse (a separate debt) or a community debt for which both spouses are liable?

3)   . Is the creditor seeking to claim separate property (property of one spouse) or community property (property of both spouses)? If it is community property, does the creditor claim rights to the entire property or only the interest of the debtor spouse?

DEFINITION

Debts incurred prior to marriage remain separate obligations of that spouse, as do debts incurred after the marriage terminates. *Community obligations* are those incurred during the marriage. Obligations are considered a *community debt* if they in some way benefitted the community, or both spouses, although not necessarily equally.

In most community property states, a creditor's right to claim marital (or community) property is not determined by its purpose nor whether a spouse contracts for himself or for both spouses. In either instance, the creditor can seize marital property. This is untrue in California, Idaho and Texas, the three community property states that do not distinguish between community debts and separate debts. You can see the importance of knowing the laws of your community property state.

The next question concerns the property targeted by the creditor. Property each spouse owned prior to the marriage continues as separate property after marriage. Gifts, bequests and inheritances made to one spouse during marriage becomes community property, as do earnings of a spouse during marriage. Certain community property states exempt earnings from the spouse's creditors.

note

Commingling separate assets during marriage confuses the assets' source identity and also makes them community property

What then are the rights of creditors? Creditors owed separate debts from one spouse can claim that spouse's separate property. Community property cannot usually be claimed to satisfy one spouse's separate debt. Since no single spouse can convert community property to separate property, a creditor has no greater right to partition and seize community property. Conversely, and except for contracts for necessities, neither spouse can jeopardize the separate property of a non-contracting spouse. Judgment creditors who hold other claims (negligence, etc.) can usually only claim separate property of the liable spouse, not community property. The asset protection features of community property laws are thus summarized:

• Property you own before you marry is exposed to your own creditors during your marriage because it remains separate property. These assets require protection. Prepare separate property agreements so there is no question as to which assets will not be subject to community property claims, whether in divorce or from creditors.

• Community property acquired during the marriage usually remains safe from creditors of each individual spouse. Community property is not safe from creditors with claims against both spouses. Re-title and further protect property where both spouses undertake joint obligations. When debts are not joint, community property laws usually offer adequate protection.

• Creditors may successfully claim that debts benefitted both spouses and can thus seize community property.

• Certain creditors, such as the IRS and other federal agencies, routinely seize community property even when it is the debt of only one spouse and was incurred before the marriage.

More reasons to avoid joint ownership

Aside from the reality that it offers questionable asset protection, there are several other disadvantages of joint ownership:

• Upon the death of one co-owner, the IRS may calculate the entire value of the jointly owned property for estate tax purposes unless the surviving co-tenant can prove his contribution. This rule applies only to non-spouses.

• Co-owners can seldom transfer their interests without the consent from the other co-owner. This may prevent the timely transfer of property, whether for asset protection, estate planning or other purposes.

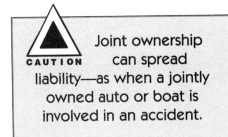 **CAUTION** Joint ownership can spread liability—as when a jointly owned auto or boat is involved in an accident.

• The death of one co-owner can impede the other owner's use of the asset. Jointly owned bank accounts, for instance, are then usually frozen.

Planning Pointers

◆ Co-ownership of assets may protect assets or expand liability and the potential loss of property—depending upon the asset, type of co-ownership, and state law.

◆ Tenancy-in-common offers no asset protection and when one co-owner has creditors, it can disrupt the tenancy and force the sale of the co-owned asset.

◆ Jointly owned property automatically bequeaths the interest of a deceased co-owner to the other co-owners, and this can avoid probate but not estate taxes.

◆ Jointly owned property is generally not protected from creditors of a co-owner, although it may, in some states, be procedurally difficult for the creditor to seize the interest.

◆ Tenants-in-the-entirety, in effect in 31 states, is a joint tenancy between husband and wife. Property so titled enjoys some immunity from the creditors of any one spouse, with the degree of protection defined by state law.

◆ Two limitations of tenancy-by-the-entirety are that its protection terminates upon divorce or death of either spouse, and it may not protect against IRS claims.

◆ Community property can be seized by creditors whose claim arose after the marriage. The husband's and wife's separate property before marriage can be claimed only by their respective creditors. Community property is not considered well-protected and stronger protection is usually required.

◆ Joint bank accounts and joint ownership of other assets are particularly dangerous as a creditor of either joint owner can possibly assert claim to the entire asset, notwithstanding the relative contribution of either co-tenant.

Trusts that protect assets

6

Chapter 6

Trusts that protect assets

What you'll find in this chapter:

⟹ The disadvantages of revocable trusts

⟹ Why living trusts may be right for you

⟹ When you need a spendthrift trust

⟹ How to use an insurance trust

⟹ Advantages of special trusts

Trusts come in a wide variety and are used for many purposes. Some trusts keep assets private and out of the probate court. Others hold property for minors or incompetent adults. Others reduce or eliminate taxes. Trusts can also protect assets against litigation, creditors, divorce or other claims. These latter trusts we will discuss in this chapter.

Understanding basic trust law

DEFINITION

A trust is an easy legal concept to understand. Trusts are created by a *settlor, grantor* or *trustor* (the terms are interchangeable) who provides the funds or other property to be held in trust. As trust creator, the grantor also establishes the terms under which the donated assets shall be managed and eventually distributed.

The grantor names a trustee(s)—in some cases, this is the grantor—and the beneficiaries who are to receive the benefit of the trust and eventually its assets. The grantor also may simultaneously be both the trustee and beneficiary. This is common with the popular living trust. However, this arrangement is not acceptable for asset protection trusts where the grantor must be neither the trustee nor sole beneficiary.

DEFINITION

Trusts can also be classified—a *living trust*, for example, as implied by its name, is set up during the grantor's lifetime. It is often called an *inter vivos trust*. Trusts that become activated upon death are called testamentary trusts.

DEFINITION

Trusts can also be classified as revocable or irrevocable. A *revocable trust* can be changed or revoked by the grantor. An *irrevocable trust* cannot. Trusts can also be domestic or U.S.-based or can be established in a foreign country. This chapter explores the various domestic or U.S.-based trusts for asset protection.

How to create a creditor-proof trust

The irrevocable trust is the only trust useful for asset protection. For maximum safety, the transfer of assets into the trust must also be made under circumstances when it cannot be set aside as a fraudulent conveyance, as this defeats asset protection.

note

The irrevocable trust, as its name suggests, cannot be revoked or rescinded by the grantor. Once you establish and fund the trust, you forever abandon your rights to reclaim your property.

CAUTION Upon the transfer of assets to an irrevocable trust, you lose both control and ownership of the property. These, of course, are serious considerations before you establish an irrevocable trust.

Because the irrevocable trust deprives you of control, you also lose the right to receive income from the trust and the right to sell or dispose of trust property. For these reasons, you should consider an irrevocable trust only when you have sufficient additional assets or independent sources of income for financial security after your assets are entrusted. Be objective. Carefully analyze your needs and resources beforehand.

An irrevocable trust, like a revocable trust, can own any property, but should only hold property that adds value to the trust. The trustee's management decisions must follow the prudent investor rule and also be guided by the investment objectives stated in the trust. You can safely make an outright gift of property to the trust, or sell assets to the trust if it has accumulated sufficient assets to pay you. But to be effective as an asset protector, the irrevocable trust must be correctly organized and operated following these criteria:

• The grantor cannot reserve any power to revoke, rescind or amend the trust. The trust should explicitly provide that it cannot be rescinded, amended or revoked by the grantor.

• The grantor can retain no rights, either directly or indirectly, to reclaim property transferred to the trust. All conveyances to the trust must be absolute and unconditional.

> *note* The more controlling your authority, the greater the likelihood that creditors can reach the trust assets. Conversely, with less control, creditors can less successfully attack the trust.

• The grantor cannot assert any authority on how the property will be managed or invested, or whether trust property should be sold or retained. These decisions must belong exclusively to the trustee.

• The grantor cannot assert authority over income generated from the trust, or how income is to be distributed, except as initially provided in the trust.

• The grantor cannot serve as trustee, nor appoint as trustee someone who is not arms-length to the grantor. Courts closely examine relationships between grantor and trustee to determine whether the trustee is the grantor's alter ego.

In sum, the protection your trust provides depends on the extent to which you relinquish control..

Two trust disadvantages

There are two obvious dangers with trusts for asset protection:

1) *The grantor must permanently relinquish all control over trust assets.* Few people will forgo control over their entire estate. They naturally seek less draconian ways to protect their assets. The limited partnership, for instance, is very popular because it provides superior asset protection over most domestic trusts, while allowing continued control over assets in the general partnership.

2) *Transfers to an irrevocable trust protect the trust assets only from future creditors.* Present creditors, whether known or unknown, can recover transfers to the trust as a fraudulent transfer. A grantor considering transfers to a domestic irrevocable trust should do so only when certain that there are no present creditors.

For these two important reasons, the domestic trust is usually not ideal for achieving asset protection objectives. Trusts should be used when they achieve some other important purpose. Asset protection should be a secondary objective.

Why revocable trusts give no protection

A revocable trust, or *nominee trust* as it is often called, is the more common trust because it is revocable and allows the grantor the comfort of changing his mind. Such trusts can be useful for estate and tax planning purposes, but a revocable trust is unsuitable for asset protection. The grantor's creditors can generally reach assets transferred to the revocable trust as easily as assets titled to the grantor.

A grantor who reserves the right to revoke the trust also reserves the power to take property back from the trust. The grantor's creditors stand in the grantor's position and can compel the grantor to re-transfer trust assets for their own benefit.

The precise rights of a grantor's creditors to property in a revocable trust differs some among states. In most states, the rights of a creditor depend upon whether the grantor retained a general power of appointment as to the remainder, coupled with a life estate. This combination of powers has been viewed by several courts as tantamount to property of the grantor.

In these states, and probably all states, it is unwise to retain both powers. Either a life estate or power of appointment standing alone may not trigger the same result. A life estate would nevertheless be an asset in bankruptcy. The life estate would then go to creditors of the debtor. The

note
Several states provide that, in the absence of a fraudulent transfer to the trust, the grantor's creditors cannot reach trust assets, notwithstanding that the grantor reserved the right to revoke the trust or claim income.

bankruptcy trustee can also claim any other interest in the trust, whether present or future, actual or contingent, that the bankrupt grantor had reserved.

If a grantor transfers assets to a revocable trust and reserves the right to revoke the trust or control the disposition of principal and interest, the grantor's creditors by common law or statute can seize assets transferred to the trust. Generally, the grantor's creditors must first seize assets in the debtor's name. When these assets cannot satisfy the claims, the creditors can seize revocable trust property.

These situations assume transfers to the trust were not fraudulent. The rights of creditors in these instances do not depend upon circumstances surrounding the transfer, but upon the powers of the grantor in respect to trust assets.

> *note* Most cases allow the grantor's creditors to reach revocable trust assets. Avoid revocable trusts if you want asset protection. The irrevocable trust is the only trust that protects you.

There are two circumstances where the revocable trust can possibly be used as an asset protector. First, when the trust shields property from an IRS lien. Property is transferred to the revocable trust before the lien is filed may not be subject to the lien. The assets, nevertheless, would be far more safely titled to an irrevocable trust or limited partnership.

A second possible use of a revocable trust offering greater safety is when you and your spouse each sets up revocable trusts and transfers to the other spouse's trust his or her property. In this situation, you no longer control your property and your creditor cannot as easily reach the assets now in your spouse's trust. This arrangement offers only marginal protection.

Advantages and disadvantages of living trusts

DEFINITION

Revocable trusts have become popular with the *living trust* (or *loving trust*). The living trust is usually nothing more than a simple revocable trust. The living trust avoids the expense, delay and notoriety of probate. It offers neither tax advantages nor disadvantages, nor significant asset protection, other than in the two instances stated earlier. An irrevocable trust can be a living trust and would be safer.

For a living trust, the grantor ordinarily names himself the income beneficiary. Upon his death, the trust assets are distributed to designated beneficiaries. However, during his lifetime, the grantor controls the trust and can freely revoke or modify the trust.

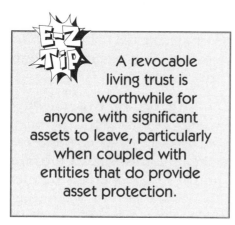

The grantor may elect to use one living trust, or several trusts, to accommodate different beneficiaries or property. The living trust may also be the beneficiary of pensions, insurance policies, Keoghs or any other cash value resources.

E-Z TIP

A revocable living trust is worthwhile for anyone with significant assets to leave, particularly when coupled with entities that do provide asset protection.

The living trust has become popular because it avoids probate. Upon the grantor's death, the trust assets pass directly to the beneficiary, which reduces the cost of administering your estate and also avoids delay in distribution and disclosure of your personal and financial affairs. This does not suggest that you can forget a will, which remains essential to dispose of assets that for one reason or another have not been transferred to the living trust. A will is also needed to name guardians for minor children.

A living trust does not reduce estate taxes, although a husband and wife can use living trusts to maximize estate tax credits. Conversely, other than for the small cost to prepare and administer, a living trust poses no disadvantages.

Millions of Americans have living trusts which, in most cases, are revocable trusts because the grantor never considered asset protection their primary objective. Others who wanted asset protection did not wish to lose control over the trust assets. One solution is to compromise with two separate living trusts, one revocable and the other irrevocable. The revocable trust holds assets you want to control. The irrevocable trust includes assets to be creditor-proofed. You will satisfy conflicting objectives with two or more trusts.

Another disadvantage of the living trust is that you lose asset protection if the trust provides less protection than how you originally titled the asset. For instance, you may lose homestead protection by titling assets as tenants-by-the-entirety.

note

The living trust is most commonly used in combination with such other asset protection structures as the limited partnership. The living trust can be the limited partner while the assets are titled to the partnership.

When you need a spendthrift trust

DEFINITION

Asset protection and spendthrift trusts are synonymous. A *spendthrift trust* insulates a beneficial interest from the creditors of the beneficiary during his lifetime. Upon the beneficiary's death, or some other specified event, that beneficial interest is distributed to second-level beneficiaries. Ordinarily, the spendthrift beneficiary only receives income from the trust during his lifetime. The amount may be specified in the trust or at the trustee's discretion.

The spendthrift trust also keeps principal intact should the beneficiary die, and thus allows the remaining principal to be gifted outright to grandchildren or an alternate beneficiary selected by the grantor.

> *note* A grantor may not be as concerned about his own child being the spendthrift who is unable to responsibly handle an inheritance, but may be concerned about the spendthrift tendencies of the child's spouse.

A spendthrift trust effectively protects the trust principal from creditors of the spendthrift because the spendthrift's creditors cannot reach the principal. Spendthrift trusts are thus ideal to fully protect inheritances for a beneficiary prone to financial difficulty.

What about the grantor's creditors? As with all other trusts, the rights of a grantor's creditor are dictated by the control the grantor retains over the trust. If the grantor can modify or revoke the spendthrift trust, then the trust assets remain exposed to the grantor's creditors.

Insurance trusts to protect insurance

The life insurance trust is another valuable weapon in the asset protection arsenal. Life insurance—both death benefits and cash value—are fully exempt from creditor attachment in several states, and nothing more need be done to protect your insurance policies in these states, except when the IRS is the creditor. Most states grant little or no protection to insurance. In all states, an insurance trust may be necessary for estate tax reasons. How can you effectively use an insurance trust?

• Borrow as much as possible against the cash value of your life insurance. Never leave the cash or surrender value of your policies exposed to creditors. Creditors in most states have a right to claim cash dividends under policies. Since no-cash policies have no value, there are no gift taxes due from their transfer to the insurance trust.

• Once the insurance policies are in trust, advance funds to the trustee to cover future premium payments.

• Decide upon the disposition of the insurance proceeds upon your death. You may designate beneficiaries under the trust as you would under an insurance policy. For example, proceeds may be paid directly to your spouse and/or children. You may prefer the funds continuously administered for their benefit under the same trust or a separate trust.

Establish an insurance trust to receive your insurance policies with your spouse or some other trusted individual as trustee. Never become trustee to your own insurance trust.

4) Insurance trusts can be either *revocable* or *irrevocable*. If the trust is revocable, you can modify it during your lifetime or you can cancel the trust and also cancel the policy at your election. You thus retain the flexibility to change the trust to coincide with new circumstances and goals. However, upon your death the trust becomes irrevocable, and the insurance proceeds automatically flow through the trust to the beneficiaries. With the irrevocable life insurance trust, you irrevocably transfer your life insurance policies to the trust. Once transferred, you lose the ability to cancel either the policies or the trust, or change or modify the terms of the trust.

The irrevocable insurance trust offers two important advantages: First, it insulates insurance policies from creditors, which is the objective with asset protection, and, secondly, it will exclude the policies from the grantor's estate under certain conditions.

To gain the added estate tax protection, the grantor must transfer the policies from his own name and live three more years following the transfer. Insurance proceeds then pass to the trust beneficiaries free of all federal and state estate and inheritance taxes. With federal estate taxes currently consuming about one-half an estate, the insurance trust preserves the entire insurance benefits for your heirs without forfeiting half—or more—to the government. The insurance trust is thus essential for anyone with a large policy and a taxable estate.

DEFINITION

An insurance trust may be either *funded* or *unfunded*. An unfunded trust has the policy either fully paid when transferred to the trust, or provisions are made for the future funding of premiums. With a funded trust, the grantor transfers to the trust both the policies and adequate income-producing assets to pay future premiums.

Sheltering assets for a charity

One of the more effective asset protection strategies is to donate property to your favorite charity during your lifetime. While it may sound too extreme as an asset protection measure, that is the essence of the charitable remainder trust.

DEFINITION

A *charitable remainder trust* is a trust established by the grantor who selects a tax-exempt charitable organization as the eventual beneficiary of the trust principal. The grantor then takes an immediate income tax deduction for the fair market value of the contributed assets. Moreover, the donated assets are no longer included in the grantor's estate for estate tax purposes. A fixed amount of at least 5 percent of the contributed assets must be paid annually to the income beneficiary, but the grantor can be that beneficiary.

CAUTION

This trust offers the advantage of insuring its beneficiaries a fixed income, even if it requires the depletion of assets. There are several disadvantages with this: A fixed income will not necessarily provide the beneficiary an adequate income during inflationary times. Also, once established, no further contributions can be made to the trust for purposes of increasing its income.

Will a charitable remainder trust adequately protect assets? Drafted properly, this trust offers total protection from future creditors of the grantor or the beneficiary. Income under the trust is subject to the claims of the beneficiaries' creditors, but only when the income is received.

note — The charitable remainder trust should be considered by individuals or couples with a net worth above $3 million and who have reached retirement age.

The concept behind the charitable remainder trust is that the grantor buys life insurance to replace the value of the donated assets. Therefore, his heirs wind up with at least as large an inheritance as they would have with the present assets intact. Moreover, there would be no estate taxes, and the tax savings would cover the cost of insurance.

There are many ways to structure the charitable remainder trust so that it is not overly restrictive. For example, the grantor may establish a family foundation as the designated charity. This provides the grantor the opportunity to direct the charitable donations, and family members may participate in the administration of the foundation.

Children's trusts for second-generation gifting

The children's trust is another popular irrevocable trust. Specifically designed to benefit the grantor's children or grandchildren, it is an ideal vehicle to hold assets you gift to them. The gift—usually an appreciating asset—is removed from your ownership and taxable estate and transferred to the children's trust, where the asset grows in value and its income is taxed at a lower rate.

note

As grantor, you cannot be the trustee of the children's trust or it will be considered part of your taxable estate. Your children receive the gift at your cost basis and do not obtain the benefit of stepped-up valuation upon your death.

Assets in a children's trust are protected from their creditors (including divorce) and also from the grantor's future creditors. But, to be an effective asset protector, the trust must be carefully drafted. For example, there can be no significant restriction on the rights of the trustee to either invade principal or accumulate income.

The children's trust has become particularly popular since the *Tax Reform Act of 1986* when a number of income splitting strategies, such as the Clifford Trusts, were eliminated. Similarly, custodianships under the Uniform Gift to Minor's Act have become less popular since they require earned income above $1,000 accruing to children under 14 be taxable at the same rate as the minor's parents. The children's trust also can be a valuable alternative to other tax-saving tactics since the children's trust has a maximum 15 percent tax rate.

> *note*   Children's trusts help to save taxes since they allow you to shift assets and income to your children.

Preserving family wealth with wealth preservation trusts

The wealth preservation trust is another irrevocable trust that also requires an independent trustee. But you can be the income beneficiary during your lifetime.

Usually highly appreciated assets, such as real estate or securities, are transferred to this trust, but qualifying assets must be debt-free. The trust then provides a tax-free environment for the assets as the assets can later be sold by the trust without a capital gains tax. The proceeds are then reinvested in income-producing assets, which the grantor can receive during his lifetime. The trust also produces tax credits to offset the grantor's other income.

 The one restriction: upon your death, the remaining assets must be transferred to a qualified non-profit organization that you, as the grantor, select.

Wealth replacement trusts reduce estate taxes

Another excellent way to reduce estate taxes while increasing asset protection is with the wealth replacement trust.

Similar to the living trust, it features two major differences:

1)   You, the grantor, can be neither the trustee nor immediate beneficiary. Your heirs can be beneficiaries.

2)   The wealth replacement trust is always irrevocable.

You can transfer up to $10,000 per trust beneficiary, per year without gift taxes. The beneficiary has 30 days to claim the gift. If the beneficiary does not directly claim the trust, which is usually a pre-arranged event, the gift becomes locked into the trust.

 The wealth replacement trust anticipates continuous lifelong gifting. Not everyone can commit to a minimum $10,000 gift each year, but a life insurance policy can be purchased to guarantee the future funding of the trust. Those who cannot commit to future funding, directly or via insurance, should not consider this trust.

The wealth replacement trust is irrevocable and thus protects assets from the grantor's future creditors and creditors of the beneficiary.

Turn your ordinary trust into a dynasty trust

The dynasty trust essentially allows you to pass considerable wealth to your grandchildren and escape estate taxes.

Two additional steps can easily convert any irrevocable trust into a dynasty trust. First, add a clause to your trust that allows the trustee the right to invest in residential real estate. Then give the trustee authority to allow the beneficiary to use trust property. Second, with the trust funded, the trustee invests in a desirable property, which can then be used by the beneficiaries rent-free. If the property's value should increase, it significantly shifts wealth from one generation to the other with huge tax savings.

Dynasty trusts also feature asset protection. For example, if your children (or grandchildren) who occupy the property divorce, the property remains protected from spousal claims. Creditors of either the grantor or beneficiaries are also unable to seize the property. The very wealthy have for years relied upon this generation-skipping strategy to escape probate taxes. Their objective: to pass wealth from grandparents to grandchildren, bypassing one level of estate tax, while each generation fully uses and enjoys the wealth.

Q-tip trusts: planning for spousal support

DEFINITION

The Q-tip or *qualified terminable interest trust* most commonly ensures a lifetime income for your spouse while ensuring the principal from your estate eventually passes to your children or another secondary beneficiary. However, the trust can qualify as an asset protection trust for the protection of the surviving spouse.

Ideal for second marriages, the Q-tip trust preserves the estate for the ultimate benefit of the grantor's children, rather than the spouse's beneficiaries, who would normally become beneficiaries if the estate were left outright to the second spouse. Of course, the Q-tip trust can also be used with a first wife, and it is commonly used in this situation when the grantor has concerns that the spouse may waste assets over her lifetime. The Q-tip trust then serves essentially as a spendthrift trust to protect the assets from the spouse's creditors or subsequent mates.

> *note*
>
> The Q-tip trust offers no asset protection against the grantor's creditors because it is a testamentary trust and takes effect only upon death.

Income from the Q-tip trust must be solely for the surviving spouse during the spouse's lifetime. This is a condition to qualify for the unlimited marital deduction. Estate taxes are deferred until the surviving spouse's death.

Land trusts create false security

Land trusts are popular in Illinois and Florida. In these two states they are valued highly for asset protection because land trusts provide privacy. Beneficiaries of the land trust cannot be easily uncovered because trust property is recorded in the name of the trustee, not the beneficiaries. While this can also be true with other trusts, the land trust offers more secrecy since there is no public record of the beneficiaries. Nor is it easy to uncover the actual beneficiaries through ordinary discovery processes. This does not suggest the beneficial interests of land trusts will always remain beyond creditor reach. If a creditor can establish a debtor as the beneficiary of the trust, the creditor can seize the debtor-beneficiary's trust interest to satisfy the debt. Beneficiaries of the land trust are still best protected by titling their beneficial interest with their less vulnerable spouse or children.

Land trusts have two disadvantages. First, it is often difficult to refinance property in a land trust. The trustees are usually banks who will refuse to execute the documents necessary for refinancing. Thus, trust property must be temporarily re-conveyed out-of-trust to its grantors or beneficiaries to complete financing with a re-conveyance to the trust. Out-of-trust property is dangerously vulnerable to creditors.

Second, for the beneficiary to take advantage of a Section 1031 tax-free, like-kind exchange, the property must again be transferred from the trust. This is because a land trust is not considered an interest in real property but an interest in personal property. Fully considered, the land trust has only marginal value for asset protection.

The pure trust fallacy

"Pure" trusts are usually nothing more than simple revocable grantor or nominee trusts. As such, they compare to the living trust and feature no extra asset protection or tax benefits.

Several organizations promote pure trusts, *common law trusts* or *constitutional trusts* as a trust for asset protection as well as freedom from income and estate taxes on trust assets. Their underlying claim: These trusts predate our laws and are thus immune or exempt from later U.S. laws that tax or allow creditors claims to the trust's assets.

There is no basis for their claim. While the trust name implies special status over other trusts, the fact is that these trusts provide no more asset protection nor tax benefits than do other trusts. Asset protection and tax benefits, in all instances, are based entirely on the terms or characteristics of the trust—not the trust title.

You cannot trust the business trust

Once popular, business trusts or *Massachusetts Business Trusts* are no longer common, whether for transacting business or asset protection. But since these trusts have been around for many years, they are discussed. The business trust is designed to engage in business and produce operating profits. More conventional trusts generally hold and invest assets for passive income.

DEFINITION

A *business trust* is an association (1) where trustees hold properties and business assets, (2) of an active, operating business that they manage and are responsible for as trustees, (3) under the terms of the trust agreement, (4) for shareholders who are the beneficial owners of the trust and share income and profits. Therefore, the business trust more closely resembles a corporation than a conventional investment trust. What are the advantages and disadvantages of a business trust over a corporation?

DEFINITION

One advantage is that a business trust may be more easily organized since it requires nothing more than a *trust agreement*, which is an entirely private agreement between the parties. A corporation, in contrast, is chartered by the state. While incorporating is not difficult, it publicly records the names of its officers and directors, and possibly shareholders. Since the business trust has no public filings, its trustees and shareholders remain private, which is helpful for asset protection.

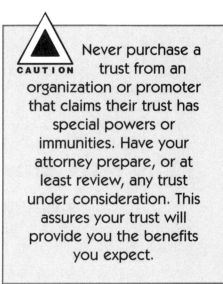

Never purchase a trust from an organization or promoter that claims their trust has special powers or immunities. Have your attorney prepare, or at least review, any trust under consideration. This assures your trust will provide you the benefits you expect.

Whether in terms of regulation and taxation, there is not necessarily an advantage with a business trust over a corporation. Many states tax and regulate the two entities alike. In some states you avoid corporate taxes with a business trust.

A business trust can present considerable disadvantage to its shareholders: They may be personally liable for business trust debts. This is no minor disadvantage and one not likely to encourage a business trust over a corporation where shareholders are personally isolated from debts. This problem is easily avoided by a clause in the trust limiting the shareholders' liability to the amount invested.

Stock ownership in a business trust is subject to creditor attachment as are corporate shares, so here the business trust offers no special advantage. One small advantage is that it is more difficult to identify shareholders in a business trust because as a private entity it does not require the same public filings as a corporation.

> *note*
>
> Because the business trust is a hybrid, there's considerable uncertainty regarding the rights of creditors. Entities that offer less speculation concerning the safety of your assets are preferred.

There is no compelling reason to use a business trust instead of a corporation if it is to engage in business, or another trust if it is to be a passive investor.

A little-known trust for disabled business owners

DEFINITION

The *standby trust* specifically protects business owners who become unable to manage their businesses. The trust activates once the business owner can no longer oversee his business. Anyone may be appointed the trustee, but it is usually a close family member or professional advisor most familiar with the business. Until the owner becomes disabled, the standby trust can be revoked. The trust becomes irrevocable only upon the permanent incapacity of the owner. The standby trust is thus similar to a durable power of attorney.

A standby trust is one of the best methods to assure competent management succession upon disability. It is also a good asset protector because it becomes irrevocable when it becomes operative. It then, but not before, safely accumulates income or assets free from creditor claims.

Shelter assets with sprinkling trusts

Sprinkling trusts are also gaining popularity and are helpful where the trust will be in force for ten or more years and the future income or tax situation for each trust beneficiary is uncertain. You can then modify the

101

distribution of trust property through a "sprinkling" provision which grants the trustee authority to either disburse or retain principal and income for the trust duration, and thus determines what each beneficiary will receive annually. As the grantor, you must specify the criteria to the trustee for determining distributions and also set minimum incomes for a spouse or dependent child.

Two key factors will determine whether the sprinkling trust offers asset protection:

1) If the grantor retains the right to modify or revoke the sprinkling trust, he loses the trust protection. As with any other trust, it must be irrevocable and beyond grantor control to shelter assets.

2) A beneficiary cannot be trustee. Although it is legally permissible, the trust assets become vulnerable to creditors of the trustee-beneficiary. When the trustee can distribute assets to himself as beneficiary, his creditors stand in his place for purposes of claiming trust funds.

 Observe these two cautions and the sprinkling trust can be very useful for both estate planning and asset protection.

Medicaid trusts for free nursing home care

The Medicaid trust is a special purpose trust used exclusively to shelter assets so the grantor can qualify for Medicaid coverage for nursing home costs. Understandably, this trust is popular with older Americans.

A Medicaid trust is similar to other irrevocable trusts. The grantor, as an individual or couple who may later want to qualify for Medicaid, transfers assets to an irrevocable trust. However, unlike most irrevocable trusts, the grantor becomes the income beneficiary and the children or spouse ordinarily become final beneficiaries for the trust's principal. The grantor continues to receive income, but since the grantor is without assets, he qualifies for Medicaid.

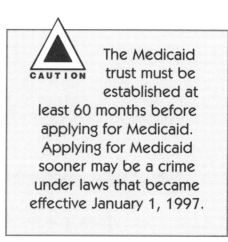

CAUTION The Medicaid trust must be established at least 60 months before applying for Medicaid. Applying for Medicaid sooner may be a crime under laws that became effective January 1, 1997.

The Medicaid trust is for this one special purpose. It does not provide asset protection beyond what can be provided by other irrevocable trusts.

Generally, Medicaid trusts prohibit using trust assets for health care purposes and also limit the beneficiary's income to an amount the beneficiary can receive without losing Medicaid benefits.

One disadvantage of this trust is that it must be created in advance of necessary nursing care, and few people can anticipate long term care far into the future. If you, or a parent, are now approaching nursing home age, then consider the Medicaid trust.

Distributing trust assets safely

The three most common ways to distribute trust assets are:

1) At a specific age

2) Outright

3) Deferred

Children should not receive distributions until reaching age 21, and most grantors prefer staggered distributions at different ages. This prevents waste of windfall inheritances at a still immature age. Distributions can be conditional upon specified criteria that establishes sufficient maturity and responsibility to receive further funds. Outright distributions are made as soon as practical after the grantor's death.

Whether it is an outright or deferred distribution, the grantor should give the trustee full discretion to delay or withhold distributions if distributions would be disadvantageous to the beneficiary, such as when he has creditors or anticipates divorce. The trust should allow the trustee to pay expenses directly for the benefit of the beneficiary.

Ways to improve trust protection

Your trusts will most likely include asset protection as only one of several objectives. Taxes, estate planning and asset enhancement are others. While your trust must balance all objectives, you can greatly increase asset protection with any trust following five strategies:

1)   **Use multiple trusts with different trustees to hold different assets.** It is considerably more difficult for a creditor to attack several trusts as opposed to one. Moreover, several trusts will give you more flexibility to accommodate your multiple objectives.

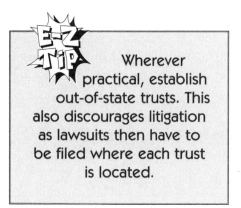
Wherever practical, establish out-of-state trusts. This also discourages litigation as lawsuits then have to be filed where each trust is located.

2)   **Transfer assets to trusts gradually** to better argue against claims the transfer was intended to defraud creditors.

3)   **Add a preamble to each trust stating purposes**, such as estate planning. This further establishes the trust was not set up primarily to protect assets.

4)   **Add beneficiaries other than yourself to your trust.** Some statutes provide that a transfer in trust for the use of the grantor is void as against his creditors. But these laws usually apply only where the grantor is the sole beneficiary. With two or more beneficiaries, there is less concern with these laws.

5)   **Remember, control is the central issue.** The more control retained over the trust and trust property, the greater the rights of the creditor to claim trust assets. Use irrevocable trusts, not revocable trusts. Appoint others as trustee, not yourself. Reserve no right to modify the terms of the trust nor dictate how assets or income will be used. And never make yourself sole beneficiary of your own trust. These mistakes are fatal to asset protection.

Planning Pointers

◆ A number of different purpose trusts are useful for asset protection. Use trusts that not only provide you asset protection, but also coincide with general investment and estate planning objectives.

◆ Use as many different trusts as is practical. This not only gives you greater flexibility, but also makes it more difficult for creditors to reach significant assets.

◆ Control is the key factor in determining whether trust assets can be claimed by creditors. The more control retained, the less protection you enjoy. Less control provides more protection.

◆ If you have considerable wealth, investigate the foreign-based trust. It gives you more ironclad protection than can any domestic trust.

◆ Add beneficiaries other than yourself to your trust. Statutes that say a transfer in trust for the use of the grantor is void as against his creditors generally apply only when the grantor is sole beneficiary.

◆ Always use irrevocable trusts, not revocable trusts, if you want asset protection. Appoint others to be trustee. Retain no right to modify the terms of the trust or distribute trust assets.

Build a financial fortress with limited partnerships

7

Chapter 7

Build a financial fortress with limited partnerships

What you'll find in this chapter:

⏮➡ Disadvantages of using general partnership

⏮➡ How to set up a limited partnership

⏮➡ What limited partners can and cannot do

⏮➡ How limited partnerships protect assets

⏮➡ Why limited partnerships frustrate creditors

The limited partnership (LP) is the foundation for most domestic asset protection plans. The LP is a valuable component for building your financial fortress because:

- the LP allows you to control your assets

- the debtor's limited partnership interest cannot be reached by creditors

- a properly structured LP can possibly protect transfers made even after a claim arises and also protect against IRS claims

- the LP is tax-neutral

- the LP provides maximum ownership and operating flexibility

- the LP gives you the opportunity to better plan your estate and reduce estate taxes. Both versatile and protective, few comprehensive asset protection plans do not include at least one limited partnership

Limited partnership versus general partnership

DEFINITION

A *partnership* is an association of two or more parties engaged in an undertaking with the agreement that they shall in some proportion share profits and losses. A partnership can be either a general partnership or a limited partnership, but never confuse the two. In a *general partnership*, the partners have equal authority to manage and act for the partnership and all partners have unlimited liability for partnership debts. A limited partnership is typically preferable to the general partnership because it protects limited partners from liability arising from the partnership's business

The major disadvantage of the general partnership is that its partners are jointly and severally liable for partnership debts. A general partner in a general partnership can easily lose personal wealth to satisfy partnership creditors if the business or other general partners individually have insufficient assets to satisfy these obligations. And, you can lose your wealth even if your partner created the liability.

Therefore, the general partnership extends liability. A general partner's interest can also be seized by the partner's personal creditors. Conversely, a limited partnership will fully protect the limited partners' assets from partnership debts, and a partnership interest cannot be seized by a partners' personal creditors. The limited partnership is thus both an excellent liability insulator and wealth protector.

The commonly called *family limited partnership* is the same as the regular limited partnership. The "family" simply distinguishes the closely owned and controlled partnership from the larger limited partnerships popular before the 1986 Tax Reform Act. This was when limited partnerships were formed as tax shelter structures for wealthy investors seeking tax losses. These tax benefits disappeared with the 1986 tax law; however, the LP's asset protection and estate planning benefits continue to establish the limited partnership as a major financial planning tool.

Structuring your limited partnership

Partners in a limited partnership can allocate their ownership interest as they choose, and this is an important feature for asset protection purposes. For instance, you can contribute personal assets to the partnership and obtain in exchange only a small partnership interest. The remaining partnership interest can be owned by other family members. However, this arrangement can create a taxable gift when the other family member is not your spouse. For example, if you contribute $100,000 to the limited partnership and your partner contributes nothing, but receives an equal share, then your partner effectively received a $50,000 gift.

There are typical LP structures for families. Frequently, mom and dad form the LP and contribute income-producing or business assets in exchange for their respective partnership interests. Mom and dad, for example, may each receive a small percent interest as the general partners. As co-general partners they equally control the partnership the same way they controlled the contributed assets. Mom and dad may

> **E-Z TIP**
>
> Have your accountant review the proposed structure of your limited partnership to avoid tax liabilities and also to determine that the LP is your most favorable entity from a tax standpoint.

additionally each receive, as limited partners, the remaining majority interest in the limited partnership. This allows mom and dad exclusive and equal ownership as well as control of the partnership, just as they had enjoyed with their assets titled in their name. The one difference is that their assets are now fully protected.

There are many other structural possibilities. Perhaps dad has creditors and therefore only mom becomes the general partner. Or mom and dad may form a corporation or LLC to be the general partner, which is particularly important if the partnership can incur liabilities for which the general partners are liable.

> **note**
>
> The LP can work very well for family estate planning, The LP structure is never permanent. Partners in an LP can always sell or gift partnership interests, subject only to those restrictions in the partnership agreement.

Mom and dad may subsequently alter their limited partnership interests. Perhaps mom will obtain the greater interest. Or mom and dad may gradually gift their limited partnership interests to their children or to a living trust, children's trust or other type of trust or entity, which may also own a portion of the limited partnership.

Key limited partnership provisions

Partnership agreements must include:

- name, address, purpose and duration of the partnership

- the combined capital contributions and ownership interests of the respective partners

- proportionate distributions of profits and losses to the partners

- general partner compensation

- duties, responsibilities and rights of the general and limited partners

- provisions for the death, retirement, incapacity or bankruptcy of a general or limited partner

- provisions to terminate and liquidate the partnership

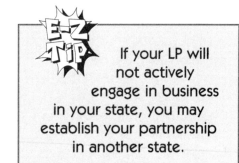

If your LP will not actively engage in business in your state, you may establish your partnership in another state.

- rights to assign or transfer a partnership interest

- provisions to replace the general partner

The partnership agreement is usually not publicly recorded. Only the certificate or articles of partnership is filed, which states only the partnership name, its address, resident agent, general partners and duration.

Laws concerning limited partnerships are reasonably uniform (all states but Louisiana adopted the Uniform Limited Partnership Act), so local taxation issues and filing fees mostly influence the filing state. Nevada is a common state for organizing LPs. Expect to pay $1,500 to $5,000 to form a customized limited partnership. As an asset protector, it is worth many times this relatively small fee.

Your rights and obligations as a partner

DEFINITION

A limited partnership has one or more general partners and one or more limited partners. The *general partners* manage the partnership. The *limited partners* must remain passive and assert absolutely no active role in managing the partnership. Limited partners who refrain from management participation remain free from personal liability for partnership obligations. Their involvement thus compares to a corporate stockholder, except that a stockholder may participate in corporate management without incurring personal liability.

 Because a general partner is individually liable for all partnership obligations, it is safest for a corporation or LLC to be appointed the general partner when the partnership can incur liabilities. This will insulate individuals from personal liability on partnership debts and the danger of losing personal assets arising from partnership activities.

The rights of a limited partner also compare to the rights of a stockholder or member in an LLC, including the right:

Definition: The Revised Uniform Limited Partnership Act defines a *person* as a natural person, partnership, limited partnership, limited liability company, trust, estate, association or corporation. Any of these may become a general and/or limited partner.

- to an accounting

- to inspect partnership books

- to obtain important partnership information

- to share partnership income when distributed at the discretion of the general partner

- to share proceeds proportionate to their ownership interest upon liquidating the partnership

A limited partner's liability is limited only to the amount invested. A limited partner incurs none of the liability of a general partner unless the

note General and limited partners can be the same parties and both can own an interest in the limited partnership.

limited partner helps to manage the partnership. Even occasional or minor management participation can render a limited partner liable. Adopting a limited partner's name for the partnership can, for example, make the limited partner liable to creditors who relied upon this representation to extend credit. Thus, to limit liability, a limited partner must avoid all involvement in partnership activities beyond those few specific authorities enumerated in the partnership agreement.

A limited partner can own or manage a corporation or LLC, which can, in turn, be the general partner. Owning the general partner entity will not create personal liability because it does not constitute management by the limited partner individually.

note While a limited partner cannot direct the general partner, a limited partner may provide advisory opinions or recommendations to the general partner. Final decisions, however, must rest with the general partner.

What authority can a limited partner assert without incurring liability? A limited partner can:

- work as employee of or independent contractor to the limited partnership

- work as an employee of or independent contractor to the general partner

- vote to amend the partnership agreement

- guarantee partnership debts

- vote to dissolve the partnership or sell, lease, exchange or encumber assets outside the ordinary course of business; change the nature of the business; or remove or appoint a general partner

Assets that an LP can protect

A limited partnership can protect numerous assets. Cash, investment securities, notes, receivables, investment real estate, patents, trademarks, copyrights and shares in a closely held C Corporation are all candidates. In exchange for transferring these assets to your LP, you receive your partnership interest. Contributions can also be made as loans, but this will offer less asset protection since a creditor can then seize the future payments due you, while the creditor cannot seize the partnership interest.

The limited partnership should only own assets intended or suitable for a business or investment. The LP should be an income-producing entity. Assets that produce neither current, anticipated income nor appreciation should not be titled in the LP. Their inclusion may disqualify the LP for asset protection.

Collectibles, such as jewelry, coins and antiques, are appropriate for an LP if their value is expected to increase. An LP cannot own shares in an S Corporation but can own an interest in an LLC. IRA and other retirement accounts cannot be owned by an LP. Annuities can be owned, but you would then lose their tax deferral benefits. Autos and boats should not be owned by the LP unless they are used in connection with a business.

Separate partnerships maximize protection

Avoid titling liability-producing assets in the same LP with such safe assets as cash and passive investments. This needlessly exposes your safe assets. The best strategy: establish different LPs to insulate your various assets.

For example, investments and cash are safe assets and can both be titled within the same LP. Commercial properties are a more dangerous asset and should be titled in one or more separate LPs. Balance the costs and administrative problems from managing multiple LPs against the benefit of reduced exposure when deciding upon the number of LPs you optimally need. Also avoid operating active businesses through an LP, particularly if the LP owns safe assets.

note It is preferable to run an active operating business through a corporation or LLC which can be owned by the LP as its stockholder or member.

Maintaining LP protection

Creditors can ignore your LP or hold you personally liable for monies or other assets removed from the LP if you personally or improperly use the partnership or its assets. The LP, as with a corporation or LLC, must be treated as an arms-length and independent entity.

The LP must maintain its own bank accounts, separate books and records, insurance, licenses and permits, and employer identification number. Its cash and other assets must also remain separated from assets of other entities or individuals and never commingled. If you should use partnership assets for personal use, then pay fair compensation. Loans to or borrowing from the LP must be properly documented. Respect the independent status of the LP if you expect it to protect you.

note

How LPs protect assets

Limited partnership law balances the rights of a partner's creditors against the rights of the non-debtor partners who want to remain free from creditor interference in their partnership dealings. Because one partner has financial problems, it should not impede the other partners. Thus, a limited partner's personal creditors are severely limited in their remedies against the debtor-partner's interest in the limited partnership.

DEFINITION

A creditor in this case can only apply to the court for a *charging order.* This gives the creditor only the right to any profit distributions from the partnership due the debtor partner. However, the creditor can seize neither the debtor-partner's partnership interest nor partnership property because the partners collectively share the partnership property as tenants in partnership. Since the partnership property does not legally belong to any individual partner, derivatively it cannot be taken by any personal creditors of that partner. Property transferred to the partnership is thus safe from a partner's future creditors.

The debtor partner's personal creditor, in essence, becomes only an assignee of the partnership interest. The creditor gains only the right to receive the debtor partner's profit distributions if and when paid, and to the extent of their debt. Limited partnership agreements generally forbid a partner's creditor from becoming a full limited partner. Thus, the creditor-assignee acquires no voice in partnership management or voting. An assignee cannot acquire rights in the partnership above that possessed by the limited partner. And, a limited partner's rights are generally restricted only to receiving income. Thus, the

> *note*
>
> The *Uniform Limited Partnership Act* limits a creditor to this charging order remedy. A creditor who seeks relief against a limited partner can neither dissolve the limited partnership nor interfere with partnership activities.

creditor-assignee's charging order remedy is nearly worthless because the general partner alone determine profit distributions.

For good measure, a well-drafted partnership agreement *forbids* an assignee (e.g., a partner's creditor) from becoming a limited partner without the consent of all partners. It also allows the general partner to withhold profit distributions from limited partners for legitimate business purposes. Therefore, the general partner may refuse to issue dividends to limited partners. Of course, the general partner can withdraw income or funds from the LP for wages, fees, loans, to transact business with affiliated entities or for a variety of other legitimate reasons.

> *note* A properly drafted LP gives a partner's creditors no practical recourse other than to await an income distribution that the creditor can neither force nor anticipate. This explains why the LP is one of the most popular domestic asset protection tools.

If more than one creditor has a charging order, the first creditor to apply for the charging order obtains priority. An individual partner's creditor has no priority over partnership creditors. If no assets remain once partnership creditors are paid, the individual partner's creditors receive nothing from the partnership.

The LP and bankruptcy

Bankruptcy trustees have greater rights against an LP than do individual creditors because federal bankruptcy law supersedes state laws concerning partnerships. Thus, while state laws concerning limited partnerships may forbid a partner's creditor from seizing a limited partnership interest, federal bankruptcy law may allow a partner's bankruptcy trustee this right because bankruptcy law allows trustees to seize all solely and jointly owned property. Thus, a debtor partner's limited partnership interest can usually be seized by a bankruptcy trustee.

Partnership assets, however, remain safe from trustee seizures because partnership assets are not jointly owned property or property of the individual partners, but instead property owned as tenancy by partnership. Moreover, the Bankruptcy Code specifically provides that a bankruptcy trustee cannot seize partnership property. However, it is important that you transfer property to the limited partnership at least one year before filing bankruptcy. Also, correctly document that the property is presently owned by the partnership and is no longer a personal asset. Proof of partnership ownership can be evidenced through a bill of sale, assignment, deed and partnership tax returns that list the property as a partnership asset.

A partnership agreement that restricts the limited partners from withdrawing their interests will similarly restrict the bankruptcy trustee. The debtor partner's interest may then be neither profitable nor marketable. If the partnership agreement assures each limited partner a fixed income, which a well-drafted partnership agreement would avoid, then the bankruptcy trustee can claim this income from the partnership. The LP agreement can also expressly keep a bankruptcy trustee from obtaining the status of a limited partner without the unanimous consent of all other partners.

> ⚠️ **CAUTION** A partnership agreement that limits a limited partner's income must do so for legitimate business reasons other than bankruptcy protection or the bankruptcy court can void the clause and grant the bankruptcy trustee unrestricted rights to the partnership income.

A bankruptcy trustee who seizes a limited partnership interest may sell that interest despite contrary contractual or other prohibitions. However, a partnership agreement that makes a limited partnership interest nonassignable without partner consent will usually find this limitation enforceable by the partners. While the bankruptcy court may order the forced sale of a limited partnership interest to cover the debtor partner's obligations, a bankruptcy trustee cannot normally assume management control over the partnership even when the debtor partner is the general partner. This is because the general partner is deemed to hold a personal services contract which cannot be transferred.

 Nevertheless, the partnership agreement may guard against this situation by expressly providing that a general partner's contract with the limited partnership is a personal services contract and therefore non-assumable by a bankruptcy trustee or any other such assignee or successor-in-interest.

Bankruptcy of a general partner can present more potentially serious consequences for the partnership than will a limited partner's bankruptcy because state laws conflict on whether a bankruptcy trustee of a general partner may dissolve the partnership and liquidate the partnership assets.

Several courts have ruled that even where general partnership interests are seized, the partnership may not be dissolved when either the partnership or the debtor general partner files Chapter 7 or Chapter 11 bankruptcy. Dissolution may also be avoided if the partnership agreement expressly provides for terminating a general partner upon its bankruptcy and the judicial appointment of a successor general partner.

Several recent cases suggest that when a bankruptcy trustee assumes a general partner's interest, the partnership must end since the general partner can no longer fulfill its fiduciary duties to the limited partners. Have your attorney check your state laws when you form your limited partnership, and discuss the specific steps your partnership can take to ensure its continuity upon the bankruptcy of a general partner. This problem can be abated by the resignation or termination of a general partner before filing bankruptcy, and this is always recommended.

To further prevent these possible problems, the partnership agreement should expressly avoid lengthy or extendible terms for a general partner and also allow for the automatic appointment of a designated successor general partner upon the seizure of a general partner's interest. Your partnership agreement should also provide that the partnership can be dissolved only with the consent of a majority of the non-debtor partners.

Clearly, a debtor general partner cannot be forcibly replaced by a creditor if that general partner possesses unique management skills essential to the partnership. And, a creditor who seizes a general partner's interest cannot automatically assume management duties for the partnership as this would interfere with normal partnership operations and the rights of the non-debtor partners to freely choose their

> *note* While a limited partner's liabilities will not jeopardize the limited partnership, problems can arise when the debtor is a general partner as it is possible his bankruptcy trustee can dissolve or interfere with the limited partnership.

management. A general partner's creditor can, at most, only dissolve the partnership, and this can be prevented through *non-assignability* and *successor general partner clauses* in your partnership agreement. Nevertheless, avoid appointing high-risk or heavily indebted general partners or allowing one to remain as the general partner.

The LP tax trap for unwary creditors

Few creditors ever obtain a charging order against a debtor-partner. Not only will such efforts prove futile for collecting, but the creditor will probably receive a huge tax bill instead.

The IRS code provides that a charging order creditor becomes automatically liable for taxes due on partnership income attributable to the debtor partner. If the partnership earns $100,000, and the debtor partner owns 50 percent of the partnership, that debtor partner would normally declare $50,000 as taxable income, regardless of whether it was received. However, the charging order creditor instead becomes liable for the tax on the $50,000 income attribution, whether or not the creditor received partnership profits under the charging order. The prospects of a tax bill instead of payment discourages creditors from pursuing a limited partnership interest. Several states do not allow the creditor in this situation to discharge the charging order without the consent of the debtor partner, who may well prefer the arrangement.

Five strategies to frustrate creditors

There are five additional strategies to further chill a creditor chasing a limited partnership interest:

1)   Inform the creditor in advance that the limited partnership shall withhold further income distributions and that the creditor cannot expect any payments. Creditors negotiate more favorable settlements once they understand the hopelessness of their situation.

2)   Reduce the equity in the partnership before the creditor charges the debtor partnership interest. One possibility: mortgage or sell partnership assets and make immediate distributions to the partners. Reducing the partnership equity produces a smaller distribution flowing to the judgment creditor. This is a particularly sound tactic when the remaining partners are cooperative, the debtor-partner owns the major partnership interest and there are anticipated distributions.

3)   Sell or encumber the debtor partner's partnership interest. One or more remaining partners can purchase the debtor partner's interest, or the partnership as an entity may acquire and redeem the interest with partnership funds.

> *note* A limited partnership interest generally has far less value to an outsider because friendly general partners can dissipate partnership profits and net worth and frustrate the creditor. The debtor with only a fractional partnership interest has an asset of questionable market value, even when the partnership has significant net worth and profits.

To prevent abuse in this situation, the court can fix the value of the limited partner's interest to avoid fraudulent transfers of that interest to the other partners for less than fair value. However, this amount may nevertheless be for considerably less than the creditor's judgment.

4)   The partnership agreement may also allow the general partners to assess the limited partners, or their charging order creditors, additional contributions for the partnership capital account. This should further discourage a creditor from obtaining a charging order if he knows in advance that the interest can be subject to assessment and forfeiture if not paid.

5)   A debtor partner with cooperative partners can also liquidate their partnership and repurchase its assets through a new entity for the liquidation value of its assets. The debtor's interest in this new entity may be through a nominee.

Combine trusts with LPs for added protection

Although a partner's creditor cannot readily seize a partnership interest, you may further frustrate creditor charging orders against a limited partnership interest by having a foreign asset-protection trust own the limited partnership interest.

The trust is normally the sole limited partner and owns perhaps 98 percent of the LP. The general partner can then liquidate a threatened LP and

> *E-Z TIP* A foreign asset protection trust is an excellent vehicle through which to hold a limited partner interest in an LP. Foreign asset protection trusts serve as additional safety nets to protect LP assets from creditors.

distribute 98 percent of the net proceeds to the more protective foreign trust. Combining an LP with the offshore asset protection trust can be an ideal way to balance control and asset protection objectives through one combined entity. The LP can similarly have other irrevocable trusts as limited partners with comparable results.

Avoid fraudulent conveyance claims

Here is a common mistake to avoid with LPs: Assume that you are sued. To protect your assets you convey them to an LP and receive in exchange no partnership interest, ostensibly because you do not want your creditor to pursue that LP interest, even with a relatively harmless charging order.

That objective is logical but can be a fatal flaw in structuring your LP. Always exchange personal assets for a partnership interest that is proportionate to your invested capital. If you donate assets for inadequate consideration, your present creditor can set aside the transfer as fraudulent and recover the asset from the LP.

However, when the value of your partnership interest approximates the value of your contributed asset, it generally is not considered a fraudulent conveyance by most courts. Your present creditor then has only the charging order remedy and cannot pursue the transferred assets under a fraudulent transfer claim.

Some courts set aside transfers to an LP when made against present creditors, even when the debtor obtains in exchange a proportionate partnership interest. More protection is needed in this situation, and the answer is usually to liquidate the assets and transfer them to an offshore asset protection entity.

Leasing from your LP to protect your business

Business owners can better protect key business assets from litigation and other claims by titling certain assets in an LP. Equipment, proprietary rights (trademarks, copyrights, patents) and real estate are frequently owned by a limited partnership. The business entity would then lease or license these assets from the partnership while the business uses the assets. LP ownership thus protects these assets from a business bankruptcy.

Limited partnership tax advantages

DEFINITION

S corporations, living trusts and LPs are all *pass-through* entities because they allocate income, deductions, gains and losses directly to each stockholder, grantor or partner in proportion to their ownership interest. The LP similarly files a partnership tax return but pays no tax on its own earnings. Instead the LP issues a K-1 to report to the IRS the profits and losses attributable and reportable on each partner's individual tax return. The LP is thus tax-neutral and presents no tax disadvantages.

CAUTION There are several tax disadvantages when titling a home to an LP. First, the LP cannot utilize the $125,000 capital gain exclusion or the two-year rollover provision for deferring gains. And mortgage interest would not be deductible.

When assets are transferred to the LP, it is not a taxable event, and the LP accepts the assets at the transferor's basis. The LP, when it sells the assets, assumes the transferor's loss or gain.

Thus, general partnerships, S corporations, limited partnerships and some LLCs all have their profits taxed only to the partners or stockholders who pay an income tax on their proportionate share of the income whether or not any profits were received. C corporation profits are taxed twice; once when earned by the corporation and again when distributed as dividend income to the shareholders. However, a limited partnership can lose its pass-through tax advantage and be taxed as a C corporation if the partnership violates certain state laws. Its tax benefits can also be lost where the limited partnership has a corporation as its general partner and fewer assets than liabilities. To avoid losing single taxation status, the limited partnership should have at least one unincorporated general partner. The primary reason a corporation is used as a general partner is to avoid personal liability for partnership debts, but this is only a necessary precaution when the partnership engages in liability-producing activity. If the limited partnership holds and manages only safe, passive assets, then risk is no longer an issue and individuals can safely serve as general partners.

Several other tax cautions to observe:

- The combined interests of all general partners must equal at least one percent of the operating income and losses, as well as capital gains and losses.

- Distributions to limited and general partners can be in any desired proportion and need not coincide with either the amount each partner invested or her percentage ownership. This can be a major advantage in asset protection planning. You may, for example, agree to accept less income from your greater share in the LP, while other family members with a lesser interest may receive disproportionately greater income.

DEFINITION

- A partner's share of partnership operating losses as a deduction on his personal return is limited by the *"at risk"* provisions of the IRS code. This limits the deductibility of a partner's share of any loss to the amount the partner actually invested, or what the partner could potentially lose from the partnership. Guaranteed partnership obligations are one example of contingent losses

With LPs becoming a more popular entity, many owners of small business corporations are now converting their corporations to limited partnerships on a tax-free basis. There are two possible ways to accomplish this:

1) *Liquidate the operating corporation and donate its assets to the limited partnership*. First, transfer all corporate assets to yourself in exchange for a re-transfer of the corporate shares to the corporation. Second, donate these same assets to the limited partnership. This increases the basis of the general partner's capital account in the partnership and keeps it a tax-free transaction provided the corporation maintains a positive net worth.

2) *Directly contribute your company shares to the limited partnership.* This also presents no tax problem as the corporation remains intact while the limited partnership becomes its new shareholder.

Limited partnerships can save estate taxes

Assets in a limited partnership may have a discounted value of 20 to 40 percent for gift and estate tax valuations. The discount will depend on the control over the partnership and liquidity, marketability and accessibility of its assets. Discounting the value is a topic under constant IRS review, with the rules subject to change.

Planning Pointers

◆ A limited partnership is an excellent vehicle for sheltering both personal and family assets from creditors.

◆ Individuals with liability concerns should own only a small percentage of the partnership, as this is all that would then be exposed to creditors. Other family members can receive the remaining interest. The debtor could still control the partnership by becoming the general partner.

◆ There are a number of possible strategies to frustrate the efforts of a creditor seeking debt satisfaction through a debtor's limited partnership interest.

◆ If you want to avoid the liability of a general partner, refrain from participating in the management of the partnership.

◆ A limited partnership can offer you tax advantages as well as liability protection.

◆ Use separate LPs to keep safe assets from "at risk" assets.

◆ General partners anticipating bankruptcy should withdraw from the management of the limited partnership.

Asset protection with an LLC

8

Chapter 8

Asset protection with an LLC

What you'll find in this chapter:

⟫ Why an LLC may be right for you

⟫ Where you should register your LLC

⟫ How an LLC protects assets

⟫ The LLC as an estate planning tool

⟫ Why you should use an LLP

The limited liability company, or LLC, has quickly become one of the most popular business entities in the United States. Once seen as a daring corporate hybrid, the LLC is now praised for its organizational flexibility and innovation. It combines the best features of corporate protection with the significant tax advantages of a partnership. It has also proven to be an effective asset protection structure as it features essentially the same shelter from personal liability and prevents seizure by a member's creditors as do the corporation and limited partnership, respectively.

Seven advantages of an LLC

While a limited liability company combines the advantages of a corporation with those of a partnership, there are many other reasons why it may be your business's best form of organization:

1) Double taxation can be avoided with an LLC. Since the LLC is not a corporation, there is no corporate income tax. Income is only taxed on the personal level, as with a partnership, if you so elect.

---

2) Personal liability is limited. The personal assets of the partners are protected from corporate creditors. Managers and officers are also protected from liability through their participation in the operation of the company.

3) There is relatively little paperwork and record keeping involved with an LLC beyond a simple operating agreement or statement of the principles of the organization.

4) You can form your own limited liability company. The forms are available from the Secretary of State in the state in which you want to form the LLC. You do not need an attorney.

5) You can easily convert your present business to an LLC and begin receiving the benefits immediately.

6) It is relatively inexpensive to establish an LLC. It often costs under $100 to register an LLC with the state.

7) Annual registration fees also are low—under $150 in most states.

 Although an excellent organizational choice, the LLC is not necessarily best for everyone. There are reasons to choose a corporation or partnership structure instead:

- There is still a narrow acceptance of the LLC because it is relatively new. Limited liability companies have been recognized by the IRS only since 1988. Two states still do not recognize LLCs, and they have been tested in few cases.

> ⚠️ **CAUTION** Multi-state businesses may have tax problems if they conduct business in a state that does not presently recognize the limited liability company or if the LLC fails to qualify to do business in another state.

- IRS rules that apply to insolvency may create problems for owners of the limited liability company.

- Limited liability companies do not enjoy the corporate advantages of prior IRS rulings when there is a sale of worthless stock or stock is sold at a loss.

- The sale of 50 percent or more of the ownership of the limited liability company in any 12-month period ends any tax advantages the LLC may have had with the IRS.

- Limited liability companies may not engage in tax-free reorganizations.

How the LLC operates

Although state statutes on LLCs do vary, most conform to the model established by the *Uniform Limited Liability Company Act (ULLCA) of 1995*. While neither a state nor federal law, it is the most comprehensive code treatment available on the subject of LLCs and contains the guidelines that most states refer to and adopt regarding LLCs.

The following highlights the general provisions of the ULLCA:

- An LLC has a legal identity separate from its members.

- An LLC may be organized for profit or non-profit.

- About half of the states allow an LLC to have only one member, all others require at least two members.

- An LLC interest is non-transferrable.

- Any interest in future distributions and return of capital can be transferrable.

- Members of an LLC enjoy limited liability.

- Managers are agents of the company and can bind the company to third parties.

- An LLC may exist for a fixed or perpetual duration.

- An LLC is dissolved upon:

    ◆ the consent of its members

    ◆ the dissociation of a member

    ◆ the occurrence of a specific event described in the operating agreement, or

    ◆ the fixed date for dissolution

note LLC members may freely transfer their rights to the distribution but not rights to membership. An LLC grants rights to membership only upon the unanimous vote of the remaining membership.

- An LLC Operating Agreement may not:

    ◆ unreasonably restrict a member's right to inspect company records;

    ◆ eliminate or reduce a member's duty, loyalty, care or good faith when dealing with or on behalf of the company;

    ◆ restrict the rights of third parties; or

    ◆ override the legal right of the company to expel any member convicted of wrongdoing, breaching the Operating Agreement, or making it impractical for the LLC to carry on business with such a member

Where to register your LLC

There are two main factors to consider when selecting a state within which to organize: financial and organizational.

When considering the financial factors, inquire about the costs of registering in the state and the ongoing annual fees. Also investigate whether your LLC will be charged state or local income taxes.

State laws governing the organization of LLCs can be another important factor. When considering the registration state, weigh state-by-state differences on six key points:

1) Is the company managed by its members or an appointed manager?

2) May the LLC merge with another business organization?

3) Who has the power to bind the company and act as its agent(s)?

4) How easily may company members be admitted and withdrawn?

5) What are the standards of negligence, malfeasance, misfeasance, misconduct, confidence, trust and confidentiality?

6) What are the rights of creditors against LLC interests held by a member? From an asset protection viewpoint, the answer to this question is the most important.

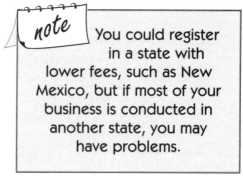

note You could register in a state with lower fees, such as New Mexico, but if most of your business is conducted in another state, you may have problems.

Next consider taxes. You may need certain organizational formats to qualify for partnership taxation at the state level, and certain states can be quite rigid in their organizational requirements.

Another factor to consider when registering your LLC is where your primary business will operate. If you register in a state other than the one in which you intend to do business, you may be forced to register as a foreign LLC under the foreign corporation statute of your primary business state. This can significantly increase filing, registration and administration costs and also require added paperwork.

Limiting personal liability with an LLC

note Limited liability does not extend to members who offer personal guarantees for leases, loans and other legal obligations.

Limited liability is, of course, essential for all members of the LLC. Often this is the very reason for forming an LLC. If this is so, then limited liability is not an element you can use to define your tax status. In this respect, there is no difference between an LLC and a corporation.

Some states allow one member of the LLC to be personally liable for the debts and obligations of the company, much in the same way a general partner has liability in a limited partnership. This person must have substantial assets that can be used to meet the obligations of the LLC.

DEFINITION The IRS has defined *substantial assets* as equalling at least 10 percent of the total capital in the LLC. This manager cannot be a mere figurehead. Such personal liability can be indemnified against by another person because the underlying liability still exists. If you require this option to qualify for partnership tax status and are willing to forsake limited liability, you *must* make it part of the Operating Agreement.

CAUTION It can be dangerous for an LLC to hire non-members as managers even when not prohibited by state law. Before your LLC contemplates this, seek qualified legal counsel or your partnership tax status may become jeopardized.

Creditor rights to LLC ownership interests

While corporate shares may be freely transferred, the LLC prevents unrestricted transfers. A membership interest in an LLC may be assigned or transferred to a third party or pledged to a creditor. However, the assignee does not become a voting member of the LLC. He may be entitled to receive distributions and a proportionate share of profits due the debtor-member, but he is not entitled to vote or participate in the management of the LLC. Admittance to voting membership usually requires a unanimous vote of the existing membership, or such percentage consent as otherwise stated in the Operating Agreement. Anyone assigning their membership may lose that voting membership.

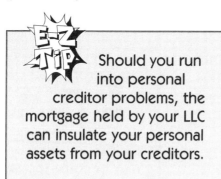

Family owned LLCs often take advantage of this limitation by further restricting membership transfers. For example, transfers may be restricted to family members. A former spouse desiring to dispose of his membership must transfer the interest back to the family. Thus, the LLC can protect an interest from seizure by an outsider—such as a creditor—and also protects assets in a divorce. The IRS agrees such provisions will not jeopardize the LLC's tax status provided only the right to share profits and not the authority to manage is being transferred.

How LLCs protect assets

There are many ways the advantages of the LLC can be used. An LLC is particularly well suited for asset protection, as well as for real estate investments, foreign investors, estate planning, creditor transactions, multi-state operations, charitable organizations and professional practices. Some examples:

> **E-Z TIP** Should you run into personal creditor problems, the mortgage held by your LLC can insulate your personal assets from your creditors.

Business owners frequently start their ventures as unincorporated sole proprietorships and become concerned about liability and the possible loss of personal assets only when their business heads for bankruptcy. One answer to this problem is to quickly form an LLC and transfer the assets from the proprietorship to the new LLC as you may do with a corporation.

Another way to shield personal assets using an LLC is to owe the LLC money. The LLC may then accept a mortgage on your home or personal property (such as a car or boat), or "blanket" mortgage all your property. Of course, your interest in the LLC would be protected from personal creditors who cannot take control of your company.

note Alternatively, you may transfer assets to different LLCs instead of transferring all assets to one LLC. The more owners there are for different assets, the harder it will be for one creditor to link and attach the assets. This insulates assets from liabilities arising from other assets.

Successor LLCs are considered to be a continuation of the original LLC if the members of the successor LLCs owned 50 percent or more interest of the prior LLC. The IRS considers this a restructuring and not a change in ownership.

E-Z TIP A single LLC may be divided into separate LLCs without risking the dissolution of the original LLC.

Be careful when transferring assets to an LLC. Many people use offshore LLCs and foreign trusts for this purpose. The trust then conducts its affairs through an LLC with the trust then owning this one asset—the entire interest of the LLC. This arrangement serves four important purposes:

1) The trust can more easily trade and do business through the LLC.

2) The LLC insulates the trust from potential liabilities.

3) The LLC creates another layer of privacy.

4) The LLC helps avoid U.S. income tax liability on most U.S. source investment income.

note The Bahamas, British Virgin Islands or Seychelles are common choices for the offshore LLCs because they are strong privacy havens.

The LLC is usually set up in a different tax haven than the trust haven, a country with favorable company laws. The trustee usually serves as the manager of the LLC and manages the entire offshore system— the trust and the LLC—as one entity. It is actually the LLC owned by the trust that conducts these activities.

As with a limited partnership, a creditor who seizes a member's interest in the LLC does not become a member of the company without the consent of the remaining members. Although the creditor receives an assignment of membership interest, the amount of membership income allocated to his share must be reported for income tax purposes. If the LLC makes no actual distribution to that member, the creditor has incurred an expense and received nothing in return. This is a powerful deterrent to a creditor seizing membership interest.

> **E-Z TIP** Make transfers of assets to the LLC well before problems arise as courts will be most concerned about attempts to avoid your obligations. The key is not to wait.

Gifts and estate planning with the LLC

LLCs are ideal vehicles for transferring real estate and other investments as gifts to children or other recipients. If the LLC owns the property, an LLC membership interest could be gifted instead of the actual property. Parents, for instance, could retain managerial control over the LLC, receive compensation for services rendered and still depreciate the gifts. Two classes of membership could be issued. Parents may have class A membership with voting rights (regardless of percentage of ownership) and children, class B non-voting membership. If the membership interest assigned each year does not exceed the $10,000 limit, no gift tax need be paid. The flexibility of the LLC's Operating Agreement can be used to anticipate voluntary and involuntary transfers, as well as a member's death.

The LLC is much more flexible than a trust that is typically used for gifting purposes. There are no limitations as to the number of members nor mandatory income distributions. Parents can eliminate third party interests by restricting membership and determine the distributive rights of members.

There are many variations of the LLC structure that may be used for any real estate, family business, closely held business or passive investments. A qualified estate or financial planner together with your lawyer can customize an LLC to your specific needs.

Protecting professional practices with an LLP

DEFINITION

Professionals, such as doctors, lawyers and accountants, may be eligible to form a special LLC known as an LLP, or *limited liability partnership.*

An LLP is similar in concept to an LLC, a professional corporation or professional tax association. It shields each partner from liabilities arising from the malpractice of other partners, but it does not protect the partner who commits malpractice. Nor does it protect those negligent employees working under a partner's supervision.

The very nature of the protection itself creates a different problem. If the manager of the LLP, under whom everyone works, is not shielded from the malpractice of a partner, who would ever agree to be manager or supervisor? A flexible Operating Agreement need not require full indemnification and may require that the LLC's assets be first depleted. It also may prohibit contributions made directly to third parties. In addition, the agreement may not require contributions in cases of fraud or other inappropriate conduct.

> *note* Most LLPs require that members indemnify the manager. The terms of indemnification must be clearly set forth in the Operating Agreement.

The risk of a malpractice suit destroying the entire partnership may be significantly reduced with an LLP, but under no circumstances should malpractice insurance be reduced or eliminated. Conversely, do not ignore the many benefits of the LLP because your firm carries adequate malpractice insurance.

Some states allow professionals to use an LLC designation instead of the LLP. Those states also tax LLCs as corporations.

Planning Pointers

◆ The Limited Liability Company features many of the benefits of a corporation and limited partnership, and as such is a hybrid company.

◆ The LLC may have certain tax benefits over other entities—or disadvantages—depending upon several factors. A tax advisor should always be involved in the choice of organizational entity.

◆ An LLC need not necessarily be organized in your own state. Selection of the organizational state also will depend upon several factors.

◆ Managers and members of the LLC have no personal liability for the debts of the LLC.

◆ A creditor of a member in an LLC can generally obtain only a charging order against that member's interest. This entitles the creditor only to any distributed profits or proceeds due that member. The creditor, however, becomes liable for all taxes attributable to that member's share of profits.

◆ An LLC can operate an active business or be used to hold more passive assets and investments.

◆ LLCs can elect to be taxed as either C corporations or as partnerships.

Any corporation can protect wealth

9

Chapter 9

Any corporation can protect wealth

What you'll find in this chapter:

➡ The C and S corporations and the LLC

➡ Why incorporate in Nevada and Wyoming

➡ How corporations limit your liability

➡ How to finance your corporation

➡ Beware of dangerous corporate obligations

How effectively can a corporation serve as an asset protector? The corporation is not always the ideal vehicle to safely hold personal assets. The two major drawbacks of the corporation as an asset protector are 1) transfers of assets to and from the corporation carries tax implications, and 2) creditors of a stockholder can claim the shares you own or any obligations due you from the corporation. The corporation then has marginal use in wealth preservation.

> **note**
> The chief value of the corporation, of course, is its ability to insulate personal assets against liabilities.

Newer entities, such as the *limited liability company (LLC)* and *limited liability partnership (LLP),* overcome some corporate disadvantages and thus assume a far more significant role in asset protection. They probably will become even more valuable in future years as professionals become more familiar with them.

Frequently overlooked corporate advantages

Notwithstanding the corporation's limitations for asset protection, a corporation offers significant benefits.

- A shareholder's liability is limited only to his or her investment.

- Employees can participate in profits and defer income in corporate retirement plans.

- Corporations traditionally enjoy lower tax rates than do individual taxpayers.

- Tax brackets can possibly be split among several corporations, or tax deductions multiplied by the same corporation.

- Social Security payments are 50 percent deductible to the corporation.

- Stock ownership in a C corporation can be owned by trusts, limited partnerships and other "safe haven" entities.

- Income and losses of one corporation can be consolidated with those of other corporations to reduce taxes.

> **E-Z TIP** Stock ownership can be anonymous when held as bearer shares, as with Nevada and Wyoming corporations.

- Appreciated shares can be used to maximize deductible charitable donations.

- Deductible fringe benefits are sometimes only available through a C corporation.

- Dividends paid to corporate shareholders may be either tax-free or nominally taxed.

- Corporate liquidations can oftentimes be advantageously structured to defer or reduce capital gains.

Select the right type of corporation

The S corporation provides the same limited liability protection as does the C corporation. The S corporation (previously the Subchapter S corporation) gains popularity with higher corporate taxes because business owners will then frequently elect S corporation status to avoid the double taxation from a regular or C corporation.

For asset protection planning, you obtain considerably greater flexibility with a C corporation because partnerships, trusts, other corporations, and other similar protective entities cannot be shareholders of an S corporation.

Because the S corporation is taxed as a partnership or proprietorship (depending upon the number of owners), it is frequently believed that the S corporation loses the limited liability feature of a C corporation. This is untrue. Consider only tax consequences when selecting your type of corporation.

Use a C corporation if corporate shares may be more advantageously owned by other entities, whether for asset protection or estate planning purposes.

S corporation or LLC?

An LLC is an entity quite similar to an S corporation because its owners have limited liability and it can elect to be taxed as a proprietorship or partnership. A member's risk would be limited to loss of investment plus liability on guarantees on behalf of the LLC. LLC profits and losses can be divided and excluded from a member's income to the extent of the member's capital contribution plus his share of liabilities. Moreover, contributions and distributions of appreciated property between shareholders and an LLC can be easily structured as tax-free exchanges.

For asset protection, the chief advantage of the LLC over the S corporation is that its ownership arrangements can be more varied.

An LLC can be owned by a family limited partnership, a trust or other corporation. An S corporation cannot be owned by these entities and is usually restricted to individual ownership. This makes estate and asset protection planning more difficult with an S corporation.

> note Most states treat member interests in an LLC as they do partnership interests in a limited partnership.

Ownership interests in an LLC are also more creditor-protected than are shares in an S corporation which can be seized by creditors. The creditor gains only a charging order against that interest, providing the creditor only the right to distributed profits or liquidation proceeds due the debtor member. But this is not universal. The laws concerning LLCs must be thoroughly reviewed to determine the rights of creditors against member interests in an LLC. The LLC, with all its advantages, will eventually obsolete the S corporation; however, there are four advantages with an S corporation:

1) An S corporation can be acquired by another business, tax-free. This is not possible with an LLC.

2) S corporation owners pay employment taxes only on their salaries. LLC owners pay employment taxes on all profits.

3) State taxes may be lower for an S corporation.

4) When a C corporation converts to an LLC, it is taxed as if liquidated. Converting an S corporation carries no such tax consequences.

 LLCs also will unquestionably replace S corporations because their ownership flexibility and greater asset protection will become more important tools in wealth preservation planning. But, this will take time. Several states still lack LLC legislation, and many do not allow professionals to use LLCs. Most importantly, because the LLC is a new type of business entity, the cautious planner will want more battle-tests before employing them extensively for asset protection.

User-friendly Nevada and Wyoming

Which states are friendliest to corporations? Most people say Delaware, but they are mistaken. Nevada offers many advantages over Delaware and all other states, except Wyoming, whose corporation laws closely parallel

Nevada's. There are many advantages in choosing to incorporate in Nevada rather than Delaware:

• Delaware taxes corporate profits. Nevada is tax-free. Delaware will be more costly if you expect significant profits.

• Nevada will not share tax information with the IRS. Other states, including Delaware, do exchange information.

• Delaware has a franchise tax, but Nevada does not.

• Delaware requires extensive annual disclosure, including stockholder meeting dates, business localities outside Delaware and the number and value of shares issued. Nevada requires no such information, only the current list of officers and directors.

> **E-Z TIP** Stockholders are not public record in Nevada, and shares may be held in bearer form with ownership anonymous.

• Nevada's corporate officers and directors have far broader protection than do Delaware's. Articles of incorporation in Nevada may eliminate or limit the personal liability of officers and directors for breach of fiduciary duty, other than improper dividend payments. Nevada also has a shorter statute of limitations to sue for improper dividends and more options for director indemnification. Delaware director indemnification is at the court's discretion. It is an absolute right in Nevada.

• Nevada also allows broader indemnities to others who incur liability on behalf of the corporation. Insurance trust funds, self-insurance and granting directors a security interest or lien on corporate assets to guarantee their indemnifications are common examples. For asset protection, the absolute authority of corporate officers and directors to place liens on their own corporate assets for indemnification purposes provides them continuing control over their corporate assets without the need to prove an exchange of funds. *This is an important strategy!* Delaware and all other states invalidate such self-serving financial and legal arrangements. Absent fraud, a Nevada board of directors' decision concerning financial arrangements is conclusive and is neither void nor voidable. This is untrue in Delaware and elsewhere.

• It is also quite easy to incorporate in Nevada. Because so many astute business owners now establish Nevada corporations, many firms offer complete incorporation and resident agent services to clients nationwide.

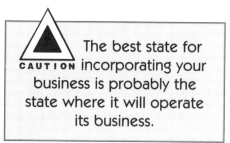

The best state for incorporating your business is probably the state where it will operate its business.

If you incorporate in another state, including Delaware or Nevada, you must also register to conduct business as a foreign corporation in your own state. Your corporation then becomes subject to the laws of your state which voids the advantages of incorporating in Nevada or Wyoming. Your business may additionally incur multiple state taxes and filing requirements.

Consider Nevada or Wyoming only when your corporation will not regularly do business elsewhere or remains a passive operating entity.

The one downside of the Nevada corporation is that they are most frequently IRS audited. Wyoming offers the same corporate advantages as Nevada, and reportedly has fewer IRS audits.

The corporation as liability shield

Physicians, dentists, accountants, lawyers, architects and many other professionals commonly conduct practices through a professional corporation. The so-called *professional association (PA)* or *professional corporation (PC)* became popular because they allow the professional to invest more into corporate pension plans.

Since the professional corporation primarily gained popularity as a tax-saver, few professionals relied upon it for liability protection. Professionals are generally less concerned than merchants about ordinary business debts, because as service providers they incur few commercial liabilities. And, as professionals operating their own practice, they correctly reason they can and will be sued personally for their malpractice. Therefore, their corporation cannot protect them personally. Malpractice insurance is still their shield to liability.

The professional corporation, however, can be a significant asset protector. While a practitioner may be the target of a malpractice suit caused by his own negligence, it may be an employee or associate who caused the injury without professional negligence. In this instance, the corporation, not the professional, would become the defendant in the lawsuit because the corporation would be the principal that employed the negligent individual.

Large legal, accounting and physician groups that operate as a general partnership or loose-knit association can greatly benefit from corporate organization. A professional corporation can insulate each partner from the unlimited liability they would otherwise incur as individuals. A still safer organizational strategy is for each professional to organize his own professional corporation with their respective corporations then forming a partnership with each corporation a partner. Should the partnership then incur a liability, the creditor could only reach the assets of the partnership and assets of the respective partner corporations. The personal assets of their principals would remain safe.

Despite this one important advantage, the professional corporation is not always the professional's first organizational choice. A business corporation offers one major advantage over the professional corporation: The professional need not be the stockholder, as is required with the professional corporation. Shares in the business corporation may be owned by the professional's spouse or another entity, such as a trust or limited partnership, which better protects the corporate shares.

Incorporate before you incur liabilities

Many business owners start their ventures as unincorporated sole proprietorships. Concern about losing personal assets arises only when their business heads toward bankruptcy. If you are that business owner, you may possibly still escape personal liability for your business's obligations, but only if you quickly incorporate your business and transfer proprietorship business assets to the corporation. The corporation should then pay first the oldest business obligations. These would be the proprietorship obligations for which you are personally liable. As your corporation pays these older debts, it incurs newer debts with the same or other suppliers. However, these debts are now corporate obligations. Your goal is to fully pay all the proprietorship debts and only then can you safely liquidate your business—when its creditors have no personal recourse against you or your personal assets.

> **note**
>
> If you now operate an unincorporated business, convert before you get into serious financial trouble. Your smartest strategy is to incorporate before starting your business.

This strategy demands careful coordination and open disclosure. For instance, you must operate your business until you fully pay all pre-incorporation debts. You must also advise creditors that your business is now incorporated. Finally, your creditors must apply your payments to the proprietorship debts that you want discharged. Earmark each check how it is to be applied.

Ways to lose corporate protection

Your corporation can be an effective liability insulator only if it functions as a corporation. You can lose your corporate protection through one of eight common mistakes that allow creditors to pierce the corporate veil and sue you personally for corporate debts:

1) *Commingling funds:* Operate your corporation as a distinct entity, separate from yourself in every respect. Segregate corporate funds from your own. Document funds transferred between you and your corporation. Example: Are your funds invested in the corporation as a loan or a contribution to capital? Conversely, are funds you take from the corporation a loan, dividends, salary or expense reimbursement? Record every transaction on both your personal and corporate records, and similarly record all financial transactions between related corporations or entities.

2) *Commingling assets:* The prohibitions against commingled cash also apply to other assets, such as inventory. You can safely transfer inventory between corporations, provided you maintain accurate records. Creditors of a corporation can throw affiliated corporations into bankruptcy when they encounter undocumented transactions between the bankrupt corporation and its affiliates.

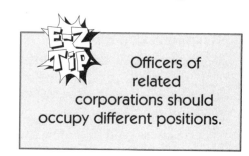

Officers of related corporations should occupy different positions.

3) *Not signing documents as a corporate agent:* If you operate as a corporation, have its legal documents say so. Clearly state the corporate name and designate your title near your signature on all documents and checks.

4) *Not operating your corporations autonomously:* Operate multiple corporations autonomously. For instance, use separate not identical or interlocking boards of directors. Conduct separate corporate meetings and maintain separate corporate books.

5) *Failing to keep adequate corporate records:* Creditors can challenge the corporate existence when records improperly document key corporate actions. Keep good records for all director and stockholder meetings.

6) *Failing to identify your business as a corporation:* Creditors must realize that they are dealing with a corporation if you are to avoid personal lawsuits from creditors and others who may think it is a proprietorship or partnership. If you use a fictitious or assumed (dba) name instead of the actual corporate name, then properly register the fictitious name according to state law.

> **note**
> Your corporate name should be on all signs, letterheads, bill-heads, checks and wherever else your business name appears.

7) *Operating a dissolved corporation:* A corporation dissolved by the state has its corporate protection voided. Pay corporate taxes and franchise fees so your corporation remains in good standing. And never voluntarily dissolve a corporation with debts. These debts then automatically become your own as its stockholder.

8) *Undercapitalizing your corporation:* Too small an investment in your corporation, or too little paid for its shares of stock compared to what you loaned your corporation, can spell trouble. Some states set minimum capitalization requirements and these should be rigidly observed.

When operating your corporation, apply five more creditor-proofing tests:

1) Does your corporation have a business address and telephone number?

2) Do you have canceled corporate checks to show that the corporation pays its own expenses?

3) Have all necessary business licenses been issued to the corporation?

> **note**
> Most lawyers and accountants recommend that at least $1 should be invested as equity (for shares) for every $4 in loans.

4) Does your corporation maintain bank accounts?

5) Does your corporation transact any significant business with unaffiliated parties?

Each point can help establish that your corporation is engaged in business as a legitimate entity, and one separate and apart from you as its owner.

Creditors frequently try to pierce the corporate veil and claim that the corporation is nothing more than a sham alter-ego of its principals. But a creditor has the burden of proof. While courts seldom dismiss the corporation's important protection, they will do so if its owners flagrantly ignore these or other basic requirements for properly maintaining their corporation as a distinct entity.

Should your creditor frivolously sue you in bad faith, countersue the creditor and his attorney. Corporate protection does not guarantee that you will not need to personally defend against a bad faith creditor claim, but you will keep your personal assets safe by observing these points.

A creditor's personal lawsuit against a corporate owner is most frequently only another bad faith maneuver to force the owner to defend the suit or settle.

Shrewdly finance your corporation

Funds that you loan to your own corporation are funds that you can easily lose. Yet, you can reduce or eliminate this risk of loss by correctly structuring your loan to your corporation.

The wrong way to finance your corporation is to directly invest in your corporation, whether it is for shares (equity) or as a loan. If your business fails, you will be only another unsecured creditor and reclaim none or little of your original investment. The bankruptcy court may even subordinate your claim to other unsecured creditors' claims, thus assuring you will receive no dividends.

Their claim then becomes superior to general creditor claims. However, your mortgage against your business may be set aside in bankruptcy without some additional steps. Strategy: Have your bank directly loan your business the funds with your business pledging its assets to the bank as collateral. Your bank will lend to the business since you can pledge personal assets as collateral for the loan. The 100 percent secured loan thus provides the bank no risk. Should your business fail, your bank will be its secured party and the first creditor to be repaid from liquidating the business's assets. Once repaid, your bank would relinquish the personal assets you pledged as security. Always safeguard your investment. Use your bank as your helpful intermediary to insure your investment will be recouped should your business fail.

Do take this strategy one step further. Bankruptcy cases routinely say that where a lender is secured by the business owner's personal guarantee, repayments to the lender from the business, within one year preceding bankruptcy, may be recoverable as an insider preference by other creditors. The courts reason that the burden to repay the lender should fall upon the business owner, not arms-length general creditors. But, you may have a friend or relative guarantee your bank loan, while you pledge your collateral to this intermediary who then pledges

The shrewd owner secures himself with the business's assets.

it to the bank. Since you are not the bank's direct guarantor, a business bankruptcy would not jeopardize the bank's secured claim against the business's assets. With the bank repaid, your collateral reverts back to you through your intermediary.

Before investing or loaning money to your corporation, review this with your attorney. It is not too complicated an arrangement and your attorney and bank can easily structure the deal. You then have two big advantages: First, funds you invest in your business are now more fully protected than if you had invested the funds for stock or made an unsecured loan. Second, you now indirectly control the mortgage on your business and can also indirectly protect your business from other creditors.

Safe ways to title corporate shares

There are five popular options for titling corporate shares:

1) A **family limited partnership** is ideal for owning shares in a C corporation.

2) An **irrevocable trust** may be desirable, particularly when the trust serves some tax or estate planning objective above asset protection.

3) **Tenancy-by-the-entirety** is an option for married couples in one of the 31 states that recognize this more protective type of ownership.

4) An **offshore trust** is particularly useful for publicly traded shares intended for long-term investment. It is not recommended for already appreciated assets, as a transfer would trigger a 35 percent excise tax on the appreciation.

5) **Another corporation or LLC** can be used when the shares of the parent company can also be protected and when the arrangement provides independent organizational or tax benefits.

Become an invisible shareholder

Corporate shares that you own in your own name can always be seized by your creditors. While an asset protection plan may attempt to conceal your identity as a shareholder to the extent legally possible, creditors can nevertheless discover the actual corporate shareholders through examination of:

• *Corporate books. A* creditor can subpoena the corporate books. This invariably lists its stockholders.

• *Bank and credit records* frequently identify the stockholders of a corporate borrower. Major suppliers may also list stockholders on credit applications. Utility companies, for instance, particularly request stockholder information on their credit inquiries.

• *Licensing applications.* Pharmacies, nursing homes, liquor stores, barber and beauty salons all exemplify the many licensed businesses where ownership disclosure is mandatory.

• *Building permits, zoning variances and other municipal applications* frequently require disclosure of the corporate shareholders.

• *Corporate tax returns* specifically list stockholders who own 50 percent or more of the outstanding shares.

> **E-Z TIP** One convenient way to conceal an ownership interest in a corporation is to use a Nevada or Wyoming corporation, the two states that allow bearer shares.

• *Personal income tax returns* show dividend income from the corporation. While small business corporations seldom issue dividends to their stockholders, more sophisticated creditors investigate personal tax returns for pass-through profits or losses from S corporations or LLCs taxed as a partnership.

You can, of course, less easily conceal ownership in a publicly owned corporation because the transfer agent must accurately record stockholders.

Unless you actually possess the shares, you can truthfully deny ownership of the corporation. If you must incorporate in your own state, have this corporation owned by a Nevada or Wyoming corporation. The ultimate shareholders thus remain invisible. Another alternative: a foreign corporation in an offshore privacy haven as the parent company. International business corporations usually allow bearer shares, or the shares can be registered to a nominee "straw."

 Have your lawyer guide you in these strategies so you do not inadvertently commit perjury concerning ownership. Also resign as an officer or director of the corporation. Creditors who discover that you are an officer or director of a small closely held corporation will more closely investigate your ownership.

Ways to poison pill corporate shares

With creditors in hot pursuit, you can quickly sell publicly traded stocks or bonds. Stockholders of a privately owned corporation cannot easily or quickly sell, but must oftentimes find ways to make their shares near-worthless to creditors. Six poison pill strategies:

1)   *Impose transfer restrictions:* Restrictions on the transfer of shares generally cannot prevent creditor seizures; however, tight restrictions may discourage the less aggressive or knowledgeable creditor. Restrictions must always be reasonable to be enforceable.

2)   *Assess your shares:* If your shares are not fully paid, or are assessable, a creditor who claims your shares takes them subject to this obligation to pay. A high potential assessment will neutralize the value of the shares to your creditors.

> **E-Z TIP**
> Dilute ownership by selling additional shares to other family members, or other family controlled entities, such as a trust or limited partnership.

3)   *Issue irrevocable proxies:* If a creditor cannot vote seized shares, it diminishes the creditor's enthusiasm and significantly lessens the value of the shares because the creditor has less control. An alternative: exchange voting shares for non-voting shares.

4) *Dilute stock ownership:* Why allow your creditor the opportunity to control your business by seizure of a controlling interest?

5) *Encumber the business:* Corporate shares have no value greater than the net worth of the business. So why hand the creditor a financially sound company that can be profitably sold or liquidated, rather than forfeit a heavily indebted business that would yield the creditor nothing? Your poison pill can be as simple as a "friendly" mortgage against your own business.

6) *Pledge your shares:* Why not borrow and pledge your shares as collateral? If the amount you borrow approximates the value of your shares, your creditor will chase worthless shares.

Spread corporate control

A creditor who gains only a minority interest in a corporation cannot control the corporation. A minority stockholder can only vote his shares and await such dividends as may be declared. Therefore, spread stock ownership in a closely owned corporation between family members so that no one family member owns more than 49 percent of the voting shares of the corporation. The bylaws should empower the remaining 51 percent, or more, to control all corporate matters.

Liability traps for corporate directors

Corporate directorships are increasingly hazardous and are a surefire way to attract liability. Directors incur civil and criminal liability in many ways other than through their negligent management; however, nine lesser known but chronic trouble spots worth noting include:

1) **Improper dividends:** Dividends that are unlawfully declared make the directors personally liable to the creditors for any resulting corporate insolvency. Delaware alone permits dividends from funds other than earned surplus.

2) **Shareholder loans:** Directors who allow the corporation to make loans to an officer or stockholder may be liable if the borrower fails to repay. Directors must prudently authorize insider loans.

3) **Unpaid taxes:** Corporate officers are usually the responsible parties for unpaid U.S. withholding taxes. Certain states also impose automatic liability on directors for unpaid state taxes. Directors can become liable for

unpaid federal withholding taxes if the IRS can prove that the directors controlled corporate funds and determined whether the withholding taxes were paid.

4) **Improper payments upon dissolution:** Directors also become liable to creditors when they authorize dissolution of the corporation and distributions of proceeds to stockholders before creditors are fully paid.

5) **Securities violations:** Directors seldom realize their liability to investors for false and misleading statements in the corporation's prospectus. Outsider or unaffiliated directors must particularly verify the accuracy of a registration because the SEC imposes this special burden upon outside directors. Directors who resign before the registration is filed cannot become liable.

6) **ERISA:** The Employee Retirement Income Security Act of 1974 imposes a director penalty of between 5 and 100 percent of the funds involved in a prohibited transaction.

> ⚠ **CAUTION** Always obtain a legal opinion before undertaking an ERISA transaction.

7) **Anti-trust violations:** Directors may be personally liable for anti-trust violations that they reasonably should have been aware of as corporate directors. Liability in these cases may be particularly costly because any recovery against the directors can be triple the actual damages.

8) **Civil rights and discrimination violations:** This is a comparatively new source of liability for corporate directors and arises when directors approve or allow corporate policies that violate these laws.

9) **Environmental law violation:** Another rapidly expanding problem for directors of companies is the potential for hazardous waste violations, particularly when the directors actually hold knowledge of hazardous waste conditions and take no action to prevent further waste.

Essential Insurance

Because corporate directors face so many potential liabilities, they must be adequately protected by insurance.

Directors need indemnification from their corporation for any lawsuits against them. The indemnification must be secured by an adequate director liability insurance policy. Most publicly owned corporations now provide indemnification and insurance for their boards, as do many more smaller, privately owned corporations with outside directors. Defending claims becomes less complicated, tax write-offs for premiums less questionable, and policies less expensive when the corporation buys the liability insurance for its board members.

A director is adequately protected only with the right insurance policy, one that satisfies eight points:

> **note**
> Few outside directors today will serve on corporate boards without insurance, and few directors will pay for this insurance out of their own pockets.

1) *Coverage:* With today's high litigation awards, the policy should provide at least $1 million coverage per occurrence ($5 million or more for larger corporations, or those with excessive risk such as hazardous waste).

2) *Exclusions:* Does the policy include such common claims as dishonesty, fraud, libel or slander, SEC violations, insider trading, pending lawsuits, ERISA, anti-trust and hazardous waste? Exclusions are negotiable and may be your deciding factor when evaluating coverage.

3) *Deductibles:* A deductible of $5,000 per director, per claim, is most common. Other policies use split deductibles—95 percent insured and 5 percent uninsured. A $5 million judgment still represents a sizeable $250,000 loss to the director. Choose affordable fixed-dollar deductibles.

4) *Negotiation:* Must the insurance company notify the directors if it cancels the policy? This is essential.

5) *Supplemental insurance:* Is other insurance available to cover deductibles, exclusions and other lapses in policy coverage?

6) *Authority:* Do the corporate bylaws allow for indemnification and the company's payment of premiums?

7) *Stability:* Is the insurer well-rated and financially stable?

8) *Legal review:* Has the policy been reviewed and approved by both the company's attorney and your own? Remember, your interests may not parallel the company's.

Tips to escape corporate guarantees

When a supplier demands your guarantee, find a more lenient supplier.

Because small business owners must frequently guarantee corporate obligations, it reduces the usefulness of their corporation as a liability insulator. Certain debts, particularly bank loans, inevitably require the owner's guarantee. But you can usually sidestep guarantees to other creditors and also escape liability on existing guarantees. Common sense, a tough attitude and these four tips are what you need:

1) *One supplier may demand your guarantee. Others will not.* A guarantee is only another bargaining point for credit. Most prospective suppliers will extend limited credit to your corporation without your guarantee.

2) *Understand your creditor's concerns and reduce his risk.* Your creditor will then willingly forego the guarantee. A supplier may refuse $20,000 on credit without your personal guarantee, but risk $10,000.

3) *Offer alternative collateral.* Your supplier may accept a security interest on business assets instead of your personal guarantee. Or perhaps a guarantee from an affiliated corporation will suffice.

4) If you do sign a guarantee, *negotiate for a partial or limited liability* to limit your exposure.

note

Insist that your creditor cancels your guarantee once your business establishes a good track record for prompt payments.

Never guarantee existing debts. You gain nothing. Once a business falters, credit managers will plead, promise, threaten and cajole for personal guarantees. But why risk personal assets to secure already shaky corporate obligations? Nor should you assume that your business will honor its obligations. A company encountering serious financial difficulty seldom fully pays its debts.

Creditors pursue the deepest pockets. When your partner's pockets are not as deep as yours, you are in trouble!

Perhaps you have already signed too many guarantees. You can possibly extricate yourself from these obligations by applying four strategies:

1) **Verify which obligations you guaranteed.** Many business people never realize, or forget, that they signed a guarantee with their original order form or as part of a credit application. Confirm with every creditor whether they have your personal guarantee—and request copies.

Make your partners sign guarantees that you sign. If your partners lack your financial resources, your creditor will chase you for payment.

2) **Immediately terminate all outstanding guarantees.** Guarantees on future credit can always be terminated, and every guarantee should be revoked to avoid further liability. Also cancel outstanding guarantees for future purchases when you sell your business.

3) **Pay personally guaranteed debts before your company fails.** If at all possible, float your floundering business until you can fully discharge every guaranteed debt. Or, secure guaranteed creditors with a mortgage on the business assets so these guaranteed creditors obtain payment priority over non-guaranteed creditors. This reduces the odds they will later pursue you for payment.

4) **Negotiate a release from your guarantee.** Use bargaining power. A creditor owed $20,000 may accept $20,000 in return merchandise. Or $10,000 in cash. Or a mortgage on the business's assets in exchange for a release on your guarantee. Do you owe your bank $500,000? It may release your guarantee if you help the bank recover more than it could on its own when liquidating your business. Secured lenders typically need the owner's cooperation to maximize their recovery. Bargain cooperation for concessions that will reduce or eliminate your personal exposure.

Apply a carrot and stick when dealing with guaranteed creditors.

If a creditor or lender with your guarantee will not release you for your cooperation, the same creditor may respond quicker to less friendly actions. For example, a Chapter 11 may forestall foreclosure and possibly dissipate collateral. This, obviously, is not to your creditor's advantage. Other bargaining chips can coax creditors to cancel guarantees.

If you personally pay a guaranteed corporate debt, you have the right to indemnification and reimbursement from the corporation. Your corporation may then give you an indemnification and security interest on its assets to secure this indemnification. You then have the right to reimbursement from the corporation ahead of unsecured creditors. Since the bankruptcy courts can set aside your mortgage as an insider preference if your business files bankruptcy within the year, then secure yourself earlier or liquidate the business without bankruptcy.

More dangerous corporate obligations

Guaranteed corporate debts and director liabilities are only two ways to become personally liable for corporate activities. Four other liability claims commonly arise against corporate officers, directors, stockholders and even employees:

1) *Unpaid withholding taxes:* Corporate officers (particularly the president and treasurer) are personally responsible for unpaid trust taxes or withholding taxes deducted from employees. There is no personal responsibility for the non-payment of non-trust taxes, or taxes contributed by the business as the employer. Your accountant or legal counsel should highlight other fiduciary taxes for which you are liable in your state.

Tax obligations can be significant. Unpaid withholding taxes can quickly became an astronomical personal liability for an officer of even a smaller business. Smart business owners realize the consequences that arise from unpaid withholding taxes.

If you cannot fully pay withholding taxes, then pay the trust portion and carefully designate this on the check so the IRS will apply the payment to the trust tax. The IRS can collect from the officers any trust taxes due if the business fails to pay.

Only one spouse should become a corporate officer.

Personal liability from unpaid withholding taxes is both a common and serious problem for owners of a failed business. The IRS then has recourse only against that one spouse while the non-liable spouse can then remain a safe haven for the family assets.

2)   ***Unpaid wages:*** Failure to pay wages can subject corporate officers to civil or criminal liability. Unpaid severance, accrued vacation and other earned pay are all "wages."

note Writing bad checks for COD purchases is a crime in most states.

3)   ***Bad checks:*** Bad checks may cause personal liability even when you sign the check as a corporate agent.

4)   ***Unemployment compensation:*** Corporate officers can become responsible if the corporation fails to pay state unemployment compensation contributions. Check your state laws to determine your individual responsibility for these obligations. Most states hold corporate officers criminally liable for unpaid unemployment compensation, sales and withholding taxes, wages and bad checks. Your attorney can advise which obligations have the most severe sanctions.

The corporate reverse mortgage

Business owners should throw friendly mortgages against their business assets as a shield against creditors. Your corporation can also mortgage and shield your personal assets. For instance, your corporation may secure your personal assets if you owe money to your business. Your corporation may hold

Use a "shell" or dormant corporation as the mortgage holder.

a mortgage on your home, car, boat or possibly mortgage all your property. This, of course, becomes a safe strategy only if your corporation remains strong financially. If your corporation goes bankrupt, your loan belongs to a bankruptcy trustee who will enforce payment against you.

Avoid passive investments

Another important limitation of the corporation is that it cannot safely own accumulated passive assets without incurring severe tax penalties. Your accountant can determine the amount and type of assets that may be safely titled to your corporation without incurring this tax; however, excess cash, investments in other entities and personal assets, such as jewelry and collectibles, may all subject the corporation and its shareholders to serious tax problems. Moreover, these assets would needlessly be exposed to the business creditors. These assets should be best owned by a family limited partnership, irrevocable trust, a limited liability company or some other entity that can hold these assets with neither tax complications nor potential creditor claim.

Planning Pointers

◆ The corporation is an excellent entity to shield its owners from the debts of a business enterprise. It has many disadvantages as an entity to shield personal assets.

◆ The C corporation and S corporation feature the same limited liability. Their only difference is in their taxation. The S corporation is taxed as a partnership.

◆ The Nevada and Wyoming corporation have many advantages over corporations organized in other states, and when the business can be headquartered in either of these states, they should be considered.

◆ Professionals require the protection of a professional corporation (or professional association) for the same reasons a business owner requires a business corporation or a comparable entity.

◆ You must operate your corporation as a distinct and separate entity and observe all corporate formalities or the courts can pierce your corporate protection and impose personal liability.

◆ Finance your corporation so that you as the owner have first claim on its assets. This protects your investment and your business from its creditors.

◆ Corporate shares can be seized by a stockholder's creditors. A limited partnership or LLC can be excellent entities to protect these shares. S corporation shares are more difficult to protect because they cannot be owned by other entities.

◆ There are a number of ways to diminish the value of corporate shares to a creditor.

◆ Corporate directors are particularly vulnerable today to liability. They require adequate liability insurance and a clear understanding of their responsibilities and acts for which they can incur liability.

◆ The value of the corporation is lost when its owner personally guarantees its debts. There are strategies to avoid personal guarantees.

Protecting your assets offshore

10

Chapter 10

Protecting your assets offshore

What you'll find in this chapter:

➡ Using offshore havens to protect assets

➡ How to use the asset protection trust

➡ Offshore protection from IRS seizures

➡ Protect against product liability claims

➡ Why the Nevis LLC is right for you

Offshore havens offer more iron-clad asset protection than domestic structures. Sheltering wealth in one or more foreign asset-protection havens may, in some circumstances, be the only way to successfully protect wealth from a creditor attack. Offshore asset protection provides considerably greater protection than does more conventional domestic asset protection strategies, such as irrevocable domestic trusts, family limited partnerships or titling assets with a less vulnerable spouse, because assets within the United States may be attacked as fraudulent transfers or recoverable under a wide range of other legal theories.

> **note**
> There is considerably less need to fear seizure when your assets are offshore and beyond the often unpredictable and arbitrary rulings of U.S.-based judges.

Offshore havens creditor-proof assets

Offshore havens more effectively protect assets for two reasons:

1)   The offshore haven provides strict financial privacy and secrecy.

2)   Money transferred correctly to such an offshore haven is exceptionally difficult for U.S. creditors or litigants to locate. U.S. creditors are powerless to discover a secretive foreign account in a secrecy haven unless you disclose it.

Of course, a judgment creditor can always compel you to disclose assets under oath. And an offshore secrecy haven should encourage neither perjury nor illegal concealment of assets. You can nevertheless protect your money through intermediaries and truthfully deny the existence of offshore assets—if your offshore accounts are correctly arranged. Nor would you necessarily know where the offshore funds are located once they flow through intermediaries.

> *note*
> It can be virtually impossible for a creditor to link offshore assets to you or your companies. But be guided by your attorney to avoid violating the law.

The offshore haven's chief asset protection advantage then is not through its ability to secrete wealth. Assume you will be compelled to truthfully disclose your offshore wealth, or that your creditor will independently locate it, most probably through your own tax returns. And if you don't report your offshore income and accounts to the IRS, your creditor may prove even more diligent than the IRS.

Secrecy can keep less inquisitive creditors from eye balling offshore assets, but secrecy is never the asset protection strategy. This forces the creditor to start a new lawsuit within the haven. This is usually futile for several reasons: The haven may not recognize the claim upon which the lawsuit is based. Or, it may be too late to start a new lawsuit. Offshore havens typically impose very short statutes of limitations, or time periods within which to sue. Most have only a two-year statute of limitations, thus requiring the lawsuit to commence within two years from when the claim arose, and not necessarily two years

> *note*
> Offshore havens chiefly protect assets because they do not enforce foreign judgments nor court orders.

from when the funds were transferred offshore. In practice, most U.S. civil cases can be stalled in litigation for two or more years. This leaves the creditor no recourse offshore.

When the creditor obtains an offshore judgment, he must then prove that the assets were fraudulently transferred offshore, an always difficult task since most havens presume the debtor acted without fraudulent intent. Even when it is possible to sue offshore, it is usually prohibitively expensive and impractical in all but those relatively few cases that involve either huge sums of money or a most tenacious or vindictive creditor.

> *note*
>
> Creditors' claims that assets were fraudulently transferred usually fall on deaf ears.

Creditors who chase offshore money through a foreign lawsuit will still have little chance to recover against an agile debtor who can continuously relocate his funds to still other offshore havens. A creditor will soon tire from the chase. Larger investors deploy their assets in several havens so their creditors cannot conveniently locate or threaten their entire wealth. A well-drafted offshore trust contains such a trigger provision that authorizes and directs the trustee to transfer the trust assets to another trust in another asset-protection jurisdiction should the trust be attacked. This never-ending game will exhaust even the most determined creditor.

> *note*
>
> No protective offshore haven will honor a foreign judgment or levy, subpoena or summons from a foreign litigant or agency, such as the IRS.

Offshore asset protection plans then are deliberately designed so creditors cannot seize offshore funds even should they obtain an offshore judgment.

However well you design your offshore financial fortress, as with domestic asset-protection strategies, no offshore arrangement guarantees complete safety. The possibility always exists that a creditor can find and seize offshore assets. But the right offshore structure will nevertheless insure your assets remain safe from all but the most clever, persistent and luckiest creditor.

Asset protection trust: the offshore financial fortress

The primary offshore asset protection structure is aptly named the Asset Protection Trust, or commonly called the International Trust, Foreign-Based Trust or Creditor-Protection Trust.

Trusts date back to Roman and Greek law. Ancient Germanic and French law had similar legal arrangements, and the trust was fundamental to Islamic law. The trust was probably the first tax shelter as feudal English trusts allowed citizens to avoid feudal taxes on property inheritances and transfers.

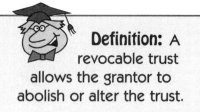 Any trust creates a legal relationship between three or more parties. The grantor or settlor creates and funds the trust. The trustee assumes legal title and manages the trust property according to the terms of the trust agreement and applicable trust law. The beneficiary receives money or property from the trust according to the trust terms.

One party can possibly assume more than one role. Many trusts enable you to be the grantor who creates the trust, while naming yourself both the trustee and beneficiary. This often happens with the popular living trust, commonly used to avoid probate. Trusts designed to reduce or avoid taxes usually have separate grantors, trustees and beneficiaries. There can be one or more beneficiaries.

Definition: A revocable trust allows the grantor to abolish or alter the trust.

A trust is either revocable or irrevocable. The grantor thus controls the trust assets, an arrangement that normally provides neither asset protection nor tax benefits.

The *Offshore Asset Protection Trust (OAPT),* like irrevocable domestic trusts, breaks the chain of legal ownership between the grantor and the trust assets. Asset Protection Trusts are also discretionary trusts, and individual beneficiaries have no vested interest. The grantor usually becomes a contingent remainder beneficiary so he has neither an immediate nor direct beneficial interest in the trust. This

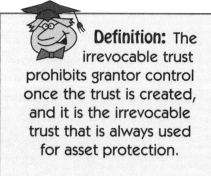

Definition: The irrevocable trust prohibits grantor control once the trust is created, and it is the irrevocable trust that is always used for asset protection.

discretionary power in the trustee thus non-vests the grantor's beneficial interest. Creditors who attempt to attach this contingent interest would unsuccessfully need to elevate their rights above those of the contingent beneficiaries. This interest is valueless because it can be destroyed by distributing principal, at the trustee's discretion; therefore, no creditor of a grantor or beneficiary can reach their interest.

note The trustee receives wide discretion to invest trust assets and also discretion to distribute assets or income to beneficiaries as he deems fit.

Assets to shelter offshore

Portable assets are most commonly transferred to the Asset Protection Trust. Cash, securities and collectibles, such as gold or jewelry, are all good candidates. To gain full protection, the asset must be physically outside the United States. The trustees and protectors must also be foreign so that they too are beyond reach of American courts. For that reason, U.S.-based or sourced assets should always be converted to foreign investments.

note You may choose not to heavily fund the trust unless it becomes absolutely necessary. Many people prefer their assets onshore, under their control and in their current investments, until the assets are seriously threatened. The Asset Protection Trust allows this. For example, the trust may become a limited partner in a limited partnership. The debtor, as general partner, decides when and if partnership assets are ever transferred to the trust, and therefore partnership assets may never be distributed to the Asset Protection Trust nor leave the United States, unless absolutely necessary. Similarly, partnership funds would remain in the partnership account until threatened by creditors, then the partnership would distribute its assets to the Asset Protection Trust as the major limited partner. The funds could be quickly wired offshore and more safely titled to the OAPT. Until then the assets may remain under the debtor's control.

note Real estate or other U.S.-based or sourced possessions, such as U.S. securities, titled to the trust remain within the jurisdiction of U.S. courts and are poorly or not protected.

While the Asset Protection Trust cannot always protect real estate or any other U.S.-based or sourced possession, you can always sell or mortgage U.S. assets so no equity is exposed to creditors. Sale or loan proceeds can then be directed to the offshore trust. The objective is never to leave assets exposed in the United States when you have creditors.

U.S. courts then lack the power to aid a creditor who attempts to seize your assets because assets physically outside the U.S. are also beyond U.S. court jurisdiction and decrees. Because it is a foreign trustee who controls the trust, a U.S. court cannot hold the grantor contemptuous for any failure to obey a court order to repatriate the funds. One cannot ordinarily be held in contempt for failure to perform acts beyond one's legal power.

> *note*
> No U.S. judge can compel you to return foreign-based trust assets to the United States if you are neither the trustee nor protector.

Using asset protection trusts for stronger domestic protection

The versatile Asset Protection Trust can accomplish more than shelter offshore wealth. Creatively used, it can simultaneously build more protection for your domestic assets. Several strategies are possible:

- ◆ The Asset Protection Trust can make loans to you and encumber your U.S. assets to secure repayment. Unattractive repayment terms can further discourage creditors from pursuing the pledged asset. Because you indirectly or informally control the trust, you can modify the payment terms or security, while the trust as lienholder can claim your U.S. asset over other creditors.

- ◆ Similarly, you can borrow from the trust with a shared appreciation mortgage. You borrow from the trust and repay the loan at a lower interest, and as the equity in your assets builds, a significant portion of that equity would be due your trust. This arrangement protects against creditors as well.

Wealth-saving OAPT features

The Offshore Asset Protection Trust (OAPT), while similar in many respects to the domestic irrevocable trust, includes several features that greatly expand its protective powers.

- *Most important, the OAPT is a foreign trust.* Since the trust is formed in a foreign anti-creditor haven, it provides special asset protection to the wealth titled to the trust. That one difference is critical. A comparable U.S. trust will remain vulnerable to creditors, but the OAPT is less vulnerable and creditors cannot easily reach its assets. This is why most OAPTs, rather than domestic trusts, are preferred for protecting larger nest eggs.

- *Foreign law governing.* The laws of the country where the OAPT is established govern trust law enforcement and interpretation. Their laws are always debtor-oriented.

- *Anti-duress provisions.* If a U.S. court compels the grantor to repatriate the trust assets, the trustee must refuse the grantor's request. This provision protects the grantor from a contempt citation.

- *Flight provisions.* This provision compels or authorizes the trustee to relocate the trust and its assets to a new trust in another haven if the trust becomes endangered by creditors in its present haven.

- *Discretionary powers.* This power grants the trustee full authority to decide all issues concerning the trust, including distributions to beneficiaries. Similar provisions may be contained in a domestic trust.

- *Provisions to alter or terminate beneficial rights.* The trustee also can alter or terminate the rights of any beneficiary with creditors, which eliminates claims against the trust by those creditors.

- *Provisions for a protector.* This provision allows for the appointment of an independent party to oversee the trustee. The protector thus protects the grantor from trustee malfeasance.

Other more subtle features characterize the OAPT. But in sum, the OAPT compares to domestic trusts the same way a modern jet compares to a World War I biplane. Both fly, but at considerably different speeds, altitudes and levels of performance.

Selecting the trustee for your OAPT

Selecting the right trustee(s) for your OAPT is particularly important because the trustee completely controls your trust.

The grantor should never be the sole trustee of his OAPT. A U.S. grantor or another American can initially serve as co-trustee but should immediately resign the trusteeship once the trust becomes threatened by creditors. A common arrangement is to start the trust with a three-trustee committee, typically an American husband and wife and a foreign trustee. Until a creditor problem arises, the husband and wife would control the trusteeship and resign only when a problem occurs and the foreign trustee becomes the sole trustee.

note For creditor protection, you must appoint at least one foreign trustee who controls the trusteeship.

Offshore trusts must, by law, have at least one foreign trustee. This is usually a resident individual or trust company within the trust haven. This is why you cannot substitute a foreign trustee only when under legal duress, as the law requires you to appoint one initially.

 Foreign trustees are plentiful and are professionally qualified to administer offshore trusts plus provide a variety of related offshore services. Most foreign trustees are chartered accountants or attorneys who passed a special examination. Some trustees work independently, but you may prefer a larger trust company or a long-established foreign bank as your institutional trustee. Qualified, well-established trustees are available to serve you wherever you establish your trust.

Strategies to safely control your OAPT

The trustee, with protector approval, has unlimited control and full discretion to manage the trust assets. The trust allows the trustee to do whatever the trustee may foreseeably need to do to protect or enhance the trust assets. This includes such common powers as are found in an irrevocable domestic trust—the rights to sell, buy, lease, encumber or invest the assets; to defend or prosecute claims; to pay debts and taxes; to hire other professionals; and to make loans and/or distribute income or principal to beneficiaries.

CAUTION When the grantor asserts significant control, the trust becomes ineffective as an asset protector.

A unique protective feature of the offshore trust is the trustee's power to establish a successor trust with an emergency trustee in another asset protection haven should the trust become threatened in its current haven.

The OAPT purposely grants the trustee the broadest powers and the grantor only negligible authority. Delegating complete control over your wealth to a foreign trustee can indeed be a frightening experience, but it becomes much less so once you realize how readily a foreign trustee will comply with your wishes on trust matters.

A grantor greatly concerned about controlling the trust assets can nevertheless take several intermediate measures to balance safety and asset protection against this desire to retain control. Of course, your attorney must ultimately decide the control you can safely retain without jeopardizing asset protection; however, this can be achieved only after he thoroughly investigates actual or potential claims against you.

 Should delegating complete control of your assets to the trustee still greatly concern you, then consider several options:

First, you may appoint a protector you know will faithfully follow your directions. Since the protector can replace the trustee, you gain alter ego control through the protector. Or, make the trust revocable until some specified event, such as when a creditor lawsuit arises the trust would automatically become irrevocable. Or, you may form a limited partnership primarily owned by the OAPT as the limited partner. As the general partner, you retain control over the limited partnership assets in the U.S. until threatened. The partnership assets would then be distributed to the offshore trust. Or, you may be the managing director of the international business corporation owned by the trust. You can also or alternatively control the trusteeship until threatened by creditors. Your spouse or another U.S. designee can serve as co-trustee. Another option is for your protector to be a co-signer with the trustee on trust accounts. Other popular control-retention techniques are available.

> **E-Z TIP**
>
> In some jurisdictions that have a short statute of limitations that commences with the trust formation, you may leave your trust lightly funded until expatriation of your wealth becomes necessary for asset protection purposes.

Protecting inheritances with the OAPT

 The OAPT can superbly shield anticipated inheritances from a beneficiary's creditors. The OAPT can be designed as a *testamentary trust* where inheritance can directly pass to the trust upon the grantor's death. Or the OAPT can be an *inter vivos trust* and funded during the testator's lifetime.

The trust beneficiaries, in either case, have their future inheritances protected against their creditors through both the trust's spendthrift provisions and the trustee's discretionary powers to withhold any distributions of principal or interest to one or more beneficiaries.

OAPTs in divorce and marital planning

Unhappy spouses who are contemplating a divorce oftentimes shelter their marital assets in an OAPT. Although they must eventually and truthfully

The divorce court can award the victimized spouse a disproportionate share of the U.S.-based assets to compensate for the trust-shielded assets.

disclose their trust assets to the divorce court, the divorce court cannot recover and divide these assets for the benefit of the opposing spouse. The court can also grant the injured spouse additional compensatory alimony or support. The OAPT then is best used to protect your share of the marital assets from a potentially dishonest spouse rather than to cheat that spouse.

Offshore protection against IRS seizures

Most offshore funds are from those who want to protect their wealth from litigation, and the next largest group is probably those U.S. taxpayers besieged by serious IRS problems. While most everyday creditors and litigants can be effectively stonewalled with standard domestic asset protection shelters, the IRS is not so easily discouraged.

The more protective offshore havens will not enforce an IRS levy, summons or cooperate with any other IRS attempts to discover or seize assets. Less-protective havens enforce IRS seizures.

E-Z TIP Taxpayer assets seldom remain safe from IRS seizure unless sheltered offshore because the laws that safeguard assets against general creditor claims are usually ineffective against the IRS.

Taxpayers who are chased by the IRS commonly sell or mortgage their assets. Their liquidated wealth is then moved offshore before a tax lien or seizure. Nevertheless, you must honestly disclose to the IRS any offshore funds or transfers. And never transfer funds offshore or try to protect against pending IRS claims unless under the guidance of an experienced attorney. Overly aggressive protection maneuvers against the IRS may trigger criminal charges under one of several federal statutes.

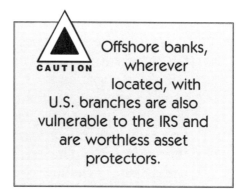

Offshore banks, wherever located, with U.S. branches are also vulnerable to the IRS and are worthless asset protectors.

Nor will the IRS quickly compromise your tax liability once it discovers you have money safely invested offshore. Still, the IRS frequently suspends collection efforts once it realizes that further efforts to seize the assets will be futile.

Offshore protection against product liability claims

Manufacturing companies frequently conduct their business through offshore companies for asset protection where they can then enjoy some

Forming an international company is your safest strategy when you produce hazardous products.

immunity against American product liability claims. In contrast, a U.S. manufacturer of a defective product is strictly liable to those injured from product defects. Goods manufactured through an offshore company create no U.S. liability because your foreign-based manufacturing company does not directly conduct its business within the United States. A plaintiff-customer can sue the U.S. distributors, but this is of little consequence for the U.S. distributor with few exposed assets. This U.S. distributor may even be a shell subsidiary of your foreign manufacturing company.

Safely repatriate foreign assets

The grantor of an OAPT cannot repatriate trust funds by revoking or dissolving the trust. But there are alternative ways to access trust funds. One way is to borrow from the trust, which is permitted if you are a beneficiary. You can borrow either directly or the trust can collateralize a loan for you from a local bank through "back-to-back" financing. The trustee also can make distributions to any beneficiary, including yourself as a beneficiary. If you are not a named beneficiary, your spouse and/or children probably will be. Trust distributions to them can then be gifted or loaned to you.

> **note** Your trust can also transact business with you or your company, and this can indirectly divert funds back to you.

> **note** There are many ways to access needed offshore funds and usually within 48 hours you can have the funds you need in your own pocket.

You can make your trust revocable, provided it has the assent of both the trustee and the protector. The grantor cannot directly exercise a right to revoke the trust or it will lose asset protection.

Six popular asset protection havens

For Americans, the most popular OAPT havens are the Cayman Islands, Bahamas, Belize, Cook Islands, Turks and Caicos and Nevis. Other good havens for OAPTs include Cyprus, Malta, Gibraltar, Barbados, Isle of Man, Guernsey, Jersey and Seychelles. Numerous factors pinpoint the one haven that is best for your own OAPT.

Are you ready for offshore protection?

You do not need great wealth to benefit from your own OAPT. A modest $100,000 nest egg can easily justify the investment. The OAPT becomes essential when you have considerably more assets at risk, and your "deep pockets" make you a prime target for litigants and others after your wealth. Significant wealth demands the most powerful offshore protection.

Middle-class Americans need the OAPT even more than the super-rich. The super-rich have the greater ability to replenish their wealth. Few middle-class Americans can recoup from a financial catastrophe.

Many articles about offshore trusts suggest a $500,000 net worth is needed for an offshore trust to become worthwhile. Still, it's wiser to establish your trust before you acquire considerable wealth because you want the trust to protect wealth as it accumulates. The trust or other offshore structure should not be an afterthought when you are running from liabilities. It should instead be a properly pre-planned wealth protector.

The Nevis LLC: the newest offshore protector

A *limited liability company (LLC)* is very similar to the family limited partnership in its ability to protect assets from creditors. The new Nevis LLC offers considerably more protection than do either domestic LLCs, LPs or even OAPTs.

A judgment creditor pursuing an interest in a Nevis LLC is limited only to a charging order against the debtor-member's share of any distribution of profits paid from the LLC. But these profits materialize only if you elect to make such distributions. Your creditor cannot claim your interest in the LLC nor replace its management. More significantly, a creditor cannot pursue a fraudulent transfer claim against assets transferred to the Nevis LLC if the debtor obtains in exchange a proportionate ownership in the LLC to the assets transferred to the LLC.

> *note*
>
> The creditor must pay U.S. taxes on your share of any earnings from the LLC, whether or not these earnings have been distributed from the LLC, or received by the creditor.

Consider five more advantages of the Nevis LLC:

1) The Nevis LLC requires minimal reporting to the Nevis government. It also avoids the OAPT's onerous reporting requirements to the IRS.

2) The LLC can be structured to achieve virtually any asset protection or estate planning objective and can also accomplish most business or investment objectives.

3) Ownership in the LLC can be registered in bearer form, thus its owners can be anonymous.

4) The LLC can elect to be taxed either as a C corporation or partnership.

5) Officers and directors of the LLC remain personally immune from liability.

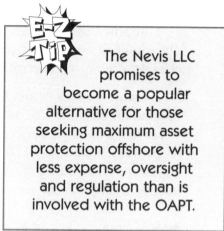

E-Z TIP

The Nevis LLC promises to become a popular alternative for those seeking maximum asset protection offshore with less expense, oversight and regulation than is involved with the OAPT.

Asset protection with offshore banks

Operating your own private offshore bank can significantly improve asset protection, and it is recommended when you have significant offshore funds or want to further block a particularly zealous creditor.

note

A bank's broad investment powers cloak the movement of assets with neither undue attention nor suspicion arising from these activities.

Owning an offshore bank also adds more privacy to an asset protection trust or offshore company. The offshore bank makes it extremely difficult for creditors to identify assets deposited to the bank's general fund and virtually impossible to link bank-invested assets to property or collateral obtained in exchange. Offshore banks are expected to widely invest their assets. Individuals are not.

Offshore bank privacy can also help if, for instance, you become immersed in a major business lawsuit and your opponent demands sensitive financial information or trade secrets.

Your own offshore bank can be the best way to protect proprietary ideas. To patent an idea in the United States requires disclosure to the U.S. Patent Office. But, this is poor protection against an inquisitive competitor who, with a few minor modifications, may steal your idea before you gain a market foothold. It is

E-Z TIP

Records stored with your own offshore bank remain protected in most havens from U.S. court orders and subpoenas.

smarter to apply for the patent through your private offshore bank. The idea would then become financial information protected under the haven's bank secrecy laws.

 note Properly structured offshore banking profits are not taxed by the United States until profits are repatriated.

Offshore banks may also be excellent tax insulators since they legally separate you from your wealth while you still control your funds in your offshore bank. Offshore bank ownership also creates more opportunity to defer U.S. taxes than other offshore structures. An investor may perpetually invest offshore to indefinitely defer their U.S. taxes.

Financial privacy in offshore havens

As an American involved in a lawsuit, your U.S. bank must provide your opponent any subpoenaed banking records. Your financial affairs are similarly exposed to the government. In contrast, offshore banking records are fully protected and remain private against U.S. court orders and subpoenas because offshore banks are jurisdictionally immune to service of process. Under no circumstance can an offshore bank in a privacy haven divulge financial information about you to any third party, except as permitted under narrow treaty provisions.

Since offshore banks are jurisdictionally immune to service of process, they equally ban U.S. writs of execution or attachment orders. Thus, the secrecy laws of most havens protect entrusted funds from creditor seizure originating from a domestic judgment and also protect the confidentiality of all financial transactions that pass through the bank.

note No circumstances, including lawsuits or routine criminal investigations, allow an offshore bank in a privacy haven to disclose protected information.

An offshore bank with no American-based branch or affiliate will not come within the jurisdiction of American courts. Thus, U.S. demands for information will be barred by both foreign and American courts if disclosure violates the secrecy laws of the offshore haven, even if the offshore bank is owned or operated by a U.S. resident. The offshore bank is considered a separate entity, obliged to protect its depositors' confidentiality.

The secrecy laws of all countries prohibit using the citizenry of a bank's principals to circumvent the privacy law that extends to the offshore bank as a separate entity.

This jurisdictional immunity explains why offshore banks guarantee against the unwanted intrusions into your financial privacy. Records that are so readily obtainable within the United States are beyond the sight of prying governmental investigators and private litigants—if your funds are deposited in the right offshore haven.

> *note* Privacy is a major benefit from offshore banking, yet many American investors overlook its importance. Consider how needlessly exposed finances can get you into serious trouble, and the privacy advantage grows in importance.

Privacy is a basic right of all free citizens. The fact that so many people search for privacy does not speak against them, but against their governments who stripped them of their privacy. Ignore those who argue that privacy encourages illegality. Financial privacy for legitimate activities should be the goal of every American. The offshore investor already has achieved this goal.

Offshore banking: myths and misconceptions

Offshore banks can be exceptionally strong or notoriously shaky. Always thoroughly investigate the bank's financial condition, even when it is large or old. You may easily review a bank's most recent financial statements with *Polk's Directory of International Banks,* available at your local library.

Americans contemplating offshore bank ownership may find measuring a bank's financial condition to be an unexpected challenge. Three key criteria can reveal an offshore bank's safety:

1) *Assets and capital.* While the bank's assets reflect its financial power, its capital even more significantly measures assets against liabilities.

2) *Age of the bank.* Longevity cannot insure future financial stability, but a long-established bank separates itself from the numerous fly-by-night operations that are here today and gone tomorrow.

3) *Management.* Study the bank's reports. What are its management philosophies? How does it view economic conditions? How sound are its policies? What is the depth and background of its management?

Offshore banks are regulated and a haven's banking regulations may be even more rigid than American rules. However, other havens impose negligible regulations on their banks. Havens that encourage private bank startups through lax regulation create less safety for the uninformed depositor.

> **note**
> Offshore banks, like American banks, publish annual reports, although their accounting rules differ from American accounting practices.

ABCs of Swiss banking

Foreign bank accounts and Switzerland are traditionally synonymous. Swiss banking, like banking in every other foreign jurisdiction, is perfectly legal for Americans. But is a Swiss bank account really superior to those other havens? Consider three points:

1) **Convenience:** You can as easily transact business with a Swiss bank as an American bank. Swiss banks are very accessible, and their proximity to all European markets a plus. Still, accounts in the Caribbean or closer havens may be more convenient.

2) **Financial stability:** Switzerland is one of the most stable money havens. The Swiss have no exchange rules on precious metals or gold-backed currency, but this may change as Switzerland restores foreign currency controls to help stabilize its economy. Swiss accounts denominated in Swiss francs may be excellent insurance against the collapsing American dollar.

3) **Privacy:** Swiss banks cannot legally disclose banking information to anyone, including the United States government. Disclosing information under Swiss law is also made more difficult since accounts are usually number coded. Still, Swiss secrecy is not absolute. Financial disclosures are routine in bankruptcy fraud and inheritance cases, unlike other havens where such information would be protected. Tax fraud is not a crime under Swiss law so records are never disclosed to the IRS when the purpose is to prosecute for tax fraud.

Swiss privacy is not as rigid as it once was. Other havens, particularly Liechtenstein and Luxembourg, now offer greater privacy. The United States has consistently pressured the Swiss to relax their secrecy, and the Swiss have acceded in a number of recent cases.

Three safe Swiss banks are the Union Bank of Switzerland (Zurich), Swiss Credit Bank (Zurich) and the Swiss Bank Corporation (Basel). All Swiss banks are strong, but avoid Swiss banks with branches or affiliates in America. An American branch or affiliate destroys privacy.

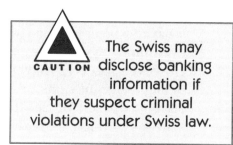

CAUTION The Swiss may disclose banking information if they suspect criminal violations under Swiss law.

Swiss banks offer a variety of savings, checking and custodial accounts for your gold, precious metals and stocks and bonds. Swiss accounts may be denominated in either Swiss or American currency.

Offshore wealth with bearer investments

DEFINITION

One of the better strategies for offshore privacy is to convert titled assets, such as real estate or stocks and bonds, into *bearer investments,* such as gold, diamonds, art, stamp collections, coins and similar collectibles. Bearer investments provide asset protection because they are easily transported offshore and are completely confidential and private.

Thousands of dollars in gold or diamonds occupy little space and can be easily transported as you travel. They can as easily be reconverted to cash all with complete confidentiality and privacy. Private vaults available in a number of countries provide even greater secrecy.

For even greater privacy, you may buy and sell collectibles through a third party, such as your own offshore corporation with its own bearer shares.

Swiss annuities for asset protection

A popular way for Americans to protect wealth through offshore investing is by buying Swiss annuities.

Swiss authorities will not allow seizure even when ordered by an American court. However, Swiss annuities remain creditor-proof only if structured correctly.

> *note* Under Swiss law, insurance policies, which include Swiss annuities, cannot be seized by creditors, the IRS or trustees-in-bankruptcy.

The first requirement for an American purchasing a Swiss annuity is that he must designate his spouse or children as the beneficiary. An unrelated party may be irrevocably named. Second, the individual must have purchased the annuity and designated the beneficiaries at least one year before a lawsuit or bankruptcy, or at least five years before a lawsuit or bankruptcy if the central purpose for buying the Swiss annuity was to fraudulently impede existing creditors. The Swiss, adopting a protective posture, rarely find this to be the purpose for investing in Swiss annuities.

Becoming private in a public world

For true financial privacy offshore, you must create two separate financial worlds.

Your public world is your home country. This is where you work, pay taxes, maintain your bank accounts and investments and expose the finances you expect the world to know about.

Your private world is offshore. That is where you keep your "invisible money," your wealth that only you know about.

This private world shelters your major bank accounts, investments, trusts, companies and all the other entities that hold assets you want invisible and private.

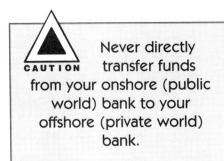

CAUTION: Never directly transfer funds from your onshore (public world) bank to your offshore (private world) bank.

The key to maintaining tight secrecy is never to mix your two worlds. Isolate each. Avoid direct transactions between the two.

How do you move your money secretly from your public onshore accounts to your private offshore bank? First understand that it remains legal for an American to move money offshore. But this may not last forever. The *Bank Secrecy Act of 1970* imposes strict reporting requirements on individuals or businesses who transport monetary instruments outside the

U.S. This includes U.S. and foreign currency, traveler's checks and any security or negotiable instrument in bearer form worth $10,000 or more. The report, filed with *Customs on Customs Form 4790,* is available to all federal agencies, including the IRS.

Balancing the objectives of legality and secrecy offers several alternatives, each with its own advantages.

Mail remains the most common way to transfer funds offshore. You can legally send a check or money order in any amount to any offshore haven without customs reporting. While this is certainly the most convenient way to transfer funds, a few additional tricks can boost secrecy.

 Avoid personal checks even for small amounts. The Secrecy Act requires banks to record all checks over $10,000. Most banks microfilm every check.

To increase privacy, directly wire transfer money market funds offshore.

Wire transfers are similarly recorded. This also forfeits privacy. Nearly all offshore banks accept wire transfers, and most have corresponding banks or foreign exchange dealers ready to process wire transfers. Speed is the one advantage of a wire transfer over mail.

Your funds would be identified by account number. A letter of instruction to the offshore bank should accompany the funds. While this provides slightly more secrecy, a diligent investigator can still discover the transfer by examining your money market account transactions.

Another possibility is to buy bonds for under $10,000 to avoid reporting the transfer to Customs. Mailing one bond daily builds a tidy offshore nest egg very quickly. Buy bonds for cash so you leave no paper trail.

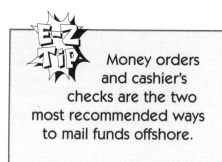

Money orders and cashier's checks are the two most recommended ways to mail funds offshore.

Money orders above $10,000 must be payable to your offshore bank or to a specific offshore individual or company. As non-bearer currency it would not be reportable to Customs. A money order over $10,000 and payable to cash is bearer currency and is reportable to U.S. Customs. Money orders under $10,000 may be payable to "cash" without reporting, provided you send only one money order at a time. For maximum secrecy, exclude your name on the money order. Use an accompanying side letter to instruct the bank to deposit the funds to your account.

Protecting repatriated funds

A convenient way to repatriate your offshore funds is to have your offshore bank issue frequent bank drafts on the account of its American correspondent banks. Every major offshore bank has correspondent banks in major U.S. cities.

To maintain strict privacy or protect your funds from a U.S. creditor, avoid depositing your funds in a U.S. bank account in your own name. Instead cash the check at the correspondent bank. Your offshore bank can send you bearer securities under $10,000. Your offshore bank may also transmit funds to a U.S. collectibles dealer who accepts the check in exchange for rare coins or other collectibles.

> *note*
> When asset protection is your goal, your repatriated funds should continuously remain under another name so they remain safe from creditors.

You may organize a Nevada or Wyoming corporation to receive the funds. Since ownership in Nevada or Wyoming corporations is usually undocumented, your affiliation may be concealed. Or, you may direct repatriated funds to a family limited partnership. Happily married? Wire the funds to your spouse's account or transfer them to a domestic spendthrift trust with you as a beneficiary. The spendthrift trust prevents your creditors from seizing your beneficial interest or any assets in the trust.

Planning Pointers

◆ Protecting assets through offshore structures is the safest asset protection strategy.

◆ The key element in offshore asset protection is not secrecy but the transfer of the assets beyond the legal reach of U.S. courts and creditors.

◆ The Offshore Asset Protection Trust is the most widely used offshore structure for asset protection.

◆ Other offshore structures that can offer asset protection include hybrid companies, foundations and limited liability companies. Each entity features advantages and disadvantages.

◆ For maximum protection, the asset should be physically outside the United States. U.S.-based assets are not well protected because they are within the reach of U.S. courts.

◆ It is not always necessary to lose control of foreign-based assets until you are under creditor attack, and then there are safeguards to insure the assets will remain well protected from mismanagement.

◆ Offshore structures can oftentimes be combined with domestic protective structures, such as limited partnerships and limited liability companies, to provide added control and tax benefits.

◆ Offshore structures can keep assets safe in a bankruptcy, divorce or even from IRS claims. However, there may be other consequences to consider arising from such action.

◆ You gain considerable privacy from offshore accounts, but you must know how to move your money secretly to retain privacy.

◆ There are a few legitimate ways to gain tax benefits offshore; however, U.S. taxpayers are generally liable for taxes on all profits earned offshore regardless of the entity used.

◆ The Swiss annuity is creditor-protected under Swiss law and is one of the safest investments.

Bankruptcy: Keep your assets, lose your debts

Chapter 11

Bankruptcy: Keep your assets, lose your debts

What you'll find in this chapter:

➠ Debts that cannot be discharged

➠ The best time to file bankruptcy

➠ When spouses should file separately

➠ Property that is exempt under bankruptcy

➠ Avoiding involuntary bankruptcy

Bankruptcy is an increasingly popular refuge for the financially troubled individual and company. Over 1.25 million individuals and companies now file bankruptcy annually. This is not a surprising statistic once you understand how bankruptcy works to eliminate debts and protect assets. You then see why more and more debtors utilize bankruptcy laws to protect their wealth in troubled times—and why it may not be your right option!

When to file bankruptcy

Debtors with serious financial problems should consider bankruptcy. However, bankruptcy isn't necessarily the right answer. Bankruptcy is the answer only in two situations:

1)   *You have too many debts to satisfy from either future income or the sale of your assets.* But why declare bankruptcy if you earn $100,000 a year with debts of only $20,000? Short-term financial sacrifices can handle excessive debts, a strategy certainly preferable to bankruptcy. Tip: If your unsecured debts total less than 60 percent of your net annual pay, then try to

avoid bankruptcy. Commit 20 percent of your net pay to past creditors. Creditors may wait two or more years for payment if you show good faith through systematic payments. You also will be proud to have avoided bankruptcy.

2) ***Bankruptcy is necessary to protect your assets.*** Once you file bankruptcy, all civil actions against you must immediately stop, whether they are lawsuits, IRS claims, seizures, levies, attachments, repossessions or foreclosures. All creditors must obey the automatic stay of continued legal action imposed by the bankruptcy code. This includes all general unsecured creditors, the IRS, secured lenders and even such creditors as landlords attempting to evict. The bankruptcy objective is to provide you the opportunity to resolve your financial problems with creditors who would otherwise seize and sell you assets. Chapter 11 reorganizations and Chapter 13 wage earner plans particularly protect assets from creditor claims.

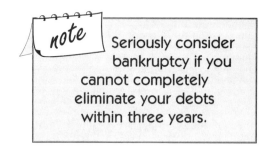

note Seriously consider bankruptcy if you cannot completely eliminate your debts within three years.

Bankruptcy is not your solution if:

◆ You filed Chapter 7 bankruptcy within the preceding six years. There is no limit on how frequently you can file Chapter 11 or 13.

◆ You primarily want to discharge debts not dischargeable in bankruptcy.

Debts you cannot discharge

Bankruptcy does not extinguish all debts. Certain debts which are usually not dischargeable in bankruptcy include:

• federal taxes less than three years old and state and local taxes

• child support and alimony

• student loans

• criminal fines and penalties (restitutions and traffic fines, for example)

• liabilities incurred through drunk driving

• withholding tax assessments

• dischargeable debts that are not listed on your bankruptcy schedules

Debts not dischargeable in Chapter 7 bankruptcy may be dischargeable or resolved in Chapter 13. The bankruptcy court can also refuse to discharge other debts in a Chapter 7 bankruptcy based upon the debtor's inequitable conduct.

Bankruptcy eliminates any remaining personal liability. The secured parties' rights become limited to the collateral and then their rights become similar to those of unsecured creditors.

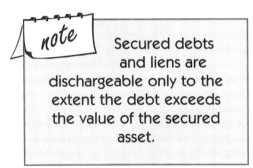

Secured debts and liens are dischargeable only to the extent the debt exceeds the value of the secured asset.

Non-dischargeable debts also include those incurred through fraud. Bankruptcy assists honest debtors. A dishonest debtor will be barred relief. Non-dischargeable debts include debts owed a creditor for $500 or more on luxury goods or services purchased within 40 days of filing, as well as debts for cash advances above $1,000 obtained within 20 days of bankruptcy. Credit card companies (Visa, MasterCard) usually contest the discharge of these debts. Also, non-dischargeable are debts incurred through intentional fraud, such as fraudulent credit applications.

Know your best bankruptcy option

Several forms of bankruptcy are available. Each is designed for individuals and businesses to handle a different financial situation. So it is important to file the type of bankruptcy that can achieve your objective.

DEFINITION

◆ **Chapter 7** bankruptcy, or *straight* or *liquidating bankruptcy,* erases all debts except those that are non-dischargeable. Conversely, you lose all assets except those few assets that are exempt. A corporation, partnership, trust or any other entity may file Chapter 7. Chapter 7 bankruptcy is the most popular bankruptcy and accounts for about 90 percent of all bankruptcies. When is Chapter 7 for you? If you have few assets to lose, other than those that are exempt, then file Chapter 7. The one big advantage of Chapter 7 is that your debts are forever extinguished. You may start life again debt free.

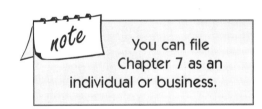

You can file Chapter 7 as an individual or business.

◆ **Chapter 13**, or the wage-earner plan, differs from Chapter 7. You keep your assets, but do not discharge your debts. You instead repay over three to five years. Your repayment plan must pay creditors at least what they would receive under Chapter 7. Priority creditors, including taxing authorities, are usually fully paid. Secured creditors must receive an amount that equals the fair market value of their collateral. Chapter 13 is your remedy if you have non-exempt assets to save, such as a home with a large equity. Chapter 7 would allow you to keep your exempt assets and eliminate your debts.

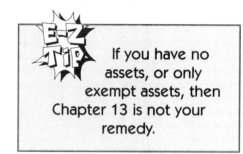

If you have no assets, or only exempt assets, then Chapter 13 is not your remedy.

◆ **Chapter 11** compares to Chapter 13. It also allows the debtor to keep his or her property while arranging a repayment plan with creditors. While a wage-earner plan is limited to employed individuals, a Chapter 11 can be filed by any debtor. There is another important difference: Debtors in Chapter 13 cannot owe over $250,000 in unsecured debt and $750,000 in secured debt. There is no debt limit with Chapter 11. Farmers file Chapter 12, which is similar to Chapter 11.

You can switch bankruptcies. A company, for example, may be involuntarily petitioned into Chapter 7 and convert their case to Chapter 11. Or a company in Chapter 11 or a wage-earner in Chapter 13 may convert to Chapter 7. This often happens when the debtor cannot negotiate a satisfactory repayment plan or defaults in other bankruptcy obligations. It is important to select the right type of bankruptcy. Make the decision only after consulting an experienced bankruptcy attorney.

Precision-time your bankruptcy

Bankruptcy timing is critical. Debtors frequently file too soon or too late. In either instance you can lose some possible benefits from bankruptcy. Timing pointers:

• Collect tax refunds before you file. Tax refunds due you when you file will be claimed by your trustee.

• Never file bankruptcy within 90 days of paying a past debt—if you want the creditor to keep the payment. Repayments made within 90 days are recoverable by the trustee as a voidable preference. Payments made within one year to relatives or other insiders are also recoverable.

• If you anticipate more debts in the near future, then wait to file until they arise and can be discharged in bankruptcy. An example: Continuing medical costs due to an extended illness.

• If you owe personal income taxes, wait at least three years from their due date, two years from their filing date and 240 days from their assessed date before you file. More recent taxes are not dischargeable.

Make certain you owned your home the time necessary to qualify, before you file bankruptcy, if you plan on claiming a homestead exemption.

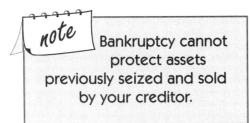

note Bankruptcy cannot protect assets previously seized and sold by your creditor.

• Wait 40 days to file if you incurred bills for non-essentials. More recent charges are not dischargeable.

Don't file bankruptcy too quickly no matter how indebted you may be. If you have only a few creditors, you may be able to settle with them without bankruptcy. Creditors settle on very favorable terms when it is their most practical option. You may also find this to be your perfect opportunity to undertake high-risk ventures. Debts from these failed future ventures can then be discharged together with your existing debts. But be careful; you also can file too late to save your assets.

When spouses should file separate bankruptcies

Spouses with common obligations frequently file joint bankruptcies. However, spouses who jointly own non-exempt assets as tenants-by-the-entirety should not necessarily file together. If spouses file jointly, the bankruptcy trustee may gain complete title to the entire asset as the trustee obtains the interest of both spouses. A trustee with complete legal title may sell the asset more easily than can a trustee with only a partial interest.

The trustee could not easily sell that interest because the property would then create a co-ownership between the non-bankrupt spouse and the buyer. Selling such a partial interest would be at a very low price, which the non-bankrupt spouse can easily acquire cheaply from the trustee.

Spouses who file joint bankruptcies may be entitled to double their state exemptions. For example, if each spouse has a $40,000 homestead exemption by state law, then spouses who go bankrupt together can apply an $80,000 exemption to the home equity. When this double exemption adequately protects your assets, consider filing jointly.

> **note**
>
> If a spouse files a separate bankruptcy, the trustee controls only the interest of the bankrupt spouse.

Save money with a low or no cost bankruptcy

Many people are so impoverished that they cannot raise the approximate $150 filing fee to file bankruptcy. But, you may make installment payments if you cannot raise the filing fee. You must obtain court approval, but this is routinely allowed if the court becomes convinced that you are without adequate funds.

Finding the money to hire a bankruptcy lawyer is more challenging. Fees for a simple personal bankruptcy are $250 to $1,000 and now average about $750 for a debtor not engaged in business. This fee is usually paid before filing. Few bankruptcy lawyers extend credit to their clients.

Check lawyer ads in your local newspaper. Bankruptcy attorneys routinely advertise their fees and any available credit terms. Bankruptcy specialists who handle many cases often charge considerably less due to their volume and their efficient use of paralegals and because their cases are usually routine.

Why not handle your own bankruptcy? This is a cash-saving option if you have no assets nor complicated issues. Best bet: E-Z Legal's *Bankruptcy Made E-Z*, available at any major stationery or office supply store. It gives you everything you need to easily process your own routine bankruptcy. If you encounter complications, then retain an attorney.

Go bankrupt and keep your assets

The one key bankruptcy strategy is to convert non-exempt assets into exempt assets before filing bankruptcy. Exempt assets are fully protected and retained in a bankruptcy. Non-exempt assets are lost to creditors in bankruptcy.

Example: Assume you live in Massachusetts and own $2 million in non-exempt assets (investment property, stock, bonds, boats, etc.). You must file bankruptcy because you owe $3 million. All your assets (except for a nominal $7,500 Massachusetts exemption) would be lost to your creditors. However, you may presently sell your Massachusetts assets for $2 million and buy a $2 million residence in Texas, where homes are entirely exempt, then you could keep your $2 million Texas home and still fully discharge your debts. After the bankruptcy, you could sell your $2 million Texas home if you prefer and have $2 million in your pocket. This one strategy legally allows bankrupts to remain full-fledged millionaires!

CAUTION You may convert non-exempt property to exempt assets in advance of your bankruptcy. Converting non-exempt assets into exempt assets is perfectly legal; however, bankruptcy courts in certain states may set aside such exchanges. Therefore, your pre-bankruptcy planning must be guided by an experienced bankruptcy attorney.

What property is exempt under bankruptcy?

Under Chapter 7 bankruptcy, the trustee liquidates the debtor's assets for the benefit of the debtor's creditors. However, an individual is allowed to keep a certain amount of property. This exempt property allows the debtor to gain a fresh start.

The classification of property as either exempt or non-exempt is important to both the debtor and the creditors. Before 1978 the area of exemptions was strictly a matter of state law, and each state had its own list of exempt properties. Then Congress decided the states could use a federal list of exemptions. Some states required the debtor to use the state list of exemptions. Others offered an option: Residents filing bankruptcies may choose the federal list of exemptions or the state's list, depending upon which is more advantageous to the resident. Exemptions include:

- a homestead exemption not to exceed $15,000

- a motor vehicle valued at $2,400 or less

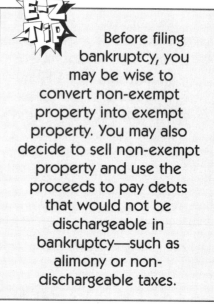

- $400 in value for specific items of household goods, furnishing and clothing or crops used by the debtor or his family for personal use up to an aggregate total of $8,000

- jewelry with a maximum value of $1,000

- real or personal property totaling no more than $800 individually and up to $7,500 of unused homestead or burial plot exemptions

- tools or professional books valued up to $1,500

- life insurance contracts

- up to $8,000 in dividends, interest or loan value on a life insurance policy

- health aids, such as wheelchairs, etc.

- future benefits, including Social Security benefits, all unemployment benefits, all veterans benefits, alimony and child support

> **E-Z TIP**
>
> Before filing bankruptcy, you may be wise to convert non-exempt property into exempt property. You may also decide to sell non-exempt property and use the proceeds to pay debts that would not be dischargeable in bankruptcy—such as alimony or non-dischargeable taxes.

- the right to compensation for lawsuits, including wrongful death benefits, insurance proceeds and compensation for bodily injury up to $15,000

Financial planning considerations are important. If you have significant assets, plan ahead for bankruptcy with your attorney or financial advisor.

Legally dispose of assets before bankruptcy

There are two more ways to protect assets in bankruptcy: sell or encumber the assets before you file bankruptcy.

1) *Sell your assets.* Prospective bankrupts frequently sell or transfer non-exempt assets before bankruptcy. But observe the fraudulent transfer

cautions discussed in Chapter 2. Transfers for less than an adequate price are voidable and recoverable by the bankruptcy trustee. Fraud, sham or straw deals to conceal assets can also be a crime. But, sell or transfer assets at least one year before you file bankruptcy. Bankruptcy courts closely investigate transfers within the prior year; however, a trustee can probe earlier transactions. And be absolutely truthful on your bankruptcy schedules and when you answer questions under oath. Bankruptcy fraud is a serious crime. You can legally protect property before bankruptcy without committing perjury or other crimes.

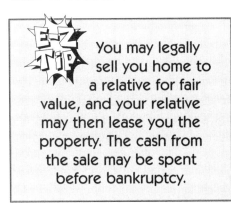

You may legally sell you home to a relative for fair value, and your relative may then lease you the property. The cash from the sale may be spent before bankruptcy.

2) ***Encumber your assets.*** Perhaps you owe money to a friend, relative or business associate. To protect and someday repay that individual, you may give your preferred creditor a mortgage on whatever property will fully secure the debt. Wait at least 90 days before you file bankruptcy because an earlier filing may void the mortgage as a preference. If the mortgage is to a close relative, wait at least one year before filing bankruptcy.

Because significant pre-bankruptcy transactions are scrutinized by the bankruptcy trustee, the trustee will certainly check the validity of the debt to make certain the mortgage is legitimate.

The most dangerous tactic is to gift property before bankruptcy. Gifts are easily recovered as fraudulent transfers. Transfers made to family members or friends, even for a fair price, will be examined closely. Make certain it is an honest and fair value transaction. Arms-length transactions are not viewed as suspiciously. However, even an innocent transaction can be wrongly interpreted in bankruptcy, cause needless aggravation and even prevent your discharge in bankruptcy. Review all major transactions within the preceding five years carefully with your attorney before you file.

note

Encumbered assets are safe from other creditors up to the amount of the encumbrance.

Sidestep involuntary bankruptcy

Most bankruptcies are initiated by the debtor. However, creditors can petition you into bankruptcy if they can prove you are insolvent and generally not paying your debts. If you have fewer than twelve creditors, any one creditor with a claim of $5,000 or more can force you into bankruptcy. When you have twelve or more creditors, three creditors with aggregate claims of $5,000 must sign the petition. How can you discourage or stop creditors from petitioning you or your business into bankruptcy?

1) *Create a preference:* Even a small payment to a threatening creditor may discourage the creditor from throwing you into bankruptcy. By putting you in bankruptcy, the creditor will forfeit any future payments other than distributions from the bankruptcy. Plus, any payments received within ninety days before the bankruptcy can be recovered by the trustee as a preference.

2) *Dispute the claim:* Only creditors with undisputed claims can force you into bankruptcy. Disputing the claims of a threatening creditor before he petitions you into bankruptcy may disqualify him as a petitioning creditor.

3) *Sell your poverty:* If you have no unprotected assets or so many debts that your creditor would get nothing in bankruptcy, then point this out to your creditor. The reality that they can obtain nothing from your bankruptcy may temper their enthusiasm.

Never admit to insolvency in writing.

4) *Never identify your other creditors:* Why allow creditors to find other creditors to join in the bankruptcy petition?

Many creditors bluff bankruptcy, but few follow through. Few creditors will pay high legal fees to prosecute a contested bankruptcy, and it is usually a poor investment since general creditors recover only pennies-on-the-dollar. Creditors may strike first, so defensively position yourself while you have the opportunity.

Debts you should pay in bankruptcy

You may want to pay a debt that was discharged in bankruptcy. While this is a noble gesture, it is usually a mistake. Bankruptcy gives you a clean start, so why burden yourself again with debts? You may reaffirm a discharged debt only when approved by the bankruptcy court. The court, in this instance, wants to be certain that you can safely handle reaffirmed obligations without future financial difficulty, and that you fully understand the consequences of reaffirming a previously discharged debt.

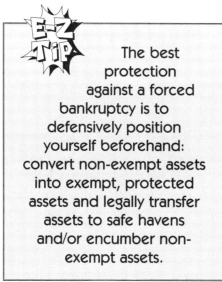

The best protection against a forced bankruptcy is to defensively position yourself beforehand: convert non-exempt assets into exempt, protected assets and legally transfer assets to safe havens and/or encumber non-exempt assets.

Creditors who you do not list on your bankruptcy schedules and who are without knowledge of your bankruptcy do not have their debts discharged. These debts require no reaffirmation because they remain enforceable after your bankruptcy. If you do not want a creditor to discover your bankruptcy, then do not list that creditor on your schedules. However, not scheduling a major creditor is usually foolish as you will remain burdened with that debt. List every possible creditor, even those who you dispute or who have contingent claims. If you become wealthy, you can pay those special creditors.

 Certain creditors are best not listed. For example, you may owe a small amount on a valuable credit card, such as American Express. If you continue timely payments to AmEx as an unlisted creditor, they probably won't discover your bankruptcy or terminate your credit card.

Tax benefits from bankruptcy

People who file bankruptcy seldom consider its important tax benefits. Conversely, the tax disadvantage if you do not file bankruptcy can be considerable.

Forgiveness or cancellation of a debt without bankruptcy creates taxable income to the debtor equal to the forgiven debt. Example: If you owe your friend $50,000 and settle for $10,000, without bankruptcy, the $40,000 difference is taxable income. There is no tax if the debt is canceled

note The tax benefit from bankruptcy is that there are no tax consequences for debts forgiven under bankruptcy.

in bankruptcy. Review with your tax advisor the tax consequences of bankruptcy compared to the tax implications of a non-bankruptcy workout.

Filing bankruptcy to stop foreclosure

Bankruptcy automatically stops creditor lawsuits, collections or repossessions. The automatic stay under bankruptcy further transfers all pending or future collection and debtor-creditor cases from other courts to the bankruptcy court. Your creditors cannot enforce prior judgments or liens against you or your property.

The automatic stay also suspends a creditor's right to repossess collateral. Still, a secured creditor can petition the bankruptcy court for permission to foreclose by requesting adequate protection. A secured creditor is any creditor who holds specific property as collateral to secure the debt. Mortgages on real estate, security interests on personal property or leases on equipment are examples.

When a secured creditor requests adequate protection, the bankruptcy court must protect the creditor so his collateral is not impaired or diminished by the automatic stay. This is important when collateral can lose value. Even a boat may decrease in value over time. The bankruptcy court then requires sufficient payment to the secured party to at least cover this depreciation. The creditor can repossess or foreclose on the collateral if there is no other way to protect the creditor. The automatic stay ends when the case is closed, dismissed or the debtor discharged.

note Criminal matters and suits to collect alimony or child support do continue during bankruptcy.

note Bankruptcy, therefore, will not always protect against a foreclosure or repossession. You may file Chapter 11, for instance, to delay foreclosure and gain the opportunity to sell or refinance the property or to develop a reorganization plan to resolve the problem loan. But you must file bankruptcy with a realistic plan on how you will protect your secured creditor who holds liens on assets you want to retain. You can always abandon unwanted assets to your secured creditor, and any deficiency will become an unsecured debt to be discharged in your bankruptcy. However, if you want a secured asset, fine tune your strategies:

◆ Bankruptcy is often filed immediately before foreclosure of an important asset, such as a home. To avoid foreclosure, be prepared to show the court why the secured creditor will not be hurt through his inability to foreclose. Will you partly or fully pay the loan? Can you show the court that the asset will not lose value and that the secured creditor would recover as much later as they would today? Your protection will be very short-lived unless you can convince the court that a delayed foreclosure will not hurt the secured party.

◆ Use your one big weapon against your uncooperative secured creditors: the cramdown. When you file a cramdown petition, the bankruptcy court reduces the secured debt to the value of the secured collateral. Excess debt is considered unsecured debt. Example: You have a $200,000 mortgage on real estate now worth only $100,000. The court will, in this instance, reduce the mortgage to $100,000. The $100,000 balance will

> *note* When you file bankruptcy primarily to stop foreclosure, then be certain that bankruptcy gives you the opportunity to solve your loan problems so you emerge from bankruptcy with the property you want.

be treated as unsecured debt. Leave the technicalities for the lawyers, but do understand your bankruptcy rights when you are overfinanced and the secured lender threatens foreclosure.

◆ Bankruptcy gives you the opportunity to cure loan defaults. A Chapter 13 bankruptcy, for example, will allow you five years to bring current the delinquent payments on secured debts. This is an important remedy if you lost your job or for some reason fell behind on your mortgage payments but can now pay punctually.

Non-bankruptcy alternatives

Do you own a business with relatively few assets and excessive debts? It may be wasting time and effort to attempt either an informal creditor workout or Chapter 11 reorganization. An easier, less costly and more sensible solution may be to voluntarily liquidate your business, re-acquire its assets through a new corporation, and leave behind the debts of your former company.

The tactic is absolutely legal if correctly handled in a fair and commercially reasonable manner because your creditors receive at least the amount they would under a non-bankruptcy workout, Chapter 11 or Chapter 7 bankruptcy. You, in turn, win back a debt-free business for pennies-on-the-dollar. The advantages of a voluntary liquidation:

- *Less costly.* Knowledgeable professionals can orchestrate it for modest fees. A Chapter 11 may consume tens of thousands of dollars in legal fees, prohibitive for the smaller business.

- *Faster.* With this arrangement, you are back in business in a few days or less. A workout or Chapter 11 will linger for months or years and distract you from your primary goal: to make money!

- *More controllable.* In Chapter 11 bankruptcy, your business is controlled by the bankruptcy court. Your creditors can also replace you with a trustee to manage the business. A buy-back eliminates the control problem.

- *Cleaner, less complex.* The buy-back also eliminates the need to resolve contested claims or engage in protracted litigation because all debts are abandoned and left for the liquidator to resolve.

The large or publicly owned corporation cannot take advantage of the informal buy-back; however, the smaller, privately owned company may find it the most practical solution to creditor problems. These businesses are unburdened by numerous stockholders, enjoy low-visibility and have the flexibility to take a legal shortcut to regain their solvency.

The strategy essentially is to liquidate your business and buy it's assets through a new corporation. You pay its liquidation value, usually a small fraction of its replacement value.

You may liquidate the insolvent business in several ways. You can appoint an assignee for the benefit of creditors. This usually does not involve court proceedings. Or you can petition the state court to appoint a receiver who, like the assignee, must sell the assets and distribute the proceeds to creditors. While you cannot choose the appointed trustee in bankruptcy, you usually can choose the liquidator in a buy-back. A more friendly lender can also foreclose on your business and sell its assets back to your new entity.

Regardless of how liquidated, the liquidator will sell your assets if you pay more than what the assets would yield at auction. But, keep it honest. Avoid impropriety. Pay more than the commercially reasonable liquidation or distress price for the assets. Creditors can challenge a transfer as fraudulent when these deals prove not to be in the creditors' best interests.

To learn more about this strategy, read *The Business Doctor,* from Garrett Publishing.

Planning Pointers

◆ File bankruptcy only after careful thought. There are alternatives to your financial problems and some may be more advantageous.

◆ Test your timing: Don't file bankruptcy too soon or too late. And file the right bankruptcy. Match the bankruptcy to your own financial situation.

◆ The key to protecting assets in bankruptcy is to convert unprotected, non-exempt assets to fully protected, exempt assets.

◆ Another key strategy is to sell or encumber non-exempt assets far in advance of bankruptcy.

◆ If you are filing bankruptcy to stop foreclosure, be realistic in whether your efforts will be successful.

◆ If your business is heading for bankruptcy, consider instead the non-bankruptcy alternatives, particularly the buy-back strategy. It can save you time, money and aggravation.

Strategies that stop the IRS

12

Chapter 12

Strategies that stop the IRS

What you'll find in this chapter:

➧ What you must disclose to the IRS

➧ Coping with a tax lien

➧ How to settle with the IRS

➧ Safeguarding your assets from the IRS

➧ Will bankruptcy solve your problems?

Is the IRS chasing you? Do you have nightmares of losing your home, savings, business and other hard-earned possessions? It happens to thousands of Americans daily. No threat to your financial future is as serious as when the IRS is after you because only the IRS has such awesome collection powers.

On the brighter side, most taxpayers eventually resolve their IRS problems. While they lose some money, most survive. IRS collection agents are tough (they have a tough job), but most are also cooperative and reasonable if you are cooperative and reasonable. The IRS may have powerful laws to help its agents collect, but as a taxpayer you also have strategies available to protect your assets from the IRS. Only when you understand and assert these rights can you have a first-line defense against the IRS.

How the IRS tracks you down

Hiding is never your answer when you owe the IRS. The IRS can find you no matter where or how often you move. Its powerful computer is linked to 50 state computers, Social Security and every other federal agency you ever

---

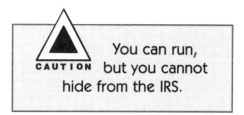

You can run, but you cannot hide from the IRS.

contacted. They also track you via state tax agencies, motor vehicle departments, unemployment offices, public welfare agencies, professional licensing boards and even voter registration records.

Despite its vast information network, the IRS computer works slowly. It may take years for the IRS to find a delinquent taxpayer. While dodging the IRS can forestall the day of reckoning, no taxpayer forever avoids it. If you owe back taxes, resolve it with the IRS now! Delay only costs you more interest and penalties. And, IRS agents are less cooperative if they believe you intentionally avoided them. Legally protect your assets first so you can bargain with the IRS more on your terms. This only happens when your assets are protected well in advance of the tax liability.

What you must disclose to the IRS

Once taxes are overdue, IRS collections agents will want you to complete a financial statement, or *"Collection Information Statement"* (IRS Form 433). This form requires you to disclose all property and sources of income for the obvious purpose of allowing the IRS to know precisely what property and wages it can seize. Your asset list and income information give the IRS whatever information it needs to work out an installment agreement or compromise if you cannot fully pay your taxes or need time to do so.

If you refuse to voluntarily provide this financial information, the IRS will summon you. If you then fail to appear and complete the form, the IRS will have the federal court compel your appearance, and the federal court can jail you for contempt or impose a fine for your failure to obey a court summons.

While the IRS can compel your appearance to answer these financial questions, you may not need to answer the IRS' questions about your assets and income. Taxpayers can rightfully refuse to disclose financial information by claiming their Fifth Amendment Constitutional right against self-incrimination. This is a technical and complex legal issue and may require advice from your counsel.

note You are certainly within your rights to refuse information if you reasonably believe you are under criminal investigation by the IRS or another federal or state law enforcement agency.

The key rule is never to lie or falsify information when discussing finances with the IRS or when you complete an IRS financial statement. Be truthful because your statements are under oath. It is far safer to refuse information than to falsify information.

Protect your assets before you disclose financial information to the IRS because the IRS quickly liens and seizes assets. Time is not on your side. The IRS can usually discover assets and income from other sources, although it cannot easily find cash, bearer investments or such collectibles as gold, jewelry or artwork. Plan ahead to honestly answer the IRS asset inquiry while disclosing nothing that will encourage IRS seizure of your assets.

The IRS will request updated collection information from you about once a year. The IRS thus tracks your future financial condition and ability to pay. Taxpayers are then triggered for renewed collection efforts when the IRS computers, which monitor your tax returns, detect your increased income.

What the IRS knows about you

Whether you cooperate or not, the IRS knows virtually everything about your finances, which may be obtained through your own tax returns or from information obtained through third parties. find assets, rather than rely strictly upon voluntarily disclosures from the taxpayer. Review your tax records as well as the information a third party may provide the IRS. Be prepared to explain any prior dispositions of assets disclosed through these records.

Avoid the IRS jeopardy assessment

DEFINITION

An IRS *jeopardy assessment* allows the IRS to lien or seize assets before it starts the usual collection procedures.

Once the IRS assesses a back tax, it can immediately collect under a jeopardy assessment. However, the IRS must follow strict procedures before and after it assesses the tax. First, the IRS must reasonably believe the taxpayer will leave the country or conceal, transfer or dissipate property, or otherwise act to imperil his financial solvency.

Requests for a jeopardy assessment are reviewed and approved by the IRS District Director. The taxpayer is then served with the jeopardy assessment, which is now immediately collectible by the IRS through enforced collection. How can you avoid a jeopardy assessment?

- Be extremely circumspect if you transfer assets for asset protection or any other purpose. Obvious transfers of endangered assets are not recommended.

- Avoid any unusual or protracted foreign travel. Don't apply for a new passport.

Do nothing out of the ordinary or that could strike the IRS as a plan to flee or render yourself insolvent.

- Cooperate with the IRS.

- Never announce your financial affairs or matters concerning your property to anyone other than your professional advisors.

- Do not completely empty your bank accounts. Gradually reduce any balances on account.

Bottom line: The IRS expects you to remain unprotected.

Jeopardy assessments are uncommon against ordinary taxpayers and are generally used against suspected drug dealers and organized crime suspects.

Never delay asset protection. It can be a costly mistake.

This does not insure that you will not incur a jeopardy assessment. The fact that the IRS can seize your assets with little or no warning must reinforce the need to shelter assets before incurring a large tax liability. Taxpayers oftentimes assume they have adequate opportunity to insulate their assets until the IRS files an unexpected jeopardy assessment.

Protect assets before a tax lien

Taxpayers frequently save assets from IRS seizure by conveying assets to a safe harbor before their assets are encumbered by a tax lien. Timing is critical. Transfers after a tax lien will not prevent the IRS from seizing the liened property later transferred to the third party as a tax lien automatically follows liened property. But when property is conveyed before an IRS lien, the transferee accepts it free and clear of IRS liens subsequently filed against you.

The IRS or any other creditor can, of course, go to court to recover property fraudulently conveyed. However, the burden to recover the asset is upon the IRS. The IRS may also file a nominee lien against property transferred fraudulently to the transferee. However, the IRS must still successfully litigate the transfer as a fraudulent conveyance, and the IRS will seldom go to great lengths to recover transferred property unless the tax liability and value of the transferred property is extensive or the transaction blatantly fraudulent.

Coping with a tax lien

How will a tax lien affect you and your lifestyle?

An IRS tax lien against you remains in effect as long as the IRS can enforce collection. Because the IRS has a 10-year statute of limitations for collections, a tax lien will remain enforceable for at least ten years from the tax assessment date. Filing a tax claim in court, submitting an offer in compromise or time out of the country automatically extends the lien and calendar period.

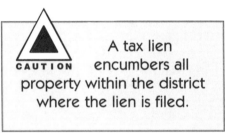

A tax lien encumbers all property within the district where the lien is filed.

The lien thus prevents the taxpayer from selling or borrowing against her property. A tax lien also makes it virtually impossible, or at least difficult, to obtain significant credit or to finance cars, homes or other major assets because the tax lien has priority over debts due other creditors. The lender is then without clear rights to his collateral. One strategy is to have your spouse take title if your spouse has no tax problem. To insure this, file separate tax returns. Another strategy is to set up a corporation to hold title to new purchases. And never become its stockholder. This strategy will not alleviate your credit problems when you must guarantee the financing.

A tax lien can also precipitate a foreclosure on your assets because an existing lender may become concerned that the IRS will seize the lender's collateral. This commonly happens with accounts receivable pledged as collateral because an IRS lien gains superiority against a loan on accounts receivables generated 45 days after the tax lien. This is particularly serious for businesspeople with receivables pledged to a lender, who loses priority rights to the receivables after 45 days. The lender then insists that you obtain a release of the tax lien, pay the loan,

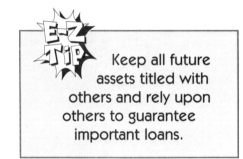

Keep all future assets titled with others and rely upon others to guarantee important loans.

substitute other collateral for receivables, or file Chapter 11. The bank would otherwise be forced to foreclose on the pledged receivables to protect its priority rights. This is one reason why many companies with serious tax problems file Chapter 11.

The IRS must release a lien once the tax is paid or upon expiration of the statute of limitations for collection; however, the IRS does not automatically do so.

note If you are entitled to a lien release, demand the release of lien from your local tax office. Your credit reports should also eliminate reference to your tax lien or you will have credit problems long after the tax liability is resolved.

How to settle with the IRS

When you have a tax bill that you cannot fully pay, you have three options:

1) Remain collection-proof until expiration of the statute of limitations on collections.

2) Stall the IRS for three years from the date the personal income tax filing was due, possibly longer if you did not file your return on time, and then file bankruptcy to discharge the tax liability.

3) Settle with the IRS under its offer in compromise program.

Since the other alternatives are discussed elsewhere, focus now only on the offer in compromise, a little-known IRS procedure that allows the IRS to accept partial payment of the overdue tax as full payment, thus discharging your tax liability, often for pennies on the dollar.

You can only negotiate an offer in compromise when the IRS is convinced that your offer is above what they could collect through enforced action over the next five years. You can convince the IRS to accept a pennies-on-the-dollar settlement if:

• You convince the IRS that collection efforts won't succeed; it often helps convince the IRS when they attempt to collect from you and fail.

• Your offer exceeds any possible recovery by the IRS from seizure of your assets. You must be either asset-poor or asset-protected if a low settlement offer is to succeed.

- Your future earnings potential as a factor does not portray too successful a future. Submit your offer when between jobs or suffering from a chronic illness that may prevent future employment. If you have good earning years ahead, you will gain little sympathy from the IRS who can patiently wait 10 years for payment.

- You know the negotiating tricks. Order *Solving IRS Problems Made E-Z* to discover the strategies.

The IRS may suspend collection efforts while considering your offer in compromise if the IRS considers your offer to be reasonable and filed in good faith.

Consider hiring an experienced accountant or tax lawyer to handle your offer in compromise. It can be a tricky procedure.

An offer in compromise effectively reduces your tax liability to what you can afford now and prospectively over the next five years.

 The two disadvantages with an offer in compromise are: 1) You must fully reveal all assets and income, and 2) the offer in compromise will add one more year, plus the time period in which the IRS is considering your offer, to the 10-year collection period.

Negotiating time to pay the IRS

You may owe the IRS more than you can immediately pay, yet not qualify for an offer in compromise. The IRS will then accept extended payments through a less formal procedure than is required for an offer in compromise. Essentially, the taxpayer submits to the IRS a financial statement and requests permission to pay the past due taxes in installments. But, the IRS does not consider itself a bank, so if your financial statement reveals easily liquidated assets, then the IRS will demand that you sell or refinance these assets rather than accept installments.

You can probably gain several months to pay the overdue tax, although a similar payment plan would have been rejected by the IRS. One-year installment plans are routine; however, revenue agents usually resist longer arrangements and prefer either an offer in compromise or bankruptcy if you need more time. Nevertheless, two and three year installment plans remain common.

IRS guidelines recommend installment arrangements to facilitate the collection of taxes. Although the IRS agrees to an installment arrangement, it can cancel it if:

- you miss a payment.

- you fail to file a federal tax return or pay any taxes you owe on time.

- you fail to give the IRS any requested financial updates.

- you provide the IRS with false information.

- your financial condition significantly improves (i.e., a large inheritance).

- the IRS finds that collection of the tax is in jeopardy

The IRS will refuse an installment plan if:

◆ You have sufficient assets to immediately pay the liability. For example, you own stocks or bonds that you can liquidate within a few days. Remember, an installment plan is a way to orderly discharge taxes over time when other means are unavailable. When you own exposed assets, the IRS will pressure you to sell or refinance those assets to immediately pay the tax.

◆ You defaulted on prior installment plans. Tip: If you honored prior arrangements, make it a selling point.

◆ Your proposed repayment period is far too long a time period.

For immediate assistance, file IRS Form 911 (the *Taxpayer Assistance Order*), which gives you an opportunity to resolve your tax problems with other IRS officials before the IRS levies or seizes your property or wages. This simple appeal procedure can significantly delay seizures.

Assets the IRS targets first

IRS collection officers enjoy broad discretion when selecting assets to seize to satisfy taxes. Agents usually consider several factors when prioritizing assets for seizure.

- the tax liability due versus the property that can most readily satisfy the claim

- ease of seizure and disposal of the various assets

- the importance of each asset to the taxpayer

The IRS usually targets assets for seizure in this progressive order:

1) savings and checking accounts

2) wages, commissions, and other income

3) cash value life insurance

4) cars, boats, airplanes and recreational vehicles with a high equity

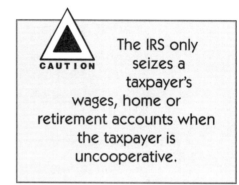

The IRS only seizes a taxpayer's wages, home or retirement accounts when the taxpayer is uncooperative.

5) accounts receivable

6) stocks, bonds, and other liquid investments

7) investment real estate

8) personal residence

9) IRAs, Keoghs, SEPs and other retirement or profit-sharing accounts

10) Social Security checks

Threatened seizure of assets often spurs the taxpayer to refinance or sell to pay the taxes. However, the IRS files tax liens against property regardless of the taxpayer's inclination to pay.

IRS guidelines for asset seizures encourage the seizure of Social Security and retirement funds only in more flagrant and aggravated cases, and then only with the prior approval of an authorized IRS supervisor.

Assets exempt from IRS seizure

The IRS need not leave you many assets; however, even the all-powerful IRS cannot seize all that you own. Certain assets are exempt from IRS seizure. These include:

- fuel, food, furniture and personal effects worth $2,500

- undelivered mail

- tools and books, valued to $1,250, needed for your job, business or profession

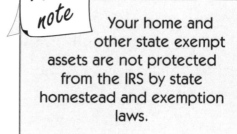

note Your home and other state exempt assets are not protected from the IRS by state homestead and exemption laws.

- income required to pay court-ordered child support

- unemployment, workers' compensation, public assistance and job training benefits

- clothing and school books

- pension payments of retired railroad employees, military disability benefits or benefits due individuals on the Armed Forces Honor Roll

- a minimal amount, which is exempted from levy on wages, salary, and other income

Social Security, IRAs, Keoghs, and 401K Qualified Pension plans are not protected, although the IRS will not quickly seize them. If you have a large tax liability, then liquidate and protect your IRAs and other retirement accounts, even if it creates a tax penalty for an early withdrawal. The penalty and deferred tax may then be handled with the original tax liability. This will be of little consequence if you do not intend to fully pay your tax liability. The IRS can ignore homestead and other state exemption laws and may in certain circumstances seize property owned as tenants-by-the-entirety.

note Relocating property to defeat seizure is not recommended no matter how desperately you want to keep the asset.

Safeguarding assets from the IRS

The IRS code rules it a felony to remove, deposit or conceal property upon which an IRS levy has been authorized, when done with the intention of defeating the collection of taxes. You must move cautiously and always follow your lawyer's advice on permissible strategies to protect assets from the

IRS. However, you need not actually surrender assets subject to seizure, nor can IRS agents force a taxpayer to produce property for seizure. However, if you state the location of an asset to an IRS agent, the disclosure must be truthful. Eventually the IRS will locate and seize your assets. The safest strategy is to sell or encumber assets before the tax lien or seizure.

Nor can the IRS enter and seize assets on residential or business premises unless you either voluntarily consent to such an entry or the IRS has a warrant or "writ of entry" from a federal court. Examine the writ of entry and confine the IRS agent to the premises described in the writ. This rule only applies to private premises. The IRS requires no writ of entry to seize assets on public property. Therefore, an automobile publicly garaged may be seized by the IRS without a writ of entry, but not an auto in your garage.

How to recover seized property

The IRS can seize your home but cannot immediately evict you. There is a minimum 90-day period between seizure date and public auction or sealed bid sale of the property. You will have another 180 days to remain in possession after your property is sold to a successful bidder. During this six-month period you can redeem or re-acquire your property for the bid price plus interest. Once the 180-day redemption period passes, the buyer can evict you, although the eviction may consume another several months. You thus live rent-free for approximately one year from the date of IRS seizure. There is no similar right to continued possession to personal property.

You may convince the IRS to release seized property in four instances:

1) You negotiate an installment agreement. A seizure often prods taxpayers to solve their tax problems by reaching agreement with the IRS or convinces them to sell or refinance the property. Taxpayers play ostrich until they are about to lose their valued assets, then often find the money.

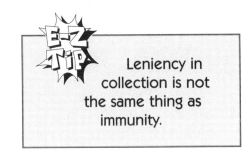

Leniency in collection is not the same thing as immunity.

2) Releasing the asset will facilitate tax collection. Business assets in operation, for instance, will usually generate more revenue than their auction price.

3) The tax liability is fully satisfied or no longer enforceable. Full payment, or payment under an offer in compromise, requires a release of seized assets as does the expiration of the statute of limitations for collections. Bankruptcy (Chapter 7, 11, 12 or 13) automatically stays further action by the IRS, unless allowed by the bankruptcy court.

4) You file a bond equal in value to the seized assets. Or you substitute collateral of equal or greater value.

When the IRS threatens your business

The IRS seizes thousands of businesses annually and yet will hesitate to seize certain businesses:

- Businesses financed by the SBA or other federal agencies. It would be foolish for one federal agency to collect at the expense of another federal agency that will then lose the opportunity to collect.

- Minority-owned businesses, or those who employ many minorities.

- Businesses engaged in sensitive defense work or those which are otherwise important vendors to the federal government.

- High-profile businesses, including major employers within the community.

If you own such a business, the tax collector may show greater restraint, even if this is not official IRS policy. The IRS expects payment of overdue taxes from every business, but these businesses apparently have the best argument against seizure.

When to encourage IRS seizures

IRS auctions generally yield a fraction of what the seized property is actually worth. So, your best strategy may be to encourage the IRS to sell your home, car, boat or other property at public auction if you can raise the money to buy your property back through a third party or straw. This strategy is practical, for example, if the

CAUTION

The IRS can immediately seize cars, boats and other property, and you have no right to redeem personal property once sold.

IRS has a $300,000 lien on your $100,000 home. You may then repurchase your home for perhaps $70,000 and wipe out all other subsequent attachments or mortgages in the process.

The IRS sets a minimum price bid on the property that it auctions. It then sells via public auction or sealed bid at no less than this minimum price bid. The IRS minimum bid accurately predicts what property brings at a distressed sale. To establish its minimum bid, the IRS establishes the asset's fair market value through a normal sale, and then deducts 20 percent, and then another 25 percent, representing the distress sale impact upon the price. A $150,000 home would thus have a $90,000 minimum bid ($150,000 less $30,000 less $30,000).

A low appraisal literally allows you to steal back your property. But beware. The IRS can instead sell your bargain property to an outside bidder and produce fewer proceeds to pay your taxes or cover the real equity you have in the property. Once you know the minimum bid, try to convince the IRS to release your property to you for that minimum bid amount. Remember, your successful offer must equal the equity the IRS can foreseeably recover on a forced sale. This amount, however, might be very nominal or non-existent.

Tips to protect bank accounts

The IRS records a taxpayers checking and savings accounts and can then easily levy these accounts. Interest payments on your accounts also go through the IRS computers. The IRS will routinely and unexpectedly levy bank accounts of delinquent taxpayers. To protect your accounts:

• Transfer funds to a corporate account which can pay your personal debts. Deposit the funds as a loan and withdraw funds as repayment.

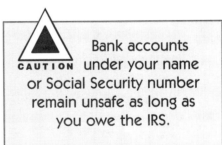

Bank accounts under your name or Social Security number remain unsafe as long as you owe the IRS.

• Open new accounts with banks the IRS will not easily discover. Smaller, remote banks work best because the IRS may levy all major banks in your area. Since the IRS periodically requires delinquent taxpayers to complete new financial statements, it will then be necessary to honestly disclose your new bank accounts. But you can open newer accounts elsewhere immediately after you disclose your present accounts. This is a perfectly legal strategy because your disclosures were truthful when made.

Keep the IRS from your safe deposit box

Your safe deposit box is never safe if the IRS suspects it contains cash or other valuables. To open your box you are forced to permit an IRS examination of its contents. The IRS also can wait until the safe deposit box rental contract expires when a bank officer can open the box for the IRS.

 Never keep cash, other valuables or important original documents in a safe deposit box. This is not always convenient because a safe deposit box is considered a safe place for these items. You may rent the safe deposit box under the name of a corporation. Since the corporation is a separate entity, the IRS cannot gain access to it to collect personal taxes. Also, do not personally hold the key to this box while undergoing enforced collection.

> ⚠ **CAUTION** The IRS can demand access to your safe deposit box in the presence of an IRS agent. Alternatively, the IRS can seal the box and deny you access.

Whether or not you are a tax delinquent, the IRS can seal your personal safe deposit box upon your death. However, because a corporation has perpetual life, your death will not invite the IRS to visit your corporate safe deposit box. Give your spouse or another trusted individual the authority to open the corporate box.

Beyond collecting overdue taxes, there are other reasons the IRS will snoop for hidden cash in safe deposit boxes. The IRS considers cash in a safe deposit box as unreported income and taxes you on these funds, with interest and penalties. Never stash cash without solid proof that it is after tax proceeds or it is money you may pay taxes on— twice!

Why spouses should never file joint tax returns

Avoid filing joint returns with your spouse. You pay less taxes when filing together, but the trade-off is that the IRS can then collect from both spouses. File individually and your spouse has no liability for your taxes and may become a safe harbor for marital assets should you run into tax troubles!

The danger from joint returns is that you cannot easily protect marital assets since neither spouse can provide that safe harbor. There are four cases when spouses should absolutely file their own individual returns:

1)   When one spouse has chronic tax problems, continuing audits, major tax liabilities or has not filed required returns.

2)   One spouse faces serious civil or criminal tax problems.

3)   One spouse owns most of the marital assets, and the other spouse has the greater tax exposure.

4)   The marriage is unstable and divorce is likely.

CAUTION When you file jointly, the entire tax liability can be collected from either spouse.

Wages the IRS can seize

The wage levy is the IRS' ultimate weapon, and is particularly effective because there is no limit on the wages the IRS can seize. The personal exemption is $75 a week, plus $25 per week per dependent, including your spouse. A wage levy remains in force until your tax liability is fully paid or the levy discharged.

Wage levies usually arise only when a taxpayer is uncooperative and does not respond to IRS requests for payment. But, even a hard-nosed IRS cannot realistically expect a single wage-earner with a net weekly salary of $500 to continuously hand the IRS $425 and survive on $75. The wage levy is then mostly used to prod a taxpayer into a payment plan when other collection efforts failed.

There are strategies to counteract an IRS wage levy:

1)   If you own your own business, you may divert income to your spouse or adult children who work in the business. They may then gift or loan you some funds. Be prepared to prove that your spouse or children actually perform services for the business, and their income is justifiable.

Negotiate payment with the IRS before a wage levy and when the IRS will be more lenient.

2)   Form another corporation to perform services for your first business. You can then be paid from this second corporation. The IRS will

eventually discover your new wage source; however, this can take a year or more when you can then repeat the process with another corporation.

If you work for someone else and you owe taxes that can be fully paid with several garnished paychecks, then your best option is to grin and bear the levy. If your tax liability cannot be quickly paid, you should negotiate an acceptable payment plan with the IRS, which was probably Uncle Sam's objective with the levy. If you cannot negotiate a reasonable payment schedule, then filing a Chapter 7 or 13 bankruptcy may be your only alternative. Bankruptcy is strong medicine and should be avoided if possible. Quit your job? It's not the answer for most people.

When collection efforts must stop

The IRS has ten years from the date of a tax assessment to collect back taxes. This has been extended retroactively in 1991 from six years. Once the statute of limitations expires, the IRS must terminate further collection unless the statute of limitations has been extended in one of six ways:

1)   *Waiver:* The taxpayer signs a waiver and voluntarily agrees to extend the time for collection.

2)   *Offer in Compromise:* Processing your offer in compromise adds one extra year, plus the time period an Offer in Compromise is under IRS consideration.

3)   *Bankruptcy:* Bankruptcy extends the statute on non-dischargeable taxes for the pendency of the bankruptcy, plus six months.

4)   *Application for Taxpayer Assistance Order (ATAO):* This application extends the statute by the time it is under IRS review.

5)   *Absence from the country:* The time period a taxpayer is outside the country for six or more continuous months.

6)   *IRS lawsuit:* When the IRS sues in court to enforce collection.

Never voluntarily extend the statute of limitations. The IRS will try to get you to sign a Form 900 Waiver when the statute of limitations nears expiration. The IRS may then aggressively try to collect or instead offer you lenient payments in exchange for the waiver. Never sign! If the IRS could not collect to date, why will it be more successful in the few remaining months? Once the statute of limitations expires you have finally ended your IRS problems. Extending the collection period only extends your tax problems.

Despite its great collection powers, the IRS allows countless tax claims to expire each year. Once yours expires, ask the IRS to abate the tax liability to acknowledge that you are in the clear. Until you receive this written abatement, keep your property fully protected.

Will bankruptcy solve your problems?

Whether bankruptcy will end your tax obligation depends upon both the type of bankruptcy and the type of tax you owe.

First, are you liable for personal income taxes or employee withholding taxes due from a business? Income taxes are dischargeable in Chapter 7 bankruptcy if more than three years old from the due date when you file for bankruptcy.

> *note* Withholding taxes are never dischargeable under Chapter 7 bankruptcy.

Next, consider the type of bankruptcy. Income taxes, whether they are more or less than three years old, are not automatically discharged under either Chapter 13 wage-earner plans or Chapter 11 reorganizations. Chapter 13 requires you to make monthly payments for three to five years to partly or fully pay your debts. Because taxes have priority over other debts, a tax claim is usually fully paid under Chapter 11 or Chapter 13.

Chapter 7 bankruptcy can end your tax problems if you plan carefully:

- Make certain your taxes are over three years old from their due date, have been filed for at least 2 years and have been assessed at least 240 days. More recent taxes are not dischargeable.

- If you negotiated an installment plan, submitted an offer in compromise or had your tax claim adjudicated in court, you must wait at least 240 days before filing bankruptcy. File earlier and your taxes will not be discharged.

- Bankruptcy will not discharge understated taxes or liabilities on false tax returns for the tax years you want discharged. Make certain all prior tax returns are accurate.

> *note* If you can fully pay your taxes over time, then Chapter 11 or Chapter 13 may be your answer.

- Filing bankruptcy will not discharge or release liens previously filed against your property. The bankruptcy court can approve the IRS seizing liened property. Remaining tax obligations will be discharged.

Chapter 13 gives you three to five years to pay your taxes, and the IRS cannot enforce collection during this period. In a business or profession? Chapter 11 reorganization allows you six years from date of assessment to pay the IRS. Still, a Chapter 13 wage-earner plan or Chapter 11 reorganization is only a possible solution if you have assets you do not want to lose. When you have few or no assets and a substantial tax liability, it is smarter to wait the three years and fully discharge the tax under Chapter 7.

While the IRS is powerful, federal bankruptcy laws are stronger. File bankruptcy and the IRS must stop all further collection enforcement. Bankruptcy can effectively protect assets and stretch your payments to the IRS, but don't wait too long or the IRS may irreversibly damage your business.

> If you cannot quickly resolve matters with the IRS, file bankruptcy before the IRS does its damage and bankruptcy becomes an empty remedy.

The IRS may, for instance, levy your cash and accounts receivable, or seize assets and close your business. Under Chapter 11 or Chapter 13, you can compel the IRS to return these assets, but this will take time. You must first file a turnover complaint against the IRS, and then obtaining relief in the bankruptcy court can take weeks or even months. Meanwhile, your business remains closed, employees find new jobs and customers flock to competitors. Customers who owe you money find an IRS levy a convenient excuse not to pay and to take their business elsewhere. Few businesses survive such serious disruptions.

Find professional assistance when you owe the IRS

CPAs, attorneys and enrolled agents (EAs) each represent taxpayers before the IRS. Consider one major difference between these professionals: What you disclose to your accountant or EA is not privileged. The IRS can subpoena records from your accountant or EA, including all documents that you provide them. On the other hand, what you tell your attorney is privileged.

If you should retain an accountant or EA, have your tax attorney or family lawyer hire them to handle your case. When they work through your lawyer, your communications to them will be as protected as your direct communication with your lawyer.

note Neither the IRS nor a court can force your attorney to disclose confidential communication without your permission. You may thus confide in your attorney without fear of disclosure.

Assert your taxpayer's rights

The newly revised Taxpayer's Bill of Rights gives you several important rights against the IRS. It explains in simple English what the IRS can and cannot do against taxpayers. Obtain your copy of the Taxpayer's Bill of Rights at your local IRS office.

Planning Pointers

◆ You cannot hide from the IRS. It has many ways to find you.

◆ If you owe the IRS, it will require complete and truthful disclosure of your assets and income to facilitate collection.

◆ Never falsify information or conceal assets from the IRS. Advance asset protection is permissible.

◆ Once a tax lien is filed, all existing assets are automatically encumbered. Assets must be protected before a lien is filed.

◆ There are a number of options available to taxpayers who owe the IRS. Ignoring the IRS is the one alternative that will most likely cause you to lose your assets.

◆ There are very few assets that the IRS cannot seize. State exemptions that protect assets do not block the IRS.

◆ It may not be too late to deal with the IRS and retain assets—even after the IRS has seized assets or levied wages.

◆ Spouses should file separate and not joint tax returns. They then will not share an IRS liability, and one spouse can become the safe harbor for family assets.

◆ Know and assert your taxpayer rights. There are solutions to tax troubles if you want to solve your problems and will cooperate with the IRS.

◆ Obtain a copy of *Solving IRS Problems Made E-Z,* by E-Z Legal Forms, and read more about what to do when you owe taxes.

Protecting your assets in divorce

13

Chapter 13

Protecting your assets in divorce

What you'll find in this chapter:

➠ Why you need a pre-marriage agreement

➠ Why you need a post-nuptial agreement

➠ How to protect assets in a divorce

➠ The importance of cohabitation agreements

➠ Community property and divorce

Divorce your spouse, but don't divorce yourself from your rightful share of your hard-earned property. Divorce can be emotionally and economically devastating and is frequently life's biggest financial catastrophe. Marriage is no longer a lifelong commitment. Over one in two marriages ends in divorce. Asset protection planning becomes essential whether you are presently married, planning marriage, happily married or anticipating separation.

Unfortunately, most divorces become adversarial. Spouses and lawyers joust for whatever marital property they can win with battle tactics nastier than those employed in most other courtroom feuds.

What can you do today to better prepare yourself financially if a divorce is in your future? This chapter highlights 1) pre-marriage and post-nuptial agreements, 2) marital financial privacy, 3) street smart tactics to win your share of the assets, and 4) your legal rights after the divorce.

Involve yourself in the family finances

Spouses who are most often cheated out of marital assets in a divorce are usually those who don't know about the family finances. Divorcing spouses can be dishonest when reporting their assets.

> ⚠️ **CAUTION** Those who are not involved with their spouses' business interests or finances during the marriage are most easily victimized when they divorce.

Nor are asset searches by professional asset search firms always successful in uncovering concealed marital assets. Assets can be cleverly hidden, particularly when the marriage had a long downturn with ample time to plan the concealment.

Develop a special alertness to your spouse's business and financial affairs. It can prevent a major asset concealment that can victimize you.

Observe your ex-spouse's financial dealings after the divorce. That is when your ex-spouse may reveal the earlier concealed assets.

Insist upon pre-marriage agreements

DEFINITION

A fair and legally binding pre-marriage agreement is the one safest way to secure asset protection in a future divorce. A *pre-marriage agreement* is a written contract between the intended spouses that specifies how property and income shall be divided in divorce. It also recites how each spouse shall share responsibilities to each other and their children. Pre-marriage agreements are often called pre-marital, pre-nuptial or ante-nuptial agreements (from the Latin prefix ante, which literally means before, and nuptial, or marriage).

> 📝 *note*
> Pre-marriage agreements are increasingly popular because they resolve in advance the many complex issues that are less easily reconciled by a divorce court.

You may believe pre-marriage agreements are only for the wealthy. But many more couples of average income and wealth now use pre-marriage agreements as an efficient and equitable way to settle matters well in advance of a future divorce.

Example: One spouse may have accumulated substantial assets before the marriage and wants his children from a prior marriage to inherit that wealth. A pre-marriage agreement is then the ideal way, and perhaps only way, to secure this wish. The pre-marriage agreement can similarly guarantee fixed spousal alimony as well as property division upon separation, divorce or death. With the agreement, both parties can marry confident that their respective post-marital needs will be fulfilled should the marriage end unhappily.

> **E-Z TIP**
> Pre-marriage agreements are particularly useful when the couple are both wealthy and do not rely upon each other financially.

Many older couples marry more for companionship than financial security. When one or both spouses has wealth and children from a prior marriage, the pre-marriage agreement insures the desired disposition of assets in divorce and death. Couples in this situation usually agree to share assets accumulated during their marriage, but assets accumulated before the marriage remain their separate property.

There are many other situations where a pre-marriage agreement is advisable. One example is the couple planning an interfaith marriage who may want a contractual understanding concerning the religion to be followed by their children. The pre-marriage agreement can be helpful in five more important ways:

1) *Avoid hostility:* Divorces become most hostile when spouses must fight over property and their children. Angry emotions then peak. A pre-marriage agreement can resolve both financial and personal matters well in advance, a time when both parties are friendly, rational and obliging. A fair and comprehensive pre-marriage agreement then allows for the dissolution of the marriage merely by filing the necessary court papers, thus avoiding costly, time-consuming and emotionally turbulent legal battles.

2) *Promote fairness:* Never assume that the divorce court will divide property equitably. Courts are unfair because judges seldom have the opportunity to hear all relevant facts. Nevertheless, without a pre-marriage agreement, the court must somehow decide how to divide the marital property. The court's judgment is necessarily substituted for what the parties themselves may have considered

equitable and fair had they contemplated such issues between themselves beforehand when they were amicable.

3) *Save money:* Contested divorces are costly. Couples with modest assets can pay attorneys tens or even hundreds of thousands of dollars to wage battle in divorce court. Lawyers pocket about one-third a divorcing family's assets, and often more. You avoid this costly conflict with a pre-marriage agreement.

4) *Divorce faster:* A contested divorce is usually a prolonged feud. Two or three year divorces are not rare. When potential disputes are resolved before the marriage through a pre-marriage agreement, the divorce is shortened to a few months.

5) *Plan properly:* Possibly the greatest benefit of a pre-marriage agreement is that it encourages, even forces, both parties to consider what they really expect and want from their marriage. This involves much more than finances. One example is an engaged couple who may unexpectedly realize that she plans a large family while he wants no children. Or, another intended bride plans a lifelong career while he assumes his wife will raise the family and not work. A pre-marital agreement encompasses such issues, compelling you to think about and discuss them and not take such important matters for granted. When you cannot agree on such basic issues before the marriage, it is unlikely that you will agree once married.

> *note*
> The pre-marital agreement forces you to express more precisely what the marital relationship will be, in terms of what you expect to give and receive from your partner.

Selling the pre-marriage agreement

One of the greatest barriers to the pre-marriage agreement is the hesitancy of intended spouses to raise such a delicate subject to their intended. Such couples believe a pre-marital agreement communicates either distrust or lack of commitment to the marriage, is unromantic and too businesslike, foredooms the marriage to divorce or is too expensive.

Lovers are optimists and few believe their marriage can fail. Others are either unassertive or too trusting. Still others are poorly organized and poorly plan most aspects of their lives. Many others simply don't realize how well the pre-marriage agreement can protect them should their marriage fail.

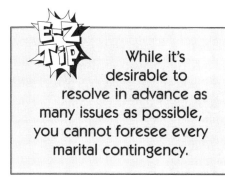

note It's never too soon to inform a prospective spouse that you require a pre-marriage agreement. The earlier your expectations are known, the sooner you may plan your wedding and post-marital finances with less concern.

A pre-marriage agreement is understandably a sensitive subject. But, it can be softened and sold to your intended spouse. You may voice concern for your children from a prior marriage, or that your lawyers insist upon an agreement. Or, you may approach the subject by suggesting that you read about pre-marital agreements in this or some other book and now want to discuss the ideas and issues routinely covered by premarital agreements. Another discussion opener is to call a pre-marriage agreement an estate plan. For example: "Carol, I think we should prepare a complete estate plan before we marry." A complete estate plan, in this instance, would include the provisions of a pre-marriage agreement. Why initially disclose this if you think it will raise objections?

Key provisions for the pre-marriage agreement

Pre-marriage agreements are not necessarily lengthy nor complicated. A simple agreement can adequately cover the basic points. Yet many couples prefer a more detailed agreement. However, a well-designed pre-marriage agreement will answer basic points:

E-Z TIP While it's desirable to resolve in advance as many issues as possible, you cannot foresee every marital contingency.

- What rights does each spouse retain to property they bring to the marriage?

- What are their respective rights to post-marital property?

- What are the spouses' rights to income earned during the marriage?

- How will pre-marital and post-marital property be divided upon the death of either spouse? Does this disposition change upon divorce?

- What insurance will each spouse maintain, and who shall be the beneficiaries during the marriage and thereafter?

- What are the work or career expectations for each spouse?

- Who will be responsible for pre-marital debts? Marital debts?

- What religion will the children observe in an interfaith marriage?

- What surname will the children adopt?

- What child support shall be provided upon divorce?

- Who will be responsible for the child's education? Medical care? Other special needs?

- Who shall have custody of the child?

- What are the visitation rights of the non-custodial parent?

- What alimony is payable upon divorce? When does it terminate?

- What surname shall the wife use? Can the wife regain her maiden name upon divorce?

- What mandatory counselling is required to resolve marital difficulties before a divorce can be filed?

- Who pays the attorney fees to enforce the pre-marital agreement? To handle the divorce?

You can consider other provisions. And pre-marital agreements are best negotiated directly by the parties. Attorneys can guide you, but don't allow them to negotiate the agreement in an adversarial manner.

Why pre-marriage agreements fail

Pre-marriage agreements are enforceable in all states. They are binding contracts guaranteed enforceable by both the U.S. Constitution and the law of all jurisdictions. However, there are limitations on what future newlyweds may agree upon.

For example: The rights and duties of spouses toward their children can always be modified by the divorce court. To insure the proper parental support for minor children, a court will modify an agreement if it determines the children will be inadequately supported. Courts also are concerned with preserving the minor children's relationships with other family members, as well as other aspects of their upbringing.

Courts closely scrutinize custody, visitation and child support provisions and freely modify those that are unreasonable and detrimental to the children, although the agreement expresses what each parent believes to be fair and necessary for the children. However, unless the agreement clearly violates the children's best interests, it will be ratified by the court.

> **note** Both parties to the pre-marital agreement must be scrupulously honest. They must disclose all relevant information or the pre-marriage agreement will be void.

Unlike disclosure requirements in ordinary business contracts, pre-marriage agreements are considered personal contracts, and the law thus requires each party to honestly, openly and fairly disclose all income, assets, debts and other matters relevant to formulating the agreement.

Spouses intending to conceal assets from a future spouse should avoid pre-marriage agreements. If you want to keep pre-marital assets separate, you must nevertheless advise your intended spouse about those assets. Failure to disclose most commonly destroys the enforceability of these agreements.

A pre-marriage agreement will not allow you to unfairly deprive your spouse of a rightful share to marital property. Divorce courts carefully examine whether both spouses are treated equitably. If the court finds otherwise, it will void the agreement. State law will then govern the disposition of the couple's property.

> **note** The validity of a pre-marriage agreement requires you to prepare it according to the laws of the state where you will reside once married.

State law governs pre-marriage agreement requirements, and their laws vary, despite efforts toward uniformity.

The *Uniform Premarital Agreement Act* is in effect in several states and is closely followed by most others. It considers a pre-marriage agreement unenforceable only under the following circumstances:

1) If the party against whom enforcement is sought proves:

   a) The party did not execute the agreement or

   b) The agreement was unconscionable when executed and before execution of the agreement that party: (i) was not provided a fair and reasonable disclosure of the property or financial obligations of the other party; (ii) did not voluntarily and expressly waive, in writing, any right to disclosure of the property or financial obligations of the other party beyond the disclosure provided; and (iii) did not have, or reasonably could not have had, an adequate knowledge of the property or financial obligations of the other party.

2) If a provision of a pre-marriage agreement modifies or eliminates spousal support and that modification or elimination causes one party to the agreement to be eligible for support under a program of public assistance at the time of separation or marital dissolution—a court, notwithstanding the terms of the agreement, may require the other party to provide support to the extent necessary to avoid that eligibility.

Issues of unconscionability of a pre-marriage agreement shall be decided by the courts as a matter of law.

Six more points are essential for an airtight pre-marriage agreement:

1) *Finalize the agreement.* Couples planning marriage oftentimes make verbal agreements. While you may testify about an oral agreement in divorce, it is never as enforceable as a written agreement.

2) *Retain separate attorneys.* Pre-marital agreements are frequently contested because the contesting spouse claims he or she did not fully understand the agreement. Separate lawyers eliminate that argument and thus insure enforceability.

3) *Check state laws.* A pre-marital agreement must coincide with how property is generally divided in your state.

4) *Negotiate fairly.* Unfair agreements are seldom upheld by courts. The agreement doesn't require equal division of property, only fundamental fairness.

5) *Agree far before the marriage.* A pre-marital agreement should not be signed under undue pressure. Both parties must have the opportunity to fairly contemplate the agreement and seek independent counsel well before the wedding when you and your future spouse are relaxed and can give the agreement your

attention without claim of last-minute surprise, distraction or coercion.

6) *Update your agreement.* Circumstances change. Review your pre-marriage agreement at least bi-annually and change the agreement to meet those new circumstances.

Agreements for the presently married

Post-nuptial agreements are similar in purpose to pre-marriage agreements but are made after the marriage.

Married couples can legally contract, however, specific marital rights cannot be bargained away as they can under a pre-marriage agreement. Some courts do not enforce post-nuptial contracts on the theory that there is no consideration to support them.

Since the laws concerning post-nuptial contracts vary between states, obtain counsel familiar with these agreements.

As with the pre-marital agreement, the enforceability of the post-nuptial agreement requires the court to find that the agreement is fair, both spouses fully understood the agreement, neither party defrauded the other, and each party had their own legal counsel.

Post-nuptial property agreements are narrower in scope than pre-marital agreements and routinely cover four important issues concerning a future divorce:

1) What property will the wife keep as her separate property?

2) What marital property will the wife receive upon divorce?

3) What property will the husband keep as his separate property?

4) What marital property will the husband receive upon divorce?

 Defining property that is considered separate versus marital property (or community property) is not always simple and frequently depends upon state law. These asset lists must be amended periodically by the couple to classify newer assets.

A post-nuptial agreement is particularly ideal for resolving the always thorny issue of valuing or apportioning business ownership in a divorce. The business often becomes the central obstacle in settlement negotiations.

Retain control over marital assets

One common and simplistic asset protection strategy is to title marital assets with the less-vulnerable spouse. One obvious problem with this

Titling marital assets in the name of one spouse is always poor planning. Spouses should jointly control marital assets.

arrangement is that this one spouse then controls the assets and can sell, encumber or conceal the entrusted assets from the other spouse.

They achieve good asset protection if, for example, both spouses hold title as tenants-by-the-entirety or as general partners in a family limited partnership. If one spouse is to hold sole title to the assets, the other spouse should at least encumber or escrow the assets to some third-party or nominee entity that he controls. This can prevent a sale or disposition of the property without his knowledge or consent.

How to divorce-proof assets

Can one spouse place his or her assets beyond the powers of the divorce court? The answer is yes if the assets are placed in an offshore asset protection trust. This devise can completely insulate assets from the divorce court.

Unhappy spouses planning for divorce frequently shelter assets in an offshore asset protection trust. While they must truthfully disclose these trust assets to the divorce court, the court cannot recover or divide these trust assets under the divorce. That hardly assures a complete victory. The divorce court can award the victimized spouse a disproportionate share of the U.S.-based assets to compensate for the trust-shielded assets. The court also can grant the injured spouse compensatory alimony or support.

The offshore trust is an excellent way to secure separate property when you have few remaining assets within the United States and your income is too insignificant for the court to even the score through an excessive alimony award.

Other offshore structures, particularly the Nevis limited liability company or a Liechtenstein or Panama foundation, offer similar protection to an offshore trust. These and newer structures should be investigated when the goal is to remove assets from the divorce proceedings.

Cohabitation agreements for lovers

Many more couples now prefer to live together without marriage. Some live together to test their relationship before marrying. Older folks frequently live together because marriage would disqualify them from social security or pension benefits. Still others prefer to avoid financial responsibility for the care of an ill partner, or the many other legal and financial complications that arise from a marriage. These concerns are particularly valid when one party is substantially more wealthy.

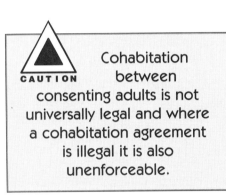

CAUTION Cohabitation between consenting adults is not universally legal and where a cohabitation agreement is illegal it is also unenforceable.

Cohabitation is now legal in Canada and most foreign countries. However, a cohabitation contract cannot be construed as a contract for sexual services. This is illegal and unenforceable everywhere.

Cohabitation agreements chiefly define the couple's rights to property. The agreement designates separate property before cohabitation and provides for the distribution of assets acquired both jointly and singly during the cohabitation. The cohabitation agreement may also resolve the responsibility for joint obligations, such as leases, utilities or insurance.

Several recent palimony cases prove cohabitation agreements to be as vital to cohabitating homosexual couples as they are to heterosexual couples. Cohabitation agreements are also advisable if one partner is considerably wealthier. This prevents the poorer partner's claim that the cohabitation was for personal care and services on the promise of substantial compensation. This claim can be dispelled by a cohabitation agreement that precisely defines the nature and purpose of the relationship and whether it includes compensation for services.

Dividing property in a divorce

Without a pre-marriage agreement or a negotiated divorce settlement, the divorce courts must decide:

- how your property will be divided. This includes property owned both before and after the marriage.

- child support

- alimony

- custody and visitation

The divorce court will divide property either through equitable distribution or as community property.

Courts in equitable distribution states have the discretion to divide all the property of both spouses. These courts consider the marriage duration, the age, health, conduct, occupations, skills, and employment and earnings potential of the respective spouses, and other factors outlined in the state divorce statutes.

Through equitable distribution, all property acquired during the marriage is considered marital property. Property acquired before the marriage is non-marital property. Gifts or inheritances to a spouse during marriage are also non-marital property. However, non-marital property is not safe from division in a divorce. Courts usually leave all or most of this property with the respective spouses, but courts in most equitable distribution states can divide pre-marital assets between spouses. The pre-marriage agreement can keep separate from the divorce procedures the pre-marital assets and also apportion marital assets.

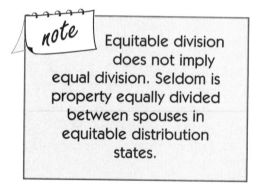

note Equitable division does not imply equal division. Seldom is property equally divided between spouses in equitable distribution states.

The equitable distribution states include:

Alabama	Alaska	Arkansas	Colorado	
Connecticut	Delaware	District of Columbia		Florida
Hawaii	Illinois	Indiana	Iowa	Kansas
Kentucky	Maine	Massachusetts	Michigan	Minnesota
Missouri	Montana	Nebraska	New Hampshire	
New Jersey	New York	N. Carolina	N. Dakota	Oklahoma
Oregon	Pennsylvania	Rhode Island	S. Dakota	Tennessee
	Utah	Vermont	Wyoming	

Community property states equally divide community property upon divorce. Community property includes property acquired by each spouse prior to the marriage, unless specifically retained as separate property through a separate property agreement.

The nine community property states include:

Arizona	California	Idaho	Louisiana	Nevada
New Mexico	Texas	Washington	Wisconsin	

Mississippi is the only title state. It awards property to spouses based solely upon who holds title to the asset. No other state considers title a conclusive factor when dividing property. Maximum asset protection in a Mississippi divorce only requires you to hold title to marital property.

Safeguarding community property

The nine community property states view marriage as an equal business partnership. Community property laws thus divide property into either community property or separate property. Community property is property acquired jointly or individually during the marriage and used in furtherance of the marriage. Separate property can be:

- property one spouse owned before the marriage and retains title to after the marriage

- property a spouse receives as a gift or inheritance either before or during the marriage

Separate property remains separate property and is not divided in divorce. If you exchange separate property for another asset, the new property continues as separate property, as do proceeds from the sale.

Liabilities that either spouse incurred before marriage can also remain separate obligations. While the parties may agree to separately pay certain debts incurred during the marriage, this does not bind creditors who can nevertheless collect from both or either spouse. Marital bills should be either fully paid or indemnified against in a divorce.

E-Z TIP Never commingle separate property and joint property. Separate property then becomes divisible joint property. Keep separate property distinguishable from joint property.

To protect property in a community property state, you must list your separate property when you marry. Your spouse must formally agree that this will remain separate property thereafter. Also keep gifts or inheritances received during the marriage separate, so these assets remain free from a spousal claim.

Concealing assets in a divorce

With an approaching divorce one or both spouses may try to hide assets. They may sell stocks or bonds or withdraw savings and claim the money was spent or lost. Or a spouse may title assets with a straw. Divorce courts routinely see these tactics and severely penalize a spouse suspected of such unfair conduct. Play fair and you will come out ahead. Nevertheless, your spouse may be less honest. Therefore, protect all marital assets until they are properly divided by the divorce court:

1)   *Secure the jewelry, artwork and other valuable or movable objects.* Provide your spouse with a complete inventory so you can't later be accused of concealing marital assets.

2)   *Secure in a safe location the cash, securities, stocks, bonds and notes or mortgages due you.* If you own assets jointly with your spouse, then notify your stockbroker or transfer agent not to transfer these investments without your written consent.

3)   *Borrow the cash reserves* on joint insurance policies for safekeeping.

4)   *Does your spouse own real estate?* File a restraining order or lis pendens to prevent transfer of the property.

> **E-Z TIP**
>
> List every asset that you and your spouse own at the first sign of marital trouble. Record the serial numbers or other means of identification. Include assets owned both individually and jointly. Your attorney will want to see how each asset is titled to determine the best way to secure it pending the divorce.

5)   *Business interests must also be protected.* A restraining order can prevent your spouse from transferring ownership in the business. And a restraining order against the business can prevent any extraordinary actions by your spouse which may diminish the value of the business.

6)   *Close all checking and savings accounts* that your spouse can access, and escrow these funds.

Timing and fast-action are key to asset protection when a divorce looms. A spouse who acts quickly leaves fewer assets to protect. Spouses do play hide and seek with property. They may transfer assets to offshore privacy havens or other states. They may camouflage ownership to assets or sell business interests to friends or partners. Fraudulent asset transfers, particularly involving business interests, are notoriously common in a divorce. While the defrauded spouse can try to prove a fraudulent transfer, the effort is usually both futile and expensive. A spouse may also delay receiving a large income, inheritance or other assets until the divorce becomes final. An accommodating employer, for instance, may defer a salary increase, bonus or large commission until after the divorce. Substantial income and assets can be secreted or diverted to others.

> Divorce courts favor the innocent spouse when the other attempts to secrete assets fail.

In a divorce, there are endless ways to hide assets or income. Remain honest. For example, if you transfer assets to an offshore trust, the court can award your spouse more marital assets available for distribution. It hardly matters that the court cannot attach certain assets when they can divide others.

How sham divorces protect assets

A staged or sham divorce can protect assets. Creditors cannot normally reach assets transferred to a spouse in a divorce as your spouse gave good and fair value for the assets: A final agreement concerning the division of assets as well as the divorce itself. Divorce is a genuine reason for transferring assets to your spouse. To make it most defensible, retain exempt assets and those assets with intrinsic value, such as professional licensure or stock in a professional practice. These assets have little or no value to creditors.

note A spouse hounded by creditors may divorce and generously give his spouse the more valuable and vulnerable marital assets as a divorce settlement.

People encountering serious financial problems often suffer marital problems as well. While most couples will not agree to a sham divorce only to keep assets safe from creditors, many others do. They may live together and subsequently remarry once the creditor disappears. Sham divorce strategists agree on three more pointers:

1) *Divorce as soon as possible.* Don't wait until the creditors are at your door. And don't file for bankruptcy too soon after your divorce. Wait at least one year.

2) *Look legitimate.* Employ separate attorneys. Keep your divorce civilized but not overly friendly. Courts can detect the obviously collusive divorce. Show hard bargaining and a few scars that finally produced the divorce settlement.

3) *Reside separately.* You and your ex-spouse can be friendly and even visit. But courts nor creditors expect a recently divorced couple to subsequently live together.

A sham divorce is a fraud on the courts. While a sham divorce can appear economically sensible when sufficient assets are at risk, do also consider the emotional turmoil. Even a temporary divorce weakens the sanctity of the marriage and will devastate the children and other family members who may not fully understand the true reasons for the event.

Protecting retirement funds in divorce

Divorce can jeopardize retirement funds. Social Security, IRAs, Keoghs, 401K plans, tax sheltered annuities, employee stock options and *self-employed person's individual retirement accounts (SEP-IRAs)* are all subject to division in divorce:

◆ Social Security benefits are never considered marital property nor divided in divorce. And the state courts cannot change these federal requirements. Married ten years or more? You are entitled to all Social Security and survivor benefits accrued while you were married, even if you later divorce. If you are approaching your tenth wedding anniversary, then

> *note* Military disability benefits are not considered marital property and are not divisible. Couples must be married at least ten years to share military retirement benefits accrued during the marriage.

delay the divorce until after your anniversary date or you will needlessly lose substantial social security benefits.

◆ Stock option or profit-sharing plans are normally considered marital property and subject to division regardless of which spouse accrued these benefits. The plan administrator can determine their present value.

◆ Military and federal pensions and benefits are usually divided in divorce.

As a general rule, all property owned by the spouses, whether singly or jointly, can be divided in divorce. However, even when the benefits or assets cannot be awarded to the other spouse, a divorce court can consider these benefits or assets for purposes of equitably dividing other property. The value of such assets may be established by formula under state law.

Assets that become big liabilities

Academic diplomas and professional licenses are considered marital assets by divorce courts, particularly when one spouse helped the other through school. Most valuable are licenses to practice high income professions. Medicine, dentistry, law and the Ph.D. degrees are all valuable.

Professional licensure and its earning power should be listed as a separate asset in a pre-marriage agreement.

Divorce courts routinely consider professional status a marital asset worth $1 million or more. To balance outcomes, the court gives the professional spouse this status, while he or she walks away from the divorce court with few other assets.

Agree to its value. Courts won't disturb such agreements if the asset's worth has been fairly considered by both parties.

Protect your credit in divorce

Good credit is the one asset you must diligently protect during a divorce. Possibly, you couldn't financially cope amidst the turmoil and expense of a divorce. Three timely steps can help protect you from unwittingly losing your good credit:

1) Immediately notify your creditors that you will no longer be responsible for debts incurred by your spouse. Use certified mail to prove proper notification.

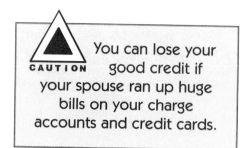

You can lose your good credit if your spouse ran up huge bills on your charge accounts and credit cards.

2) Destroy and revoke all credit cards for which you have liability. Never assume you have no liability for your spouse's credit card debts. You may have guaranteed the credit without realizing it. Verify this with the credit card company.

3) Publicly disclaim liability for your spouse's future debts. Many states consider a public notice to be sufficient notice to third parties that you reject liability for debts subsequently incurred by your spouse. Check your state laws and precisely follow the required procedures.

Creditors will cooperate if you cooperate.

Accept your own credit responsibilities. If you cannot punctually meet obligations during the divorce, communicate this fact to your creditors before you default. Inform the creditors of the reasons behind your financial problems. Send small but timely installment payments to show good faith. Most importantly, request that your creditors not report any defaults to the credit bureau. Finally, make certain that you receive every bill and statement on which you have liability. Months may pass otherwise before you know about a long overdue bill and your ruined credit.

Losing wealth to your divorce lawyer

You may fight to keep your assets from your spouse while losing them to your lawyer. Like every legal battle, divorce can be unbelievably costly. Limit these costs before you do battle or you lose the war even if you do win in divorce court. To reduce costly legal fees:

1) *Avoid the big name lawyers:* Every community has at least one lawyer reputed to be the best hired gun in town. Few attorneys with this reputation are worth their steep fees. Junior associates still handle much of your case, while you pay those fancy fees. Hire an attorney who is well-experienced with divorces and someone who respects your desire for an economical, fast and relatively painless divorce.

2)   *Shorten the battle:* You save a fortune in legal fees when you complete the divorce quickly! These tactics only generate horrendous legal bills without providing a corresponding benefit. Tell your lawyer in advance that you expect fast resolution without legal fanfare or unnecessary legal cost.

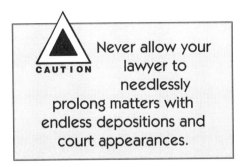

Never allow your lawyer to needlessly prolong matters with endless depositions and court appearances.

3)   *Arbitrate or mediate:* Arbitration and mediation are both quickly gaining ground as cost-effective alternatives to divorce court. Your spouse is probably as anxious as you are to resolve the divorce and save legal fees. Arbitration or mediation can be an ideal solution; particularly when you have no children.

4)   *Settle the points you can:* Negotiate directly with your spouse. Resolve yourself whatever issues you can. You then reach agreement more quickly on unresolved issues.

Confront your lawyer should you feel overcharged. If you remain unsatisfied, refuse to pay or have the fee arbitrated through the fee arbitration committee of the state bar. Most lawyers will adjust their bill when challenged.

5)   *Watch your lawyer's clock:* You can largely control the legal costs by controlling your demands on your attorney. Phone your lawyer ten times daily and you will be billed for ten phone calls. Fifty-dollar to $100 phone calls are expensive conversations.

6)   *Change lawyers:* Seemingly "unreasonable" legal fees can be reasonable if such fees provide for a fast, equitable divorce. But, beware of lawyers who pad bills or churn needless work and billable hours. Unfortunately, few non-lawyers can determine what is a reasonable fee. Have an impartial lawyer review both the legal services performed and the fee. Obtain the opinion from someone who may candidly evaluate the bill without a stake in what you do with that advice.

File your own divorce—save a fortune

You can quickly and easily file your own divorce if your divorce is uncontested and you are without minor children. A divorce is not a difficult process. You and your spouse can prepare the few necessary documents:

- Petition or complaint

- Answer and affidavit in response to petition

- Proposed final judgment or decree

- Certificate of divorce or dissolution of marriage

- Marital settlement agreement

- Financial statements for each spouse

Some states will require incidental forms, and you will probably need child support/visitation orders if you have minor children.

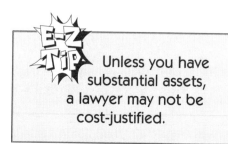 Unless you have substantial assets, a lawyer may not be cost-justified.

Why process your own divorce? The obvious reason is that lawyers are expensive and may charge several thousand dollars for even a routine divorce. Another important reason to handle your own divorce is because lawyers frequently incite conflict and adversity. This is counterproductive when your objective is to complete the divorce quickly, equitably, pleasantly and inexpensively. And when you and your spouse handle your divorce collaboratively, you become more cooperative and can develop a friendly future relationship. This is critical when you have children.

Can you handle your own divorce?

 1)   Buy one or two do-it-yourself divorce books or kits at your local bookstore. E-Z Legal Forms' *Divorce Made E-Z* is an excellent resource for filing your own uncontested divorce.

2)   Paralegal or document preparation centers are now popular, and they can be found in most communities if you walk through the yellow pages or check legal services in your local newspaper. These paralegal services prepare divorce papers for under $150. While paralegal services can prepare the necessary legal documents, they cannot offer legal advice.

3)   If you do hire a lawyer, then select one who will reduce to agreement what you and your spouse had agreed upon. Look for a non-adversarial divorce. Lawyers who advertise frequently depend upon case volume and may readily provide you with an inexpensive and fast divorce as opposed to a fight, the trademark of more prominent divorce lawyers.

Protecting assets after you divorce

Asset protection cannot end with the divorce. Ten additional protective steps are needed after you divorce:

1) **Obtain from the divorce court certified copies** of your final divorce decree. This will be needed to transfer property, divide bank accounts, etc.

2) **Exchange with your ex-spouse all personal and household property** as soon as possible after the divorce. Jewelry, tools, furnishing and other personal property due you under the divorce agreement may otherwise disappear.

3) **Close all joint checking and savings accounts**, but first verify their balances. Obtain certified checks so you know you have a good check.

4) **Close all joint credit accounts.** Estimate and pro-rate utility and other bills pending a final statement. Destroy or surrender joint charge cards and notify the credit company that you will no longer be responsible for your ex-spouse's debts. Finally, establish new accounts for yourself.

5) **Notify the lenders on loans on which you and your spouse are jointly liable.** Request a release from these obligations if your spouse will agree to pay the loans as part of the divorce settlement. If you must remain on the loan, and your spouse indemnified you for any liability arising from the loan, then ask the lender to immediately notify you if your spouse defaults. You then institute timely legal action against your spouse and pay the lender before the lender seizes your assets or destroys your credit.

> *note*
> Releases are generally not granted unless the lender is sufficiently comfortable with the collateral or your spouse's creditworthiness.

6) When you and your spouse agree to **transfer titles** to cars, boats, airplanes or recreational vehicles, change all registrations, license plates and insurance and titles as soon as possible after the divorce.

7) **Review all life insurance policies.** Change the beneficiaries with your insurance company or agent. Similarly review all accident and health, disability and homeowners insurance.

8) **If real estate is to change ownership, have your attorney convey the property.** If the real estate is mortgaged, then first notify the mortgage holder. When property is to be transferred between spouses, then lender consent is normally not required.

9) **Will you and your spouse file a joint tax return for the current year or will you file separately?** If you do file jointly, then decide beforehand who will pay the taxes or receive refunds. Caution: To file jointly, you must be married on the last day of the tax year. Because of liability reasons, you may want to file separately.

10) **Change your last will and testament.** Some states automatically revoke wills upon a divorce. Others do so only upon remarriage. In certain states, neither divorce nor remarriage will cancel a prior will. However, it's safest to prepare a new will and it is not difficult. Try E-Z Legal's *Last Wills Made E-Z.*

Asset seizures in child support cases

There are eight ways a spouse or the state can compel child support payments from a recalcitrant father. Child support remedies have increased in recent years as more state governments attempt to shift the support burden from taxpayers to the responsible parent under a court ordered child support decree. Their arsenal includes:

1) *Levy of income tax refunds:* If you owe more than $150 in child support and your spouse collects welfare, she can have the state prosecutor charged with enforcing child support payments and they can notify the IRS to intercept your tax refunds. You will receive notice of the intercept. Objections succeed only if you can establish that you don't owe the support. Other non-payment excuses are futile.

 If you are now re-married and filed a joint return anticipating a refund, then your ex-spouse can intercept only your share of the refund. Your new spouse must notify the IRS so the entire refund is not improperly applied.

2) *Posting bond to insure payment:* Some states require parents under a support order default to guarantee future child support payments by posting a bond. This may require pledging stocks or bonds, or escrowing deeds to real estate.

> *note* You will have the opportunity to explain why your payments are in default.

California, Michigan, Mississippi, New York, Oklahoma, Rhode Island, Tennessee, Vermont and Wyoming provide for such bonds by statute. Bonds are discretionary with all other courts.

3) *Property liens:* Liens can be placed on real or personal property of ex-spouses behind on child support payments. The custodial parent can then foreclose on the lien to collect. Most states require a support judgment before filing the lien.

4) *Contempt proceedings:* Violating child support orders constitutes contempt of court. Your ex-spouse can then petition the court for a contempt hearing. Without a reasonable explanation for non-payment, the court can hold you in contempt and jail or fine you. The court's objective is to throw its authority behind child support so the errant parent pays rather than incur criminal sanctions.

5) *Wage garnishment:* Child support judgments are enforced like other judgments. Most popular is the wage garnishment which is authorized after a judgment is issued. The sheriff will serve this upon your employer who must then directly remit part of your net wages to satisfy the judgment. Most states allow a creditor to attach only some of your net wages. With child support garnishments, the court can garnish any amount. Seizure of your car, boat, savings and checking accounts, or even your home or business interests remain a possibility.

> **note** Aside from the wage garnishment, your spouse may attach and sell other property as can other judgment creditors.

6) *Reporting you to the credit bureau:* In addition to seizing your assets to enforce child support, there are three lesser-known remedies. First, your ex-spouse can ruin your credit if you fall behind on your support payments. If you owe $1,000 or more for child support, the support enforcement agencies must report this to the credit bureaus under the Child Support Enforcement Amendments of 1984. But the credit bureaus can reveal child support defaults, even when you owe less than $1,000.

7) *Most-wanted lists:* More embarrassing still is the practice of certain states to publish in newspapers the names of parents who defaulted on child support payments. Delaware, Florida, Virginia, Maryland and Pennsylvania routinely follow this process. Others are considering this as child support defaults climb. The controversial strategy does encourage many more fathers to pay child support when all other efforts fail.

8)   *Criminal prosecution:* Your spouse may also seek criminal prosecution. Or the state can independently commence a criminal proceeding if you default on child support.

Bankruptcy protection against child support and alimony

Child support and alimony obligations cannot usually be discharged in either Chapter 7 or Chapter 13 bankruptcy. Chapter 13, however, can protect you from collection efforts on overdue alimony or child support payments. Your spouse cannot demand faster collection but can enforce all support or alimony payments due after you file Chapter 13.

There are three situations when a Chapter 7 or Chapter 13 bankruptcy will discharge child support or alimony obligations:

1)   *Support between unmarried persons:* With only an agreement but no court order for support, the obligation is dischargeable in bankruptcy—if the parties never married.

2)   *Support assigned to a third party:* If your spouse assigns and transfers her right to receive income support to a third party, that obligation is then dischargeable in bankruptcy. One exception is when support payments are assigned to a state welfare agency.

> *note*
> Chapter 13 allows you to pay child support arrearages over three to five years as part of your repayment plan.

3)   *Support payments not under court order:* Support and alimony are dischargeable unless there is a court order. Conversely, court-ordered support and alimony obligations are never dischargeable.

Planning Pointers

◆ Asset protection planning is essential for anyone in a relationship—or expecting a relationship.

◆ Stay in tune with your spouse's finances. Unless you know what assets your spouse has, you can be too easily cheated should you divorce.

◆ Insist upon a premarital agreement if you are planning to marry, particularly if you have significant assets or children from a prior marriage.

◆ The courts will not enforce marital agreements that are fraudulent, coercive or contract away the rights of the couple's children.

◆ Couples who live together may face many of the same financial problems as married couples. They need cohabitation agreements for their protection.

◆ Protecting assets offshore is the safest method in a divorce.

◆ Keep the divorce as amicable as possible or the lawyers will wind up with most of the wealth.

Strategies to stop foreclosures and repossessions

14

Chapter 14

Strategies to stop foreclosures and repossessions

What you'll find in this chapter:

- ➡ The four most common lender concessions
- ➡ How to refinance your way out of trouble
- ➡ How to cover negative cash flow
- ➡ Why you should avoid balloon mortgages
- ➡ How to recover foreclosed property

A foreclosure or repossession of your property may result in the loss of your family home, business or some other valuable property or important asset. It may also produce a large deficiency that you will owe the secured lender, which may jeopardize even more assets.

Debtor strategies when dealing with a lender are similar whether the foreclosure involves real estate, a boat, car or an apartment complex. In each instance the lender is secured by certain assets as collateral. When you default on your obligations, the lender can sell the collateral and apply the sale proceeds to the loan. Any surplus is yours. A deficiency may mean that you will continue to owe the lender until the underlying debt is fully paid.

A secured lender with adequate collateral is obviously in a much stronger position than is an unsecured creditor who must first obtain a judgment before seizing assets. If a debtor files bankruptcy, the unsecured creditor can only hope for dividends. The secured creditor, on the other hand, retains all rights to the pledged collateral even when the debtor files bankruptcy.

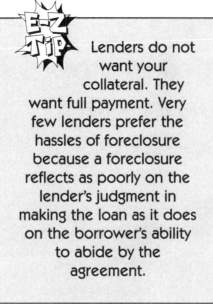

Lenders do not want your collateral. They want full payment. Very few lenders prefer the hassles of foreclosure because a foreclosure reflects as poorly on the lender's judgment in making the loan as it does on the borrower's ability to abide by the agreement.

While secured lenders enjoy a very powerful bargaining position, you may negotiate an asset-saving deal with your lender when you cannot punctually pay your loan. But, no lender can forever remain idle when a loan falls further and further into default. Both the lender and borrower in a loan workout must understand their opponent's position, compromise and cooperate until their mutual problem is resolved. Final resolution may be through new terms, new financing or the debtor's voluntary surrender of the collateral to the lender.

Loan workouts are often creative. There are many ways to convince a lender that you are proceeding in good faith and trying to protect the lender as much as saving the collateral. However, a borrower must protect himself from his secured lender. Many lenders are unreasonable or violate the lending laws, so you must know when to cooperate and when to fight. You must know how to do both quite well if you expect the outcome you need and want.

The less experienced you are with problem loans, the more you will fear your problem. Playing ostrich is too common, and it is also a costly mistake. Lenders cooperate more with borrowers who anticipate their difficulties, negotiate fair interim arrangements and search for long-term solutions which are advantageous to both seller or buyer.

Scan newspapers. They constantly feature many homes, investment properties, businesses, equipment, cars, boats and nearly every other asset that can fall beneath the auctioneer's hammer. The reasons for this are as varied as the causes of financial trouble. A poor economy, rising interest rates, business failure and personal problems head a long list.

Lenders are less forgiving of borrowers who hide from their problems.

Most common is borrowing too much. Loans either exceed the value of the collateral or are so poorly structured that the borrower cannot pay. The borrower must then adjust the loan terms to accept payments the borrower can afford. Most default situations require a significant loan restructuring, which reduces the debt, extends payments or otherwise modifies payments to parallel the debtor's cash flow, assets and financial abilities.

Negotiate loan terms you can afford

The fair market value of the pledged collateral always determines the maximum amount of your loan. Secured lenders negotiate debt restructuring agreements chiefly based upon the collateral's liquidation value plus any recovery available from the loan's guarantors. Try these four tips to negotiate your new deal:

1) *Anticipate disagreement on your collateral's liquidation value.* The type and condition of the collateral, auction efforts and seasonal demand for the collateral are only three factors that influence what lenders recoup through a forced sale. Timing and even whether interested buyers appear before the collateral is sold are others. There usually is substantial difference between what you and your lender estimate the collateral to be worth at a forced sale.

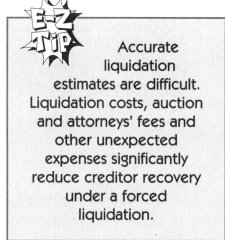
Accurate liquidation estimates are difficult. Liquidation costs, auction and attorneys' fees and other unexpected expenses significantly reduce creditor recovery under a forced liquidation.

2) *Recognize that lenders will pursue every option to maximize recovery.* For example, lenders frequently seek buyers willing to pay above the auction price for the secured assets. The one danger of a delayed settlement is that the lender then gains valuable time to find a buyer willing to pay the price that weakens your own negotiating position. Conversely, when your primary objective is to fully pay the loan, you share the lender's objective and may sell the collateral for the highest possible price.

Always consider your lender's alternatives before you negotiate.

3) *Beware that lenders resist re-negotiating loans for many reasons.* For instance, a lender secured by the SBA or some other wealthy guarantor can take that hard stand because the lender relies as much on the guarantor as their collateral to secure their loan.

4) *Understand that low interest loans are often the easiest workouts.* A lender may more willingly accept a $30,000 settlement on a $50,000 loan when the interest rate is significantly below the current market rate. Lenders prefer a new loan at a higher rate than a loan tied up in bankruptcy court.

Negotiate your cents-on-the-dollar settlement when poverty is on your side.

Lenders strongly resist reducing their loan balance. They prefer to extend the payments to eventually secure full payment. The more optimistic lender realizes that a troubled business or distressed real estate project may eventually turnaround and fully pay the loan. The lender may believe your settlement offer is preferable to the forced liquidation that will produce less.

Become bullet-proof before you battle your lender

Never battle your lender when you have other assets unprotected. Your lender may pursue these assets to secure a shaky loan and fully collect. If you are not judgment proof, begin by protecting money on deposit with your lender. Banks can, without notice, apply the funds in your checking or savings accounts to their loan. Deposits from any loan guarantors are also vulnerable.

note

Protect all assets from your lender before you borrow. This protects you against a fraudulent transfer claim.

A lender who questions whether his collateral will cover his loan probably believes it will not. Why jeopardize more assets which only improves your lender's bargaining position and weakens yours?

Once a loan becomes shaky the lender inevitably requests additional collateral. Refuse!

Withholding additional collateral will not trigger a faster foreclosure. Only the well-secured lender confidently forecloses because he has ample security to cover his loan. The undercollateralized lender hesitates to foreclose. Time alone gives him the opportunity to recover more.

You can gracefully refuse a lender's demand for more collateral. For instance, other properties may be titled with your spouse. While you would grant the lender's request, you may be experiencing marital problems and your spouse will refuse to encumber other assets. This is one face-saving way to politely refuse a lender and still appear cooperative.

Poverty is power. When a lender has too few assets to fully recover a loan, it builds your own negotiating power.

Four common lender concessions

There are four points you and your lender can quickly negotiate when you cannot punctually or fully pay your loan:

1) **Extend the loan:** This concession is most acceptable to the lender because your loan remains classified for full payment. Lenders frequently extend loan payments well beyond their original term to recoup what they are owed.

2) **Defer principal payments:** This is another common solution to reduce stranglehold payments because monthly payments are mostly allocated to the principal rather than interest. This concession will provide less relief on the newer loans where payments are mostly interest.

> *note* Loan workout terms frequently change. Both you and your lender must be flexible and constantly reassess the situation to insure that fair and orderly workout.

3) **Reduce interest:** A more severe situation may force the lender to reduce the interest. Alternatively, the loan balance may be restructured to what can be fully but immediately repaid.

4) **Freeze loan payments:** This is the most difficult proposition to sell a lender, but lenders whose borrowers suffer acute cash shortages may temporarily suspend all payments. Lenders more willingly suspend payments when they are adequately secured and the freeze is only temporary.

The option-to-equity solution

This is another possible solution when you need more money each month to pay your loan. For instance, your rental property rents for $800 and your mortgage costs $1,000 monthly. You must either cover the $200 deficiency or lose your property.

Perhaps $800 a month is the highest possible rent for your property — unless your tenant considers it more than a mere rental. An option-to-equity is then your answer. Your tenant may pay $1,000 monthly if in a year or two your tenant owns an interest in the property paid by the extra $200 a month. You can structure this arrangement many ways and eventually offer the tenant complete ownership of the property.

Options-to-equity work particularly well when you have a small cash flow shortage and you can find a tenant interested in acquiring all or part of the leased property. Try present tenants first. They may not be ready to buy today but may be interested in future ownership.

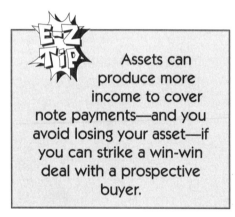

Assets can produce more income to cover note payments—and you avoid losing your asset—if you can strike a win-win deal with a prospective buyer.

This strategy is not limited to real estate. It works equally well with other assets. Would someone pay something each month to occasionally use your boat if they could later purchase your boat by applying part of the rental payments to the sale price? Do you have plant equipment, such as a printing press, with downtime someone else could utilize? Think creatively.

Refinance your way out of trouble

Refinancing your property is a popular way to save property from foreclosure, particularly if you have sufficient equity in your property to support additional borrowing. Proceeds from a new second mortgage can pay the arrears on your first mortgage. Or, refinancing with a larger first mortgage may produce sufficient surplus to cover future payments on your new loan until cash flow becomes stabilized.

Why replace a 9 percent mortgage with a new 12 percent mortgage? Refinancing with a lower interest mortgage can considerably ease cash flow.

A new second mortgage may also bail you out. Default on a first mortgage, and you are in serious trouble. So are your subordinate or

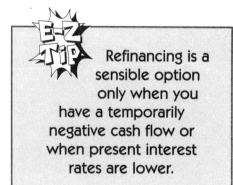

Refinancing is a sensible option only when you have a temporarily negative cash flow or when present interest rates are lower.

secondary lenders. Under foreclosure, they must pay the first mortgage or lose their own mortgage. Subordinate mortgage holders can assist you and themselves by helping to subsidize your first mortgage.

The interim second mortgage is a particularly good financial solution when the negative cash flow is temporary and the second mortgage holder foresees no further need to cover the first mortgage. Offer the second mortgage holder a bonus: Some equity? Higher interest? Faster repayment on his mortgage? Negotiate!

Always consider involving others potentially hurt through foreclosure. It may be a key business tenant whose lease would then be in jeopardy. When your own business is under foreclosure, your primary suppliers may help rather than lose your business and whatever you owe them. A landlord may help pay a tenant's lender rather than lose that good tenant. When you have a problem loan, others inevitably share your problem. Make them part of the solution.

Attract cash-rich partners

If you have a real estate project or business deal in deep financial trouble, your headache venture may be just the right medicine for wealthy investors seeking tax breaks and long-term capital appreciation.

To find investors to save your property from foreclosure:

1)   *Advertise.* Physicians, attorneys, executives and successful business owners are your top candidates.

2)   *Form a limited partnership.* A limited partnership, or limited liability company, limits the investing partners' liability to the loss of their investment while they fully participate in profits and the tax write-offs.

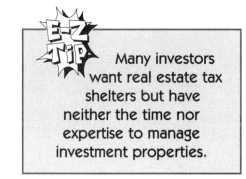

Many investors want real estate tax shelters but have neither the time nor expertise to manage investment properties.

3)   *Give your investors 100 percent of the tax benefits.* When investors can deduct the entire loss on their tax return, they have a hefty tax savings to justify a generous investment.

4)   *Your investors must cover any negative cash flow.* But split profits 50/50 when you sell, even if you own a paltry percentage of the partnership.

As the general partner you would manage the properties for a fee. This puts more money in your pocket.

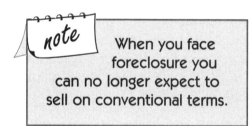

This type of deal attracts many passive real estate investors—even to properties operating in the red. Your accountant can show the benefits that investors may reap, and the benefits you must sell. Unfortunately, real estate limited partnerships are not nearly as attractive an investment after the 1986 Tax Reform Act, but a creatively structured deal can still dazzle investors because there are far fewer deals now available for interested investors.

Sell for "no cash down"

Another cure for the poor cash flow property is a buyer who can afford to cover the negative cash flow. But who would buy such a deal? Someone who can buy your property on "no cash down" terms and cover the loan for a potentially far bigger long-term gain.

> **note**
> When you face foreclosure you can no longer expect to sell on conventional terms.

For instance, the buyer who foresees a $300,000 negative cash flow before revitalizing the property and breaking even will enthusiastically tackle the project if his down payment covers these future losses and he sees a big gain.

Forget the high price and down payment. Your objective is simply to sell your property before you lose it. Sacrifice price, down payment, or both, but sell it. Find yourself a reliable buyer and secure yourself as best you can with a mortgage on the property. You will sell fastest offering a small or no down payment. This is more important than price to most buyers.

Reverse your priorities. A speedy sale is more important when racing foreclosure than is a higher price or down payment because your one priority is to sell quickly. A high price or large down payment only discourages buyers. The greedy seller is the one who usually ends up in foreclosure owing the lenders even more.

Avoid dangerous balloon mortgage

Mortgage defaults are most common with the dangerous balloon mortgage. These require the borrower to pay the entire principal on a fixed date. Sellers grant balloon mortgages to buyers who can initially afford only the interest payments and assume that the buyer can refinance the balloon mortgage before its due date.

> **note** Balloon mortgages are sensible when the parties anticipate increased property values, allowing the buyer to refinance and fully pay the balloon mortgage.

Unfortunately, not all properties increase in value. These buyers, unable to refinance and pay their balloon mortgage, then have two options: Offer the lender additional interest or other concessions for extending the loan—when there is sufficient income to pay more interest—or find an equity investor who can replace the mortgage.

The poison pill strategy

How can you discourage foreclosure when a new deal cannot be arranged? Lenders avoid foreclosure on properties with hazardous waste problems because the lender shares liability for the hefty cleanup costs plus other damages. The lender will find it exceptionally difficult to resell the property because no buyer wants the mammoth cleanup costs unless the buyer can steal the property. The lender's losses from abandoning the property and the mortgage may be substantially less than what the lender is liable for under toxic waste laws.

> **E-Z TIP** If your property has hazardous waste problems, try to quickly eliminate the problem but also remember the poison pill strategy and use the problem to your advantage.

Wave the lender liability club

Lender liability lawsuits are more difficult for borrowers to win, but still remain a major weapon in the beleaguered borrower's arsenal against lenders. Courts sanction lenders for possible violations when dealing with borrowers. Lenders detest lender liability claims because borrowers may be awarded considerable damages and cancel their loans due overbearing lenders. The seven most common violations are:

1) Fraudulent lender conduct or misrepresentations when soliciting or administering a loan.

2) Changing loan terms without borrower consent.

3) Unreasonable control over a borrower's collateral, or the lender asserting excessive management authority over his business.

4) Failure to make agreed loan advances.

5) Derogatory comments against the borrower.

Carefully review your lender's conduct.

6) Defaulting loans without good cause.

7) Negligent disposal of collateral.

Underscore questionable lender practices. A good lender liability lawyer can review the merits of your claim. A strong case may put your lender on the defensive and is powerful leverage when negotiating with your lender.

Discover loan defects

Another self-defense tactic is not to assume that your lender has an enforceable mortgage. It may significantly delay foreclosure until the defect is corrected. Whether a mortgage is defective usually requires a thorough review by a good attorney who should check for nine common loan defects:

note Legal defects in a mortgage may render the mortgage entirely worthless (but not necessarily the obligation).

1) incorrect name of the borrower

2) missing mortgagor signature

3) incorrect property description

4) incorrect filing in the public records

5) failure to file in the public records

Faulty security interests (mortgages on personal property) are more common than are defective real estate mortgages.

Security interest problems include:

6) lapsed security interests from not timely re-filing

7) incorrect debtor's name

8) collateral incorrectly described or deleted

9) financing statements incorrectly filed

Some defects render the mortgage or security interest void against third parties, but not the debtor. A bankruptcy Chapter 11, assignment for the benefit of creditors, or similar insolvency proceeding is considered a transfer to a third party and will void the defective security interest. This mortgage holder will also lose his security to subsequent lien holders.

Uncovering a serious mortgage defect will give you enormous bargaining power over your lender if your cooperation is necessary to correct the problem. But cooperate only if you achieve your own objectives in the bargain.

When to encourage foreclosure

Foreclosure on your real estate, personal property or business assets may be a smart way to transfer your property to a new entity while raising fewer questions from creditors whose debts are eliminated by the foreclosure.

With your lender as your ally, you both win. Your lender may cooperate only to keep your property and his mortgage out of bankruptcy court. This approach works when a secured lender holds a high-balance mortgage on real estate, a car, boat, airplane, business or some other asset.

> **E-Z TIP**
> A lender cooperates faster if you offer attractive incentives such as higher interest or partial ownership.

How to spot a sham foreclosure

Always attend a foreclosure auction on your assets. You must check that the auction sale was conducted in a commercially reasonable manner to yield the highest possible price. Close observation is vital when you are responsible for any deficiency on the loan and therefore want the property sold for the best possible price or at least a price to cover the mortgage. Lenders frequently conduct bad auctions to suppress the price. They win back the property at a bargain price, and you end up with a huge deficiency on the note. Do not be victimized by:

1) **Rush bidding**—or allowing too-little time for counterbids.

2) **Discouraging bidders**—through negative remarks about the property.

3) **Unrealistic terms**—such as an unreasonably high deposit or closing date.

4) **Insufficient notice**—auction ads that inadequately announce the sale or that appear too soon before the auction.

 Protect yourself from these and other auctioneering gambits. Hire another auctioneer to attend and record the entire auction proceedings. Let the lender know he cannot steal your property. For your efforts you may avoid a big deficiency and even pocket a surplus from the sale.

Strategies to recover your property after foreclosure

Property is not necessarily lost even when your lender has completed the foreclosure. Why would a lender sell you back foreclosed property after your lender incurred the expense and trouble to foreclose? Here are three compelling reasons:

> **note** You may possibly convince the lender to sell you back your home, auto, boat or other foreclosed asset.

1) The lender may have anticipated selling the property for much more. If that sales price fell too far short, the lender may sell the property back to you for the note balance, or less.

2) The lender may now see you as a better credit risk, particularly if the foreclosure eliminated other liens against the property, you filed bankruptcy or otherwise cleared your other debts.

3) The lender may want to quickly dispose of the property to avoid further costs or liability from holding the property.

To recover your property, you must convince the lender that you will not default again. If it is your home, your lender can rent the house to you for the mortgage payments until you prove your future ability to pay. Timely payments will give the lender sufficient confidence to deed you back your home or other property you once considered irretrievably lost.

Two ways to avoid a deficiency

DEFINITION

Foreclosed or repossessed property can cost you more than losing your property. In most states, you also remain liable for any *deficiency,* which is the difference between what you owe your lender, including attorneys' fees and costs, and the lender's recovery from selling the collateral.

Your lender will typically sue for a deficiency judgment; however, this is generally easily and quickly obtained. The lender may then enforce this judgment. To avoid a deficiency judgment:

1) Offer the lender the collateral without foreclosure. Waive foreclosure and all rights of redemption. Be cooperative. A lender who can avoid hassles and legal costs may accept the property rather than chase deficiencies, particularly if the lender considers you judgment-proof.

2) Find a buyer for the collateral. You will get a higher price and escape deficiency or incur a smaller deficiency if you sell the property without foreclosure.

E-Z TIP Watch your timing. Negotiate when your lender remains vulnerable to your interference or possible opposition to a foreclosure. Cooperation is a bargaining chip before, and not after, the foreclosure. By then, your leverage is lost.

Avoiding a deficiency judgment is only one goal. Maintaining good credit is another. Besides negotiating a release from any deficiency, your lender also must agree not to damage your credit. Always obtain lender concessions in writing.

How to recover a repossessed car

Most states allow a borrower some opportunity to redeem an auto (or boat or plane) after repossession. However, this redemption right is not absolute.

You cannot reinstate the contract and reclaim your vehicle if you:

- once had the installment contract reinstated

- concealed the property to avoid repossession

- damaged or neglected the property

- physically interfered with repossession

- misrepresented your creditworthiness

Your lender must give you notice of your right to reinstate or you can reclaim the property without making overdue payments. But you must punctually pay all future installments. If you choose to reinstate, then quickly notify your lender. If you fail to reinstate the contract or loan with the time stated in the installment agreement, usually 60 to 90 days, the lender can hold you responsible for the loan balance but must nevertheless notify you of his intent to sell the repossessed property. You can then reclaim the property by full payment on the loan.

note You can usually reinstate your loan and reclaim your car by paying all overdue installments, plus late fees and reasonable legal repossession costs.

What about your right to reclaim personal items left behind in a repossessed car, boat or plane? If your vehicle is repossessed with your personal objects, you can demand the return of these personal items if you notify the lender within the time stated in your contract, or a reasonable time if no specific time period is stated.

When bankruptcy stops foreclosure

Bankruptcy immediately stops foreclosure. Once bankruptcy is filed, the lender must immediately halt all foreclosure or repossessions. But bankruptcy may not be your solution if you are now in good financial shape, aside from this one problem loan. A bankruptcy to stop or delay foreclosure only makes sense when:

- The property has substantial equity, and you need time to turnaround or sell the property and recover your equity.

- Bankruptcy is necessary to cram down or reduce the mortgages to the property's fair market value. This frequently solves the overfinanced property problem, especially when new financing is available to replace the present loan.

Secured lenders can combat the bankruptcy filed to avoid foreclosure. A bankruptcy (Chapter 7, 11, or 13) temporarily stops foreclosure or repossession but will not necessarily prevent it. The lender may obtain court permission to foreclose if the lender is not adequately protected. A court imposed delay cannot hurt the lender. The lender would be hurt if the loan balance increases in bankruptcy (you did not make interest payments or the collateral is decreasing in value; examples—real estate prices decreased, property became neglected or receivables diminished.)

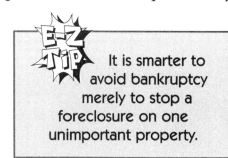

It is smarter to avoid bankruptcy merely to stop a foreclosure on one unimportant property.

Planning Pointers

◆ Never assume you cannot cooperatively work out a problem loan with your lender. There are many ways a lender and borrower can restructure a loan to their mutual advantage.

◆ Make certain other assets are not exposed if you run into trouble with a loan. You may owe your lender money even after the collateral is sold.

◆ It's usually wiser to sell the property for a low, low price or on lenient terms rather than lose it through foreclosure.

◆ Watch out for lender liability. It can give you considerable leverage when negotiating with lenders.

◆ It may be wise to voluntarily surrender property to the lender rather than have it foreclosed upon and produce a large deficiency.

◆ Carefully check your loan documents. You may have ironclad defenses to a foreclosure.

◆ Bankruptcy can stop a foreclosure, but it's not always your best solution.

Creditor and disaster-proof your business

15

Chapter 15

Creditor and disaster proof your business

What you'll find in this chapter:

➠ Why corporate protection is essential

➠ Use professional organizations for protection

➠ Assets a business should never own

➠ Making your banker your ally

➠ The advantages of non-bankruptcy workouts

Asset protection is not only necessary for individuals. Businesses are even more vulnerable to creditor problems and need their own brand of financial protection.

Unfortunately, too few business owners go through the advance drill necessary to successfully block creditors and the many other inevitable financial threats that can sink a business. This is because business start-ups are the products of entrepreneurs and entrepreneurs are typically fueled by over-optimism. Success-oriented, they ignore even the possibility of failure and overlook even the most obvious precautions essential to protect themselves and their businesses should their rosy predictions fade. Realistic business people don't see through rose-colored glasses. They reduce their risk, and defensively plan to safeguard their enterprise. They prepare both themselves and their business for battle long before inevitable battles with creditors and other litigants erupt. These are the businesses best positioned to survive.

> **note**
>
> Some entrepreneurs journey into business happily envisioning only the upside of their venture. Seldom do they see the downside.

You can transform your own business into a creditor-proof enterprise, and through a good defensive plan:

- you and not your creditors always remain in full control

- you more effectively negotiate with creditors the business-saving deals you may need

- you reduce your personal risk if your business should fail

 Creditor-proofing a business is not complicated. It requires only common sense and a desire to have a creditor-proof business following several strategies.

Corporate protection is essential

No business can become a fortress unless it operates with the correct business organization. Why venture into business without corporate protection? Why gamble personal wealth on the success of your enterprise? Since most small companies will eventually fail, this is an extremely poor gamble.

Nevertheless, over three million American businesses remain unincorporated. Small business owners, frequently unsophisticated in business and legal matters, seldom appreciate the importance of a corporation for personal protection. Attorneys also overlook the hazards of business and fail to incorporate their clients' ventures. Accountants who typically are more concerned with

 The corporation and limited liability company are preferred entities because they protect personal assets from the debts of the business.

 additional corporate paperwork than liability protection may also discourage incorporating.

But, incorporating your business is your best insurance because only a corporation (or similar business organization) limits your potential losses to your investment in your business. Operate as a sole proprietorship or partnership and you and your business are legally one and the same entity. Should your business fail, your business's creditors can claim your personal assets. Protect your personal assets from any entrepreneurial misadventure with a corporation or limited liability company.

Business entities that protect you

Corporations are historically the preferred business entity for limiting liability but now compete with several newer entities.

• *S Corporations:* The S Corporation is a corporation that elects to be taxed as a partnership or proprietorship. Whether or not this is preferable from a taxation viewpoint, the S Corporation features the same limited liability protection as a regular C Corporation.

• *Limited Liability Companies (LLCs):* The newer LLC usually offers limited liability benefits comparable to the corporation. Whether a corporation or LLC is preferable usually depends more upon tax-related factors than liability protection.

• *Limited Partnerships:* Protects the limited partner from debts of the enterprise. However, general partners are personally liable for partnership debts. This is a disadvantage of the limited partnership when compared to the LLC, where management avoids personal liability for LLC debts. This disadvantage can be overcome if a corporation with few assets serves as the general partner.

Defensive planning for professional practice

Several organizational options are also now available for professionals and are widely used by doctors, dentists, lawyers and accountants.

◆ The *professional corporation (PC)* or *professional association (PA)* limits liability for the professional in the same way a corporation protects the business owner. While the professional corporation protects the professional from debts incurred by the practice, the professional corporation does not protect the professional owner from claims resulting from his own malpractice. However, it will insulate the professional from other employee errors as well as all other corporate liabilities. Moreover, the professional corporation's assets cannot be directly seized by the professional's personal creditors. Nor can the professional's personal creditors easily liquidate the professional's stock ownership in the professional corporation because shares in these entities must be owned by professionals from within that profession.

◆ *Limited liability partnerships (LLP)* are similar to LLCs but are available only to professionals. The LLP is thus an excellent option when professionals want to participate in the management of the practice while insulating personal assets from the partnership liabilities.

The professionals' asset protection improves when they conduct their practice through a professional corporation or limited liability partnership. Each professional operating as a partner in a general partnership should, at the least, organize his own professional corporation. The respective professional corporations may then become partners in the partnership. While this creates a more cumbersome arrangement than a limited liability partnership, the structure provides certain tax, regulatory or organizational advantages.

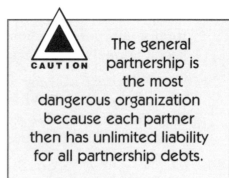

CAUTION The general partnership is the most dangerous organization because each partner then has unlimited liability for all partnership debts.

No professional today can rely solely upon insurance for protection. There are now many other opportunities for a professional to incur liability arising from their practice. The need for sound organizational protection for professionals clearly matches that of the commercial business owner.

Protect profit makers from problem makers

Dividing your "eggs" into separate baskets is your second protective strategy. If one corporation is sensible, two are more sensible if you operate two businesses. Separately incorporate each business you own. If one business should fail it will not endanger the others. Multi-corporations limit losses and defensively organize an expanding enterprise when the failure of some entities become inevitable.

note Always isolate your potential losers from present winners by compartmentalizing your ventures into separate corporations (or similar entities).

Many once-thriving companies vanished because their "eggs" were all in one proverbial corporate basket. Example: A successful restaurant quickly expands into three successful restaurants, owned by the original corporation. But its fourth restaurant fails and quickly bankrupts the three financially healthy restaurants. Even smart entrepreneurs make mistakes and become saddled with losers. You can then safely shed your losers while building on your winners.

Operating your business through one entity may offer some tax or operational benefits, but never structure your business on these factors alone. Asset protection is far more important, particularly when you are small, growing and vulnerable. Only when your business grows to the point you cannot shed your losers will tax, financing, creditor relations and operational factors parallel liability protection as a planning objective. At that point, you may then substitute parent company guarantees for your own, gain certain tax benefits and operate like a major corporation in many different ways.

Perhaps you own a troubled company that can be severed into separate companies. With your financially strong operations insulated as separate corporations, you can either liquidate or attempt the rehabilitation of your sick business without jeopardizing these healthy ventures. However, for your failing business to be viewed by creditors as a separate entity, you must quickly untangle it from your healthy operations.

> **note**
>
> You can own multi-corporations through one holding company. Each operating corporation then becomes a subsidiary.

CAUTION Properly organized separate entities may also lose their protection because they don't operate as separate entities. Affiliated companies, for instance, may share bank accounts or commingle cash, inventory or other assets. They may utilize one payroll account, combine corporate meetings and generally operate as one large entity, not the distinct entities that they should be. If one entity then goes bankrupt, its creditors can also force the affiliated entities into bankruptcy, pierce their corporate veils and claim their assets. This is the price you pay when entities do not operate independently.

While it may be more cumbersome to operate different businesses through separate legal entities, the effort is worthwhile. You will be more confident that one failed venture cannot jeopardize your overall organization.

Review your business organization. Can you isolate your more risky business activities into separate corporations? Can you restructure your present organization so one failure will not produce a domino effect for total organization failure?

Assets no business should own

Unthinking business owners title valuable assets to their operating company. But, why needlessly lose valuable assets if your business fails when these assets may be safely titled with another entity, safe from the business' creditors? Assets owned by another entity may always be leased or licensed back to your operating company for its use or used to start a fresh venture, or perhaps sold.

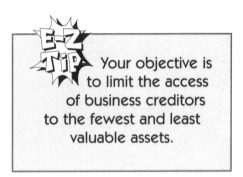

Your objective is to limit the access of business creditors to the fewest and least valuable assets.

Real estate is one asset that should be titled separately. You may, for instance, own and operate a restaurant and the valuable building your restaurant occupies. If the real estate is owned by the restaurant corporation, the restaurant's creditors may claim the building as a corporate asset if the restaurant fails.

Why needlessly expose the real estate when you can safely own the real estate through another entity, such as a limited liability company, a trust or a limited partnership? Separately titled, the real estate remains safe no matter what happens to the business. You should similarly title equipment, furniture and fixtures, trademarks, tradenames, copyrights, patents and other proprietary rights to separate, independent entities.

Whether these valuable and protected assets are used to start another business, sold or leased for your personal profit, you win either way.

 Never title valuable business assets in your individual name. You may have personally guaranteed certain business debts, and these creditors then have recourse to your assets.

Debt-shield your business with friendly mortgages

A mortgage against your business' assets is another vital strategy to help shield your business from creditors.

 A mortgage may be your best friend when you need an ally to fight creditors. Should you fully mortgage your business to a friendly lender and later run into creditor problems, your lender may then foreclose and sell you back your assets to start again.

Example: Assume your business owns assets worth $100,000; however, a friendly creditor has a $100,000 mortgage against these assets. Also, assume that your business owes $200,000 to unsecured creditors. Your friend's mortgage has priority, whether in bankruptcy or any other liquidation, and the unsecured creditors recover nothing if your business fails. They may not fully recover their debts, but nevertheless, control your enterprise because they may seize your business.

Conversely, a friendly mortgage allows you to control your business. Regardless of what unsecured creditors do to collect, a cooperative mortgagee may always foreclose and re-sell your business's assets to your newly formed corporation. No funds need change hands because your mortgagee can finance the purchase with a substituted loan. But, avoid a sham mortgage. The friendly mortgage must withstand close scrutiny. A legitimate, well-documented mortgage is as vital as is total honesty.

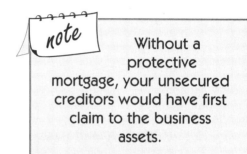

note Without a protective mortgage, your unsecured creditors would have first claim to the business assets.

How can you establish that friendly mortgage?

• Secure your investment in your own business. Don't simply invest in your business. Your investment would then be subordinate to all creditor claims. Instead, invest indirectly through a cooperative friend or relative who can make a secured loan to your business using your own money.

• An affiliated entity may perform consulting or other services to your operating company and be owed a substantial amount which may be secured.

• Have you transferred valuable personal assets to your corporation? This creates another opportunity for a friendly mortgage on your business to secure payment.

• Do you have a friendly or important supplier you want to protect should your business fail? A mortgage can secure this debt, but enlist this creditor's cooperation if you must combat less-favored creditors.

As the owner of your business, do not directly encumber the business. Bankruptcy courts routinely void self-serving owner-mortgages.

There are many variations on the theme. If your business is either unencumbered or secured to an unfriendly mortgagee, then structure that one friendly mortgage that insures you continued control in all structures.

The friendly mortgage is also a business-saver against the IRS, who generally will not seize the fully encumbered business.

Your mortgages against the business should ideally exceed the liquidation value of its assets. Tax and other creditors without equity in the assets to cover even their costs of seizure seldom try. Still, the IRS or other creditors sometimes seize the heavily encumbered business if they too-optimistically appraise its assets as worth more than its mortgages, or they may also seize if they believe the owner will pay rather than lose the business.

Three ways to safeguard your lease

A most valuable business asset may be a favorable lease. Your lease needs special protection when your location is important to your business.

The key strategy is never have the business entity hold the lease as the lessee. If your business has the lease and later fails, the bankruptcy court can transfer the lease to a buyer even without the landlord's consent and when the lease prevents assignments or sublets. When you no longer control your important location you essentially lose your business. And when your lease is valuable and in jeopardy, you also lose negotiating power against creditors who can enlist the bankruptcy court to sell your business as a going concern.

Here are the three best strategies to protect your lease:

1)   Lease through another entity who then assigns or sublets the lease and location to your operating company on a month-to-month tenancy at will. You, not your creditors, then control the location should your business fail. If you hold the lease through another entity, you can evict your failing business and sublet to a new tenant or establish a successor business at the same location under a new sublet agreement.

2)   Alternatively, you can, with the landlord's permission, pledge the lease as collateral security to a friendly mortgagee. Upon a loan default, the mortgagee may claim the lease and similarly re-let to your successor business or other nominee.

3)   When you face business troubles, you can arrange for your landlord to cancel your current lease but continue to rent to you on a monthly tenancy. The landlord, under this arrangement, can give you an option to lease the premises through another entity should your existing business fail. This

insures your continued control over the lease. Your landlord benefits from this arrangement because either you renew your tenancy or your landlord can seek a new tenant, unencumbered by your tenancy.

These businesses survive only when their owners have the foresight to control the location as their most important asset and the foundation for rebuilding.

> *note*
>
> Safeguarding a valuable location is a vital defensive strategy for restaurants, gas stations, retail businesses and the many other businesses that depend upon high traffic or are difficult to relocate.

Recruit your banker to protect your business

Maintain good banking relationships because your banker may be in the strongest position to protect your business against other creditors.

For instance, your bank can protect your business from IRS levies by applying funds from your levied account to your outstanding loans. The bank can then return the IRS levy and later replenish your account by re-loaning you the funds.

Your banker ally can best diffuse IRS and other creditor attempts to seize your business because your banker may demonstrate that there is insufficient equity beyond the bank's own mortgage for other claimants. Creditors listen to lenders long after the business owner loses all credibility.

Never bank where you borrow

A big mistake is to bank where you borrow. Of course, this is never a problem when you and your banker are on good terms, but extremely dangerous once your business becomes shaky and your bank nervous. Your bank can automatically apply funds in your account against your loans — and at the worst possible time—when you desperately need the cash! Creditors, particularly the IRS always ready to levy bank accounts, may also assume that you deposit with the bank that financed your business. A lien search quickly reveals your secured lenders.

Lenders expect you to bank with them, an arrangement that is sensible while banking relationships are good. However, once the relationship cools, transfer your funds to another bank.

Protect trade secrets

Protecting tangible business assets is only a half-way measure. You must also protect trade secrets and other proprietary information, such as operating procedures, marketing studies, business plans and customer lists.

You cannot always completely protect ideas and proprietary information, but you can significantly reduce or discourage their misappropriation with four simple steps:

1) *Identify your important trade secrets:* List the specific information you consider trade secrets. You and your employees then both know what is protected.

2) *Require all employees to sign confidentiality and non-disclosure agreements:* The courts will protect proprietary information that is backed by reasonable confidentiality and non-competition agreements.

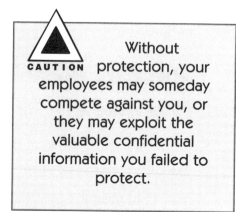

CAUTION Without protection, your employees may someday compete against you, or they may exploit the valuable confidential information you failed to protect.

3) *Establish and control all procedures:* Asset protection planning requires you to carefully review how confidential documents are produced, circulated, handled by others, stored and finally discarded. Controlling confidential documents is critical to security.

4) *Expand trade secrets protection to non-employees:* Vendors, consultants, franchisees, licensees, sales agents, customers and even potential buyers are examples. What access to trade secrets is each allowed? What restrictive covenants and non-disclosure agreements should they sign? How can you more effectively monitor confidentiality when dealing with these people?

Trade secrets law is complex, so enlist an attorney to help you protect key information through proven legal methods.

Recoup your investment from your failing business

Once a business turns bad the owner naturally thinks of ways to recoup his investment before the business closes. Stealing cash receipts may avoid detection, but such tactics remain dishonest. Also, excessive withdrawals may trigger repayment claims from a bankruptcy trustee.

To legally and safely recoup what you have invested from your failing company:

1)   *Repay yourself on loans due from your company,* but keep your business out of bankruptcy for at least one year. As an insider, creditors can recover preferential payments you have made to yourself (or any relative, officer, director or stockholder of your company) if within one year of the bankruptcy.

2)   *Stagger repayments.* Avoid large, easily detected payments to one or two individuals. Sprinkle smaller payments to more individuals. Smaller withdrawals are less easily spotted, and a bankruptcy trustee won't quickly start lawsuits against numerous individuals repaid a variety of different obligations—from reimbursed expenses to wages to consulting fees.

3)   *Withdraw funds as wages.* Excessive wages are considered a fraudulent transfer and a misappropriation of funds when the amount greatly exceeds fair and reasonable compensation.

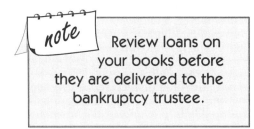

note Review loans on your books before they are delivered to the bankruptcy trustee.

CAUTION

Do your company's books show loans outstanding to you or your family? You can easily forget about old loans from your business; however, your financial statements gives the bankruptcy trustee little choice but to pursue their collection from you.

You may, however, deduct from the loan due you any obligations the business owes you. Perhaps you once transferred personal assets to the business toward repayment? You see the point. Or, if you had personally guaranteed certain business debts, you may possibly transform the loan into a payment for serving as a guarantor on the business loan. It may create taxable income to you, but it offers you a safe, legal way to claim re-payments.

What creditors must never discover

Never needlessly publicize your business's financial troubles. Creditors with such information can only improve their chances to collect at the expense of your business. What information can you safely reveal to creditors when your business is in trouble?

◆ You may admit to a temporary financial difficulty, but never admit insolvency, whether verbally or in writing. Creditors can use your admission of insolvency to bankrupt your business.

◆ Never reveal other creditors to a creditor, nor furnish creditor or vendor lists. Without this information, one creditor cannot easily locate the two other creditors necessary to file a bankruptcy petition.

◆ Never disclose prior payment arrangements with other creditors. Creditors who are not receiving preferential payments have good reason to force you into bankruptcy.

The better strategy is to encourage creditor support when your business is in trouble:

• *Communicate.* Creditors become angriest with debtors who won't communicate. Accept creditor phone calls. Take the initiative. Notify creditors if you need time to pay your obligations. Candid communication will greatly increase your credibility and reduce creditor anxiety. Still, never reveal more than is absolutely necessary.

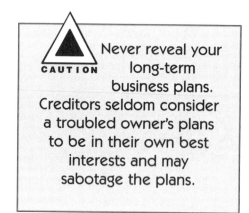
CAUTION Never reveal your long-term business plans. Creditors seldom consider a troubled owner's plans to be in their own best interests and may sabotage the plans.

• *Anticipate creditor concerns.* Assure creditors that they will be treated equally with all other creditors. Creditors rightfully become most hostile when they find another creditor has an advantage.

• *Stay scrupulously honest.* Creditors fight game-playing debtors. Bad checks, violating promises, preferring other creditors, diverting business assets or embezzling funds are most serious offenses. Creditors usually cooperate with honest debtors, and you need creditor cooperation when you want to save your troubled business.

Three advantages of a non-bankruptcy workout

A business in serious financial difficulty should never rush headlong into Chapter 11. An out-of-court workout may be preferable. A non-bankruptcy debt restructuring offers you and your creditors a few important advantages:

1) An out-of-court workout is **much less costly** than a Chapter 11 reorganization.

2) **Privacy.** An out-of-court workout keeps financial information relatively private. This is particularly important if you may lose vital clients because of your financial instability. Employees also seek more secure employment once their company files Chapter 11. The out-of-court workout gives you considerably more confidentiality because it involves only you and your creditors. A bankruptcy court and the possibilities of adverse publicity are largely alleviated.

> **CAUTION** You can may $50,000 or more in professional fees to navigate even a small business through Chapter 11. An equivalent out-of-court creditor arrangement may cut fees by 80 percent.

3) **You avoid a Chapter 11's rules and restraints.** The non-bankruptcy workout gives you greater flexibility for designing your repayment plan and the way you operate your business during the workout.

> **note** The pre-packaged Chapter 11 may save you time, aggravation and huge legal fees associated with a prolonged Chapter 11.

Still, the out-of-court workouts may not be your best alternative. One drawback is that a dissenting creditor can reject your settlement and sue your business or petition it into bankruptcy. Holdout creditors often upset workout plans between a debtor company and its assenting creditors.

note One alternative to this likelihood is the pre-packaged Chapter 11. Under this arrangement creditors, when accepting your proposed non-bankruptcy repayment plan, agree that if you should be forced to file Chapter 11, they agree to the same reorganization plan under the Chapter 11. A majority of your creditors can then accept an out-of-court plan, and in Chapter 11 automatically force the same settlement upon all dissident creditors. Your company then successfully and quickly emerges from Chapter 11 rather than lingering in bankruptcy court a year or two as is typical in Chapter 11 reorganizations.

When chapter 11 reorganization is your right remedy

Although too many troubled smaller companies file Chapter 11 when a simpler out-of-court workout would rehabilitate their business more efficiently and economically, Chapter 11 can be the right solution in four situations:

1)   When the IRS threatens seizure or has already seized, and you cannot reach agreement to pay the back taxes. Chapter 11 allows you six years from the date of assessment to repay back taxes.

2)   When a secured lender threatens foreclosure. Chapter 11 (and other bankruptcies) automatically stops foreclosure or repossessions. The bankruptcy court may eventually allow the lender to foreclose; however, until then your business is safe.

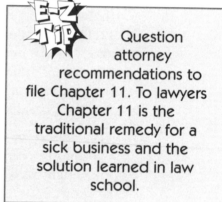

Question attorney recommendations to file Chapter 11. To lawyers Chapter 11 is the traditional remedy for a sick business and the solution learned in law school.

3)   Your business has been petitioned into bankruptcy by creditors and you cannot avoid the bankruptcy. You can then automatically convert the Chapter 7 liquidating bankruptcy to a Chapter 11 reorganization.

4)   You have too many creditors with conflicting interests to successfully reach agreement without the protection of Chapter 11.

Chapter 11s may generate big legal fees. Check other solutions in *The Business Doctor* (Garrett Publishing), listed in the Appendix. You will discover several overlooked strategies to bail out your business faster and cheaper!

Negotiate a workable workout plan

Whether through Chapter 11 reorganization or an out-of-court workout, a creditor repayment plan must be feasible, fair and equitable.

Unless your plan is feasible, your business can't repay what you promised. Your plan is equitable when assenting creditors within their respective class receive proportionately equivalent repayments on their claims. Six more key points must also be negotiated:

1)   *How much will you pay?* Creditors want to recover as much as possible. Your lowest possible settlement must equal what creditors could recover if they liquidate your business. Offer creditors more and your creditors will want to keep you in business. What is the maximum amount your business can pay? Calculate surplus cash flow over the next two or three years, plus surplus funds immediately available.

> *note*
> Your plan is fair when you promise to repay more than what the creditors could obtain through a forced liquidation of your business.

2)   *How much now, how much later?* Creditors also want fast repayment. But, you still cannot pay more cash now than is available, nor can future payments exceed what your business can afford. Conservatively project cash flow. Never allow creditors to pressure you to invest more of your personal funds to produce those faster or larger repayments. Let your business stand on its own.

3)   *Length of payments?* Creditors can demand never-ending payments if it will repay the debt. Never let creditors mortgage your future beyond the next two or three years.

4)   *Will you personally guarantee payments?* The answer may chiefly depend upon the total debt, your personal finances, your risk or exposure, and how important the business is to you. Bargain, if you must, for a limited guarantee which limits your exposure. Convince creditors your effort is your commitment to see the business succeed.

> **E-Z TIP**
> A creditor who is offered one plan must decide whether to accept. When you offer alternative plans, the creditor will more likely think in terms of which plan to accept, not should he accept. Psychology can tame angry creditors.

5)   *Will you secure repayments with a mortgage on your business?* Secured creditors can more easily enforce their rights if you default. And your current creditors, once secured, gain priority for repayment over future creditors if you subsequently fail.

6)   *There are still other points to negotiate.* Will you give your creditors part ownership in your business? This may be sensible if your company can grow rapidly and go public. Will

you pay a bonus dividend if your company should earn more than you anticipate? Be creative. Consider all possible terms when approaching creditors.

 Offer options. This is an even more powerful way to coax creditors to accept a payment plan. Examples: 1) 20 percent of their claim payable in four annual 5-percent installments, 2) a lump sum 10-percent payment, or 3) 5 percent now and a share of the profits over the next three years. Each creditor can then accept the option he wants. This strategy works because it's good psychology.

Six chapter 11 survival tips

Nine out of ten Chapter 11 companies eventually fail and are liquidated under Chapter 7. Most fail within three years of reorganization. Only a tiny handful of Chapter 11 companies survive beyond three years. Why so many failures? How can you improve the odds for survival?

1) One common cause of reorganizational failure is that few smaller businesses can finance themselves through Chapter 11. While Chapter 11 allows credit and innovative borrowing, there can be acute and fatal cash shortages. Companies entering Chapter 11 must understand how their business will stay afloat, with a negative cash flow and no lender support.

2) Companies in Chapter 11 as a safe harbor from foreclosing creditors will find their protection short-lived if the bankruptcy court concludes the lender is inadequately protected. Can you convince the bankruptcy court that your secured creditors will not lose more because you filed Chapter 11?

3) Creditors can force the sale of the business's profit-makers to raise more cash for themselves. This is counterproductive to the business's long-term profitability and survivability.

4) Chapter 11 bureaucratic rules and restrictions create a quicksand. Bureaucratic death often befalls the smaller business which is taken less seriously by bankruptcy courts.

5) Creditors stay hostile and unreceptive to even overly generous reorganizational plans when the owner is dishonest.

6) Companies mistakenly believe they solved their problems with Chapter 11 and exit bankruptcy court losing as much money as

before. Chapter 11, or any other business reorganization, only gives you one more opportunity to redirect your business toward profitability and a positive cash flow.

Can your company survive Chapter 11? Examine key characteristics of long-term survivors:

• Survivors file Chapter 11 with their assets intact and a core business activity needed to successfully rebuild. Losers dwindle their assets and customer base until there is no business upon which to rebuild.

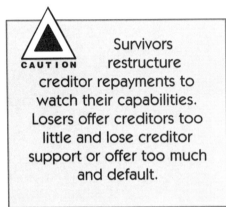

Survivors restructure creditor repayments to watch their capabilities. Losers offer creditors too little and lose creditor support or offer too much and default.

• Survivors win and maintain creditor cooperation and support, and frequently new credit and financing. Losers lack credibility and thus forfeit creditor cooperation.

• Survivors prioritize cash flow throughout the reorganization. Losers hemorrhage.

• Survivors quickly and decisively cure their underlying problems and design realistic plans for new profitability and growth. Losers see their future as an extension of their past.

Squeezing equity from your business

A good defensive strategy for the troubled business is to strip its equity. Turn assets into more easily protected cash, which can be distributed to stockholders, or invested in protective offshore companies or other asset protection entities. Equity stripping follows basic strategies:

1) Sell or factor accounts receivable. Accounts receivable can be sold or factored if due from solid business customers and the amount owed is sufficiently large. A factor pays immediate cash for these receivables and your unsecured creditors then lose claim to these receivables. Factoring also protects against IRS levies on your receivables. Few businesses with substantial receivables can survive an IRS levy because of the cash flow crunch and its effect on customers. Faced with an IRS levy, your alternatives are to either factor your receivables or file Chapter 11.

2)   Reduce inventory to the lowest level you need to operate without losing sales. Businesses frequently reduce inventories 50 percent or more without hurting sales. This can release considerable cash for sheltering.

3)   Sell or encumber the business's capital assets. Borrow against real estate and equipment, or sell under a sale-leaseback arrangement. Many lenders will buy your equipment, vehicles or real estate and lease them back to you. Your exposed equity in fixed assets is then turned into instantly protectable cash.

4)   License or sell proprietary assets. Tradenames, copyrights and patents can also be sold and your company can retain exclusive marketing rights, which is of little value to creditors.

Proceed carefully. Avoid civil or criminal problems and recognize that creditors also have rights. Have a good lawyer guide you on these matters so that you stay on the right side of the law.

Planning Pointers

◆ Businesses need perhaps more asset protection than individuals because they are more likely to incur creditor and legal problems.

◆ Entrepreneurs starting and expanding their business must emphasize asset protection in their organizational planning so that they are always defensively positioned.

◆ Every business venture should operate within an entity that insulates the owners and managers from the debts and liabilities of the enterprise.

◆ The professional practice is no less immune to liability and its owners require the right organizational structure to limit personal liability.

◆ Always divide business operations into as many separate entities as possible so that the failure of one will not jeopardize the other businesses.

◆ Title as few valuable assets as possible in a high-risk, creditor-prone business entity.

◆ Shield those few assets in a high-risk business with friendly mortgages so little or no equity remains exposed to creditors.

Glossary of useful terms

A-B

Adequate Protection

The standard of protection granted a creditor by the trustee or debtor-in-possession in order to avoid court sanctioned foreclosure on its property.

Automatic Stay

An injunction, or court order, that takes effect when a bankruptcy petition is filed. An automatic stay prohibits all collection against a debtor.

Avoidance Powers

The powers used by a trustee to reverse transfers of the debtor's property.

Balance Sheet

A statement of financial conditions as of a specific date. It is different from a cash flow statement, which summarizes income and expenses.

Bankruptcy Code

The body of a federal statutory law that governs the bankruptcy process.

Bankruptcy Petition

The legal instrument filed with the bankruptcy court that commences a bankruptcy proceeding.

Bar Date

The last date for filing a proof of claim.

Ch-Co

Chapter 7

In a Chapter 7 proceeding, the debtor's business is liquidated and its assets are distributed to creditors with allowed proofs of claim.

Chapter 11

Normally, a Chapter 11 proceeding is a reorganization proceeding. The debtor continues to operate its business after the bankruptcy is filed. Chapter 11 liquidators are not uncommon and usually are the result of an unsuccessful reorganization attempt.

Chapter 11 Plan

In a Chapter 11 proceeding, the reorganization plan sets forth the rights of all classes of creditors. It may also include various repayment schedules pertaining to the various creditors.

Chapter 13

May only be filed by an individual debtor with limited debt. In essence, it allows a payment plan for an individual's financial and/or business debts.

Closing

When a bankruptcy case is closed, it is no longer in the court's docket.

Collateral

Property of a debtor in which a creditor has a lien securing its debt.

Complaint

A pleading that is filed to initiate a lawsuit or an adversary proceeding.

Composition

Out of court agreement to pay a percentage of a debt in full settlement.

Consumer Credit Counseling Services

Non-profit organizations established to help debtors make payment arrangements with creditors.

Conversion

The conversion of a bankruptcy case from one chapter type to another.

Cr-F

Cram-Down

The confirmation of a plan to reorganize over the objection of a creditor or class of creditors by the votes of other creditors.

Creditor

One to whom you owe money.

Debtor

One who owes debts. In bankruptcy, the bankrupt business that is under the control and protection of the bankruptcy court is the debtor.

Debtor-in-Possession (DIP)

The business debtor in a Chapter 11 reorganization. In a Chapter 11, the debtor retaining possession of the assets involved in the bankruptcy.

Discharge

A discharge in bankruptcy relieves the debtor of the dischargeable debts incurred prior to filing. Discharge is the legal term for the elimination of debt through bankruptcy.

Dismissal

The dismissal of a bankruptcy case, for all intents and purposes, returns the debtor to the same place it was before bankruptcy was filed.

Examiner

An officer of the court sometimes appointed to investigate the financial affairs of the debtor.

Exemption or Exempt Property

Property of an individual debtor that the law protects from the actions of creditors, such as the debtor's residence or homestead, automobile, and the like.

Foreclosure

A debt-collection whereby property of the debtor is sold on the courthouse steps to satisfy debts. Foreclosure often involves real estate of the debtor.

G-Pe

General, Unsecured Claim

A claim that is neither secured nor granted a priority by the Bankruptcy Code. Most trade debts are general, unsecured claims.

Involuntary Bankruptcy Proceedings

In an involuntary bankruptcy proceeding the debtor is forced into bankruptcy by creditors. Involuntary bankruptcies are relatively rare.

Judicial Lien

A lien created by the order of a Court, such as the lien created by taking a judgment against a debtor.

Jurisdiction

The power and authority of a court to issue binding orders after hearing controversies.

Levy and Execution

A judicial debt-collection procedure in which the court orders the sheriff to seize the debtor's property found in the country to sell in satisfaction of the debtor's debt or debts.

Lien

An interest in property securing the repayment of a debt.

Motion

A request for the court to act. A motion may be filed within a lawsuit, adversary proceeding, or bankruptcy case.

Personal Property

Moveable property. Property that is not permanently attached to land is considered personalty.

Petition for Relief

The papers filed initiating a bankruptcy case.

Po-R

Possessory Security Interest

A security interest or lien on property that requires the creditor to have possession of the property, such as a pawn or pledge.

Preference

A transfer of property of the debtor to a creditor made immediately prior to the debtor's bankruptcy that enables the creditor to receive more than it would have received from the bankruptcy. A preferential transfer must be made while the debtor was insolvent and as payment for a debt that existed prior to the transfer of property.

Priority

Certain categories of claims are designated as priority claims by the Bankruptcy Code, such as claims for lost wages or taxes. Each classification of claims must be paid in order of priority (the claims in one class must be paid in full before the next class receives any payment).

Priority Proof of Claim or Priority Claim

A proof of claim of the type granted priority by the Bankruptcy Code.

Proof of Claim

The document filed in a bankruptcy case that establishes a creditor's claim for payment against the debtor.

Realty or Real Property

Immovable property, such as land and/or buildings attached to land.

Redemption

The right of a debtor in a bankruptcy to purchase certain real or personal property from a secured creditor by paying the current value of the property (regardless of the amount owed on the property).

S-U

Secured Creditor

A creditor whose debt is secured by a lien on property of the debtor.

Secured Proof of Claim

A proof of claim for a debt that is secured by a lien, a judgment, or other security interest.

Security Interest

A lien on the property in possession of the debtor that acts as security for the debt owed to the creditor.

Statutory Lien

A lien created by operation of the law, such as mechanic's lien or a tax lien. A statutory lien does not require the consent of the parties or a court order.

Trustee

An officer of the court appointed to take custody of the assets of a bankruptcy estate.

Unsecured Creditor

A creditor without security for its debt.

Index

A-C••••

Annuities 66

Assets

    Concealing 42, 242

    Disclosing 43

    Distributing trust.............103

    Exempt 215

    Locating...........................47

    Safeguarding 216

    Asset protection havens ..176

Bank accounts

    Joint 79

    Protecting.......................219

Bank relationships...............283

Bankruptcy 189, 252

Bearer investments..............182

Child support enforcement

act of 1975 64

Consumer credit protection

act (CCPA)............................64

Corporation........................141

Corporate shares.................151

Creditors 285

D-J••••

Divorce..............................229

Employee Retirement Income
Security Act of 1974 (ERISA)155

Enrolled agents (EAs)..........224

Fair consideration 29

Fair value.............................29

Family limited partnership..110

Federal wage exemption.......64

Financial privacy 53

Foreclosures 257

Fraud claim 30

Fraudulent transfers 28

Friendly mortgage 280

Homestead protection 57, 63

Indemnification...................155

Insolvent 29

Insurance exemptions 66

Internal Revenue Service (IRS)
....207

Invisible shareholder...........152

Jeopardy assessment 34, 209

Joint tenancy.......................74

L-S ·····

Liabilities	29, 80
Limited liability company (LLC)	129
Limited partnerships	109
Nevis LLC	177
Non-bankruptcy workout	286
Offshore asset protection trusts (OAPT)	168
Offshore havens	166
Options-to-equity	261
Partnership	110
Pre-marriage agreement	230
Property,	
Community	81, 241
Co-owning	71
Foreclosure	267
Recovering	216
Protected income	63
Real estate foreclosure	267
Refinancing	262
Reorganization	287
Repatriated funds	185
Repossessions	257
Secrecy	42
Social security payments	63
Sham transfer	35
Safe transfers	36

T-W ·····

Tax liens	210
Tenancy by-the-entirety	76
Tenancy-in-common	72
Trade secrets, protecting	284
Trusts	
Asset protection	168
Business	100
Charitable remainder	95
Children's	96
Creditor-proof	88
Dynasty	97
Insurance	93
Irrevocable	88
Living	91
Medicaid	102
Nominee	90
Q-tip	98
Revocable	88
Spendthrift	93
Standby	101
Wealth replacement	97
Wages	
Garnishment of	64
Levy of	220